STATUTES

OF THE

UNIVERSITY OF CAMBRIDGE

CAMBRIDGE UNIVERSITY PRESS
C. F. CLAY, Manager
London: FETTER LANE, E.C.
Edinburgh: 100 PRINCES STREET

New York: G. P. PUTNAM'S SONS
Bombay and Calcutta: MACMILLAN AND CO., Ltd.
Toronto: J. M. DENT AND SONS, Ltd.
Tokyo: THE MARUZEN-KABUSHIKI-KAISHA

STATUTES

OF THE

UNIVERSITY OF CAMBRIDGE

WITH THE

INTERPRETATIONS OF THE CHANCELLOR

AND SOME

ACTS OF PARLIAMENT

RELATING TO THE UNIVERSITY

EDITED BY

THE REGISTRARY OF THE
UNIVERSITY

Cambridge:
at the University Press
1914

Cambridge:
PRINTED BY JOHN CLAY, M.A.
AT THE UNIVERSITY PRESS

STATUTES OF THE UNIVERSITY OF CAMBRIDGE

STATUTE A

Approved by the Queen in Council, 27 *February* 1882

CHAPTER I

CHAPTER II

CHAPTER III

CHAPTER IV

CHAPTER V

CHAPTER VI

CHAPTER VII

CHAPTER VIII

CHAPTER IX

CHAPTER X

CHAPTER XI

DECLARATIONS

STATUTE B

Approved by the Queen in Council, 29 *June* 1882

CHAPTER I

CHAPTER II

CHAPTER III

CHAPTER IV

CHAPTER V

CHAPTER VI

STATUTE C

Approved by the Queen in Council, 10 March 1882

STATUTE D

Approved by the Queen in Council, 10 March 1882

STATUTE E

Approved by the Queen in Council, 10 March 1882

OTHER STATUTES

STATUTES PRIOR TO 1877

INTERPRETATIONS OF STATUTES BY THE CHANCELLOR

I. STATUTES APPROVED BY THE QUEEN IN COUNCIL, 31 JULY 1858

II. STATUTE A. APPROVED BY THE QUEEN IN COUNCIL, 27 FEBRUARY 1882

STATUTE B. APPROVED BY THE QUEEN IN COUNCIL, 29 JUNE 1882

ACTS OF PARLIAMENT

STATUTES

OF THE

UNIVERSITY OF CAMBRIDGE

Deum timeto: regem honorato: virtutem colito: disciplinis bonis operam dato.

STATUTE A

Approved by the Queen in Council, 27 *February* 1882.

This Statute is declared to be a Statute for the University of Cambridge.

CHAPTER I

TERMS.

There shall be three Terms in the year, called respectively the Michaelmas Term, the Lent Term, and the Easter Term, and they shall include two hundred and twenty-seven days at least. The Michaelmas Term shall commence on the first day of October. The Lent Term shall not end later than the Thursday next before Easter Day. The Easter Term shall not commence earlier than the Tuesday next after Easter Day, and shall end on the twenty-fourth day of June.

Terms shall be kept by residence within such boundaries in or about Cambridge, and during such part, being not less than three-fourths of any term, as the University may from time to time prescribe by Grace.

The University shall have power to determine by Grace from time to time what constitutes residence.

CHAPTER II

DEGREES

SECTION 1. *Students in Arts.*

Students in Arts shall keep by residence at least nine Terms. They shall pursue such studies and pass such examinations as the University may from time to time prescribe by Grace.

Having done all that is required by the Statutes and Ordinances of the University, they may be admitted to the title of Bachelor Designate in Arts, and shall afterwards be inaugurated Bachelors of Arts at the time prescribed by the University.

[SECTION 1 A. *Research Students in Arts.*

Research Students in Arts shall keep by residence at least six terms. They shall pursue such studies and satisfy such conditions as the University may from time to time prescribe by Grace.

Having done all that is required by the Statutes and Ordinances of the University, they may be admitted to the title of Bachelor Designate in Arts, and shall afterwards be inaugurated Bachelors of Arts at the time prescribed by the University.][1]

SECTION 2. *Bachelors of Arts.*

[Bachelors of Arts, who have done all that is required by the Statutes and Ordinances of the University, may be admitted Inceptors in Arts at the end of six years from the end of their first term of residence, provided that not less than two years have elapsed from their inauguration: and after such admission they shall be created Masters of Arts at the time prescribed by the University.][2]

[1] Grace 5 of 9 May 1912, and Grace 6 of 23 May 1912, confirming a Report of the General Board of Studies (*Reporter*, 5 March 1912, page 678). Sealed, 14 June 1912. Approved by the King in Council, 11 February 1913 (*Reporter*, 25 February 1913, page 686).

[2] Grace 12 of 24 May 1894, and Grace 6 of 8 November 1894, confirming a Report of the Council of the Senate (*Reporter*, 1 May 1894, page 691). Sealed, 21 November 1894. Approved by the Queen in Council, 29 June 1895 (*Reporter*, 2 October 1895, page 2).

Section 3. *Masters of Arts.*

Masters of Arts wishing to graduate in Divinity shall study Divinity until the Feast of St Barnabas in the seventh year from their creation[1].

Having done all that is required by the Statutes and Ordinances of the University, they may be admitted to the Degree of Bachelor of Divinity on the said Feast of St Barnabas or on any later day.

Section 4. *Bachelors of Divinity.*

Bachelors of Divinity shall continue to study Divinity for five years[1].

Having done all that is required by the Statutes and Ordinances of the University, they may be admitted to the title of Doctor Designate in Divinity.

[Moreover Bachelors of Divinity who have previously been Masters of Arts or Masters of Law may by special Grace, at the end of twelve years from their creation, be admitted to the title of Doctor Designate in Divinity, even though five years have not passed since their admission to the Degree of Bachelor of Divinity provided that they have done all that is required by the Statutes and Ordinances of the University.][2]

Persons admitted to the title of Doctor Designate in Divinity shall be created Doctors at the time prescribed by the University.

Section 5. *Students in Law.*

Students in Law shall keep by residence at least nine Terms. They shall pursue such studies and pass such examinations as the University may from time to time prescribe by Grace.

Having done all that is required by the Statutes and Ordinances of the University, they may be admitted to the title of Bachelor Designate in Law.

[1] The omission from this paragraph of the words "and shall preach once in the University Church" was approved by the King in Council, 14 May 1914. For further references see the note to the third paragraph of Section 4 of this Chapter.

[2] Grace 2 of 22 November 1912, and Grace 13 of 25 April 1913, confirming a Report of the Council of the Senate (*Reporter*, 7 October 1912, page 42). Sealed, 5 May 1913. Approved by the King in Council, 14 May 1914 (*Reporter*, 26 May 1914, page 1007).

After such admission they shall have the same rank and privileges as Bachelors Designate in Arts. They shall be inaugurated Bachelors of Law at the time prescribed by the University, and shall have then the same rank and privileges as Bachelors of Arts.

Bachelors of Arts, also, who have done all that is required by the Statutes and Ordinances of the University, may be admitted to the title of Bachelor Designate in Law, and shall afterwards be inaugurated Bachelors of Law at the time prescribed by the University.

[SECTION 5 A. *Research Students in Law.*

Research Students in Law shall keep by residence at least six terms. They shall pursue such studies and satisfy such conditions as the University may from time to time prescribe by Grace.

Having done all that is required by the Statutes and Ordinances of the University, they may be admitted to the title of Bachelor Designate in Law.

After such admission they shall have the same rank and privileges as Bachelors Designate in Arts. They shall be inaugurated Bachelors of Law at the time prescribed by the University, and shall have then the same rank and privileges as Bachelors of Arts.][1]

SECTION 6. *Bachelors of Law.*

[Bachelors of Law, or Bachelors of Arts, who have done all that is required by the Statutes and Ordinances of the University, may be admitted Inceptors in Law at the end of six years from the end of their first term of residence, provided that not less than two years have elapsed since their inauguration.

After such admission they shall have the same rank and privileges as Inceptors in Arts. They shall be created Masters of Law at the time prescribed by the University, and shall have then the same rank and privileges as Masters of Arts.

[1] Grace 5 of 9 May 1912, and Grace 6 of 23 May 1912, confirming a Report of the General Board of Studies (*Reporter*, 5 March 1912, page 678). Sealed, 14 June 1912. Approved by the King in Council, 11 February 1913 (*Reporter*, 25 February 1913, page 686).

Masters of Arts, also, who have done all that is required by the Statutes and Ordinances of the University, may be admitted Inceptors in Law, and shall afterwards be created Masters of Law, and shall not thereby lose their rank and privileges.][1]

SECTION 7. *Masters of Law.*

Masters of Law, who have done all that is required by the Statutes and Ordinances of the University, may be admitted to the title of Doctor Designate in Law at the end of five years from their creation, and after such admission they shall be created Doctors at the time prescribed by the University.

Masters of Law may also be admitted to the Degree of Bachelor of Divinity on the same conditions as Masters of Arts.

SECTION 8. *Students in Medicine.*

Students in Medicine shall keep by residence at least nine Terms. They shall pursue such studies and pass such examinations as the University may from time to time prescribe by Grace.

Having done all that is required by the Statutes and Ordinances of the University, they may be admitted to the title of Bachelor Designate in Medicine.

Bachelors of Arts, also, who have done all that is required by the Statutes and Ordinances of the University, may be admitted to the title of Bachelor Designate in Medicine.

All persons so admitted shall be afterwards inaugurated Bachelors of Medicine at the time prescribed by the University.

SECTION 9. *Bachelors of Medicine.*

Bachelors of Medicine who have done all that is required by the Statutes and Ordinances of the University may be admitted to the title of Doctor Designate in Medicine in the ninth Term after their inauguration.

[1] Grace 12 of 24 May 1894, and Grace 6 of 8 November 1894, confirming a Report of the Council of the Senate (*Reporter*, 1 May 1894, page 691). Sealed, 21 November 1894. Approved by the Queen in Council, 29 June 1895 (*Reporter*, 2 October 1895, page 2).

Masters of Arts, also, who have done all that is required by the Statutes and Ordinances of the University, may be admitted to the title of Doctor Designate in Medicine in the twelfth Term after their creation.

All persons so admitted shall be created Doctors at the time prescribed by the University.

SECTION 10. *Students in Surgery.*

Students in Surgery shall keep by residence at least nine Terms. They shall pursue such studies and pass such examinations as the University may from time to time prescribe by Grace.

Having done all that is required by the Statutes and Ordinances of the University, they may be admitted to the title of Bachelor Designate in Surgery.

Bachelors of Arts, also, who have done all that is required by the Statutes and Ordinances of the University, may be admitted to the title of Bachelor Designate in Surgery.

All persons so admitted shall be afterwards inaugurated Bachelors of Surgery at the time prescribed by the University.

They shall have the same rank and privileges as Bachelors Designate in Arts and Bachelors of Arts respectively.

SECTION 11. *Bachelors of Surgery.*

Bachelors of Surgery who have done all that is required by the Statutes and Ordinances of the University may be admitted Inceptors in Surgery at the end of three years from their inauguration.

Masters of Arts, also, who have done all that is required by the Statutes and Ordinances of the University, may be admitted Inceptors in Surgery.

All persons so admitted shall be created Masters of Surgery at the time prescribed by the University.

Inceptors in Surgery and Masters of Surgery shall have the same rank and privileges as Inceptors in Arts and Masters of Arts respectively.

SECTION 12. *Students in Science.*

[Students in Science who, having already taken a Degree in Arts, Law, Medicine, Surgery, or Music, have given proofs of distinction in Science by some original contribution to the advancement of Science, and have done all that is required by the Statutes and Ordinances of the University, may be admitted to the title of Doctor Designate in Science, and shall afterwards be created Doctors at the time prescribed by the University. Provided that only those graduates in Music shall be qualified for such admission and creation who had before graduation kept at least nine Terms by residence.

SECTION 13. *Students in Letters.*

Students in Letters, who, having already taken a Degree in Arts, Law, Medicine, Surgery, or Music, have given proofs of distinction by some original contribution to the advancement of Learning, and have done all that is required by the Statutes and Ordinances of the University, may be admitted to the title of Doctor Designate in Letters, and shall afterwards be created Doctors at the time prescribed by the University. Provided that only those graduates in Music shall be qualified for such admission and creation who had before graduation kept at least nine Terms by residence.

SECTION 14. *Students in Music.*

Students in Music shall keep by residence at least nine Terms. They shall pursue such studies and pass such examinations as the University may from time to time prescribe by Grace. Having done all that is required by the Statutes and Ordinances of the University they may be admitted to the title of Bachelor Designate in Music, and shall afterwards be inaugurated Bachelors of Music at the time prescribed by the University.

Bachelors of Music who have, previously to graduation, kept by residence at least nine Terms, and who have done all that is required by the Statutes and Ordinances of the University, may be admitted Inceptors in Music at the end of three years from their inauguration; and after such admission they shall be created Masters of Music at the time prescribed by the University.

SECTION 15. *Bachelors of Music.*

Persons not being less than thirty years of age who have already graduated in some Faculty of the University, have given proofs of distinction in musical composition, and have done all that is required by the Ordinances of the University, may be admitted to the title of Doctor Designate in Music, and shall afterwards be created Doctors at the time prescribed by the University.][1]

SECTION 16. *Terms not kept by Residence to be counted in special cases.*

The University shall have power by special Grace to allow a Term to be counted as kept by residence by a candidate for a Degree, though he may not have resided the whole or any portion of the prescribed part of it, provided that the cause of absence be considered sufficiently grave by the Council of the Senate, and be clearly stated in the Grace proposed for the Degree.

SECTION 17. *Admission of Students from other Universities.*

The University shall have power to make such regulations as may seem fit for admitting Students *in statu pupillari* who have kept Terms by residence at another University, and for counting the Terms so kept instead of Terms kept by residence in Cambridge, provided that such University has obtained from the Senate a special privilege to that effect, and that the whole time of residence for a Degree in every case be not less than that which is required in these Statutes.

[1] Grace 16 of 7 June 1894, and Grace 8 of 8 November 1894, confirming a Report of the Special Board for Music (*Reporter*, 15 May 1894, page 747). Sealed, 21 November 1894. Approved by the Queen in Council, 29 June 1895 (*Reporter*, 2 October 1895, page 2).

The University shall have power also, under such conditions as may be prescribed by Grace, to admit by incorporation Graduates of other Universities to the same Degrees as those which their own Universities have conferred upon them.

[SECTION 18. *Degrees and Titles of Degrees conferred without the fulfilment of the usual conditions.*

The University shall have power to grant admission to complete Degrees *honoris causâ* without fulfilment of the usual conditions imposed by Statute or Grace to the following persons, namely, Members of the Royal Family, Privy Councillors, Bishops, Bishops Designate or Elect, including persons designated for Colonial or Indian or Missionary Bishoprics and approved by the Archbishop of Canterbury, Peers, Members of the Supreme Court of Judicature, Deans of Cathedral Churches or the Abbey Church of Westminster or the Royal Chapel of St George, Windsor, and Heads of Colleges in the University.

The University shall have power also to grant admission to complete Degrees *honoris causâ* without fulfilment of the usual conditions to persons who, having already been admitted to a Degree in the University or obtained some University office, are distinguished by conspicuous merit.

Titles of Degrees in Arts, Law, Medicine, Surgery, Science, Letters, or Music may be granted to foreigners of distinction, and to British subjects who are of conspicuous merit or have done good service to the State or to the University.][1]

SECTION 19. *Affiliated Colleges.*

[The University shall have power to adopt as an affiliated College in any place within the United Kingdom or in any part of the British dominion any institution founded for the education of adult students, with such conditions as to the provision of lectures, and as to the rules and arrangements for the students, as may be determined from time to time by Grace.

[1] Grace 1 of 13 June 1889, and Grace 3 of 25 February 1892, confirming a Report of the Council of the Senate (*Reporter*, 4 June 1889, page 798). Sealed, 26 February 1892. Approved by the Queen in Council, 16 May 1893 (*Reporter*, 30 May 1893, page 876).

[Students of the institution who shall have continued Members of it for such length of time, not less than two years, and shall have attended such lectures and passed such examinations as may be required from time to time by Grace of the Senate, shall, if admitted as Members of the University, be deemed, for such purposes and under such conditions as the Senate may from time to time by Grace determine, to have already kept by residence one or more terms (not exceeding three in number).][1]

The University shall have power also to terminate at any time by Grace the connexion of the University with the institution as an affiliated College.

The University shall have power also to admit on like conditions to the privileges of students of an affiliated College adult students attending a course of education conducted by a Committee in concert with the University in places where there is no affiliated College.][2]

[The University shall also have power to admit to the same privileges members of Universities which have not been adopted as Affiliated Institutions.][3]

SECTION 20. *Admission to Degrees in absence.*

[The University shall have power to admit any student who has done all that is required by the Statutes and Ordinances of the University to the title of Bachelor Designate in Arts, Law, Medicine, Surgery, or Music in his absence, if his special circumstances shall require it; but the name of the candidate shall be published to the University at least three days before the proposal of the Grace for his Degree.

[1] Grace 4 of 1 March 1906, and Grace 1 of 15 March 1906, confirming a Report of the Council of the Senate (*Reporter*, 6 February 1906, page 476). Sealed, 23 March 1906. Approved by the King in Council, 26 March 1907 (*Reporter*, 30 April 1907, page 791).

[2] Grace 2 of 10 December 1885, and Grace 23 of 17 December 1885, confirming a Report of the Local Examinations and Lectures Syndicate (*Reporter*, 9 June 1885, page 809). Sealed, 17 December 1885. Approved by the Queen in Council, 26 June 1886 (*Reporter*, 5 July 1886, page 870).

[3] Grace 5 of 9 May 1912, and Grace 6 of 23 May 1912, confirming a Report of the General Board of Studies (*Reporter*, 5 March 1912, page 678). Sealed, 14 June 1912. Approved by the King in Council, 11 February 1913 (*Reporter*, 25 February 1913, page 686).

The University shall also have power to admit any graduate to a further or to a higher Degree in his absence; but the name of the candidate shall be published to the University at least three days before the proposal of the Grace for his Degree[1].][2]

CHAPTER III

Graces of the Senate

Section 1. *Congregations and Graces.*

The University shall have power to prescribe from time to time by Grace the form and manner of holding a Congregation, the conditions under which Graces having received the sanction of the Council may be offered to the Senate, the mode of taking votes and recording the results, and generally to regulate its own proceedings.

There shall be a meeting of the Senate for the discussion of proposed Graces, or of Reports made by the Council of the Senate, Boards of Study, or Syndicates, or of any other question strictly Academical, whenever the Chancellor or the Council of the Senate think fit, but no vote shall be taken at the time of such discussion. It shall be the duty of the Council to consider any proposals or amendments pertinent to the subject discussed which may be offered at the time of the discussion by any Member of the Senate.

Section 2. *Repealed*[3].

[1] The omission from this paragraph of the words "and if his Degree be a Degree in Divinity he shall first make the usual subscription" was approved by the King in Council, 14 May 1914. For further references see the note to the third paragraph of Section 4 of this Chapter.

[2] Grace 2 of 27 February 1902, and Grace 3 of 13 March 1902, confirming a Report of the Council of the Senate (*Reporter*, 28 January 1902, page 481). Sealed, 27 May 1902. Approved by the King in Council, 28 March 1903 (*Reporter*, 21 April 1903, page 614).

[3] Grace 2 of 22 November 1912, and Grace 13 of 25 April 1913, confirming a Report of the Council of the Senate (*Reporter*, 7 October 1912, page 42) Sealed, 5 May 1913. Confirmed by the King in Council, 14 May 1914 (*Reporter*, 26 May 1914, page 1007).

SECTION 3. *Right of Voting.*

[The following persons shall have the right of voting in the Senate, namely, the Chancellor, Vice-Chancellor, Doctors of Divinity, Law, Medicine, Science, and Letters, Doctors of Music who before being admitted to their first degree have kept by residence at least nine terms, Bachelors of Divinity, and Masters of Arts, Law, Surgery, and Music.][1]

The right shall not, however, be granted to any one who has been admitted to a Degree *honoris causâ*, or who has migrated from another University, unless either before or after his admission to such Degree or his migration he shall have kept by residence in Cambridge the greater part of each of three terms.

No one who has been admitted to the title of a Degree only shall thereby gain the right of voting.

The names of all persons entitled to vote shall be inscribed by the Registrary in a Register or book provided for the purpose. No one shall be allowed to vote or have his name inscribed in the Register who has either refused, or after due warning neglected, to pay any fees, fines, or other dues required by the University.

Persons who have continued to be members of the University from the time of admission to their first Degree shall have their names inscribed in the Register at the time of completing their Degree by creation.

If any one has not continued to be a member of the University from the time of admission to his first Degree, his name may be inscribed in the Register at the time of completing his Degree by creation, or at any later time, if he pays all fees, fines, and other dues which he would have been called upon to pay if he had been a member of the University continuously from the time of admission to his first Degree.

Any one whose name has been inscribed in the Register and afterwards removed may have his name inscribed again if he pays all fees, fines, and other dues which he would have

[1] Grace 16 of 7 June 1894, and Grace 8 of 8 November 1894, confirming a Report of the Special Board for Music (*Reporter*, 15 May 1894, page 747). Sealed, 21 November 1894. Approved by the Queen in Council, 29 June 1895 (*Reporter*, 2 October 1895, page 2).

been called upon to pay if his name had continued on the Register from the time at which it was removed.

The University shall have power to prescribe by Grace a sum or sums of money to be accepted in lieu of the fees, fines, and other dues mentioned in the two preceding cases; but in neither case shall the person whose name is so inscribed in the Register be entitled to vote within a period of one hundred and eighty days after the inscription of his name.

Those persons who have the right of voting in the Senate shall be deemed to be the Members of the Senate.

CHAPTER IV

Elections

Section 1. *Election of Chancellor.*

The office of Chancellor shall be held, in accordance with the ancient laws and customs of the University, for two years complete, or so long as the silent consent of the University permits.

When a vacancy of the office is certainly known to the Vice-Chancellor, he shall call a Congregation as soon as possible, and openly declare the fact through the Senior Proctor, and assign a day, not before the seventh nor after the twelfth day next following, for another Congregation for the election of a new Chancellor. The election shall be completed before the fifteenth day after that on which the vacancy was declared.

If the vacancy becomes known in the Vacation after the end of the Easter Term, the Congregation for declaring the vacancy and assigning the day of election shall be held on the first day of the Michaelmas Term ensuing.

On the day assigned for the election the Vice-Chancellor and Proctors shall stand in scrutiny. They shall first give their own votes in writing, and then take the votes in writing of all other persons present who have the right of voting. The person for whom the greatest number of votes is given shall be declared by the Vice-Chancellor to be elected.

An instrument of election of the Chancellor shall be sealed and delivered to him without delay.

The Commissary shall be appointed by the Chancellor by Letters Patent.

SECTION 2. *Election of the Vice-Chancellor.*

The Vice-Chancellor shall be elected yearly some time before he enters upon his office, and the day of election and the day of entering upon office in every year shall be prescribed by Grace from time to time as the University may find expedient.

On the day preceding the day of election the Council of the Senate shall assemble in the Senate House. The Members of the Council in order of seniority of Degree shall severally nominate one of the Heads of Colleges for the office. They shall then severally mark two of the persons so nominated for election. The two persons to be proposed to the Senate for election must be so marked that in a first, or second, or third scrutiny each of them has more marks than any of the other persons nominated. If in none of these three scrutinies two, but in the third scrutiny one, shall be found to have the required greater number of marks, the Regius Professor of Divinity, or, if he be a member of the Council, the Vice-Chancellor of the next preceding year who is not a member of the Council, shall nominate one of the persons who have each an equal number of marks next less than the highest.

If in the third scrutiny neither two nor one of the persons nominated be found to have more marks than any other, the said Regius Professor, or the said Vice-Chancellor of a preceding year, shall nominate two of those who have each an equal number of marks greater than any other.

The Chancellor shall on the same day publish the names of the two persons thus nominated to the members of the Senate.

On the next day the election of the Vice-Chancellor shall be made as follows:

The Proctors shall stand in scrutiny with the two senior Doctors then present in the Senate House, or if no Doctors be present, the two senior Bachelors of Divinity present. They shall first give their own votes in writing and then take the votes in writing of all persons present who have the right of voting. That one of the two persons nominated, for whom the greater number of votes is given, shall be declared to be elected.

If the election of a Vice-Chancellor becomes void before the day of entering upon office by the death of the person elected, or by any other cause, or if the office of Vice-Chancellor becomes vacant during his year of office, a new Vice-Chancellor shall be elected as nearly as possible in the same manner, as soon as possible after certain knowledge of the vacancy.

The Vice-Chancellor may nominate one or more Deputies at his discretion.

SECTION 3. *Election of the High Steward and his Deputy.*

Upon a vacancy of the office of High Steward the election of a new High Steward shall be made in the manner prescribed for the election of the Chancellor; and an instrument of his election shall be sealed and delivered to him without delay.

The Deputy High Steward shall be appointed by the High Steward by Letters Patent; but the appointment shall be subject to the approval of the Senate.

SECTION 4. *Election of the Proctors.*

The Proctors shall be nominated by the Colleges in turn, two for every year, according to the Cycle prescribed in these Statutes; and when the series of years named in the Cycle is ended, the order of nomination shall proceed as in the beginning of the Cycle and until the end of it, and so on continually.

The persons nominated shall be Members of the Senate who shall at the time of nomination have completed three years at least from their creation.

The Head of each College, or other person in his name, shall present the person nominated to the Chancellor in the presence of the Registrary before the end of the Easter Term, together with a Certificate under the hand and seal of the said Head that the person nominated has resided in the University during the last two years for the greater part of each of three Terms at least.

The Proctors shall retire from office on the first day of the Michaelmas Term in every year at 10 o'clock in the morning, and the Members of the Senate shall vote respecting the persons nominated without delay, as follows:

The two senior Masters of Arts present shall stand in scrutiny and take their own votes and the votes of other persons by the words Placet or Non Placet, and if the greater part of the voters approve the persons nominated, the senior who stood in scrutiny shall declare them to be elected.

Each Proctor elect shall give the Chancellor a Bond, binding himself to give a true account at the end of his year of office of all money received by him by virtue of his office and to pay to the Chancellor at the end of every term what is then due to the University, and to all other persons at the usual times what is due to them severally.

If a Proctor desires leave of absence he must have a Deputy approved by Grace, who shall bind himself by public declaration to the faithful discharge of the duties of the office.

If the nomination of a Proctor, having been duly made by a College, becomes void before the day of election by the death of the person nominated, or by some other cause which shall be deemed sufficient by the Chancellor and two senior Doctors present in the University, the College shall be allowed to make a second nomination. But if the cause be not then deemed sufficient, or if the College whose turn it is to nominate fails to nominate and present at the prescribed time, or if the Senate decline to elect the person nominated, or if the person elected do not duly undertake the office, the nomination and election shall be made in the manner prescribed in the fifth section of this chapter, except that the two senior Masters of Arts shall stand in scrutiny with the Chancellor.

If the office of Proctor become vacant after election by death, resignation, deprivation, or any other cause, Trinity Hall shall nominate and present a person for election, in manner as nearly similar as possible to that described above, and the person elected shall hold office until the first day of the Michaelmas Term next ensuing.

[SECTION 5. *Election of Orator, Registrary, and Esquire Bedell.*

The nominations and elections of persons to fill the offices of Orator, Registrary, and Esquire Bedell shall be conducted in the same manner as the nomination and election of the Vice-Chancellor, except that the Chancellor shall stand in scrutiny with the two Proctors. The election shall be made in every case within fourteen days (exclusive of any vacation) from the vacancy being known.

SECTION 5 A. *Election of Librarian.*

1. The election to the office of Librarian shall be made by a Board consisting of the Vice-Chancellor and ten persons elected by the Senate, five of such persons being nominated by the Council of the Senate and five by the Library Syndicate. One of the electors nominated by the Council of the Senate and one of those nominated by the Library Syndicate shall be when elected persons who are not resident in the University nor officially connected with it and of the remaining eight electors the four nominated by the Library Syndicate shall be when elected members of that Syndicate.

2. The first election of the Board shall take place as soon as conveniently may be after the passing of this Statute; at this election the members who are elected as being not resident in the University nor officially connected with it shall hold office for four years; one of the four other members nominated by the Council of the Senate shall hold office for one year, one for two years, one for three years, and one for four years, and the four other members nominated by the Library Syndicate from their own body shall hold office for like periods. All other and future elections (save in the case of elections under paragraph 3) shall be for periods of four years. The periods for which office is held (save in the case of elections under paragraph 3) shall be reckoned in all cases from the twentieth day of February next after the date of the election.

3. In case of a vacancy on the Board occurring from any other cause than the expiration of time of tenure a new

member shall be elected to fill the vacant place. He shall be nominated by the body which nominated the person whose substitute he is and under the same conditions, and he shall continue a member of the Board as long as the person whose substitute he is would have continued.

4. If a member of the Board be a candidate for the office of Librarian he shall be thereby disqualified from acting in the matter of the appointment and the other members of the Board shall have power to act without him.

5. If an election to the Board be made in the interval between the vacancy of the office of Librarian and the election of the new Librarian, the member so elected shall not have any voice in the election of the Librarian, but the person into whose place he was elected, if not a candidate for the office of Librarian, shall retain his right to vote in that election.

6. In the event of a vacancy in the office of Librarian, the Vice-Chancellor shall give public notice of it by fixing a written or printed paper on the door of the Public Schools immediately after the vacancy is made known to him if in term time, or on the first day of the following term if the vacancy is made known to him out of term time; and within fourteen days after the date of the notice of the vacancy the Vice-Chancellor shall in like manner give notice of the day for electing a new Librarian, such day to be not less than twenty-eight days after the date of the notice of the vacancy. The names of candidates shall be sent to the Vice-Chancellor not less than five days before the date of election.

7. In the event of a vacancy in the office of Librarian occurring after the division of any term and before the beginning of the next ensuing term the day for electing a new Librarian shall be some day before the end of the next ensuing term, and in the event of a vacancy occurring after the beginning and before the division of any term the day for electing a new Librarian shall be some day before the division of the next ensuing term.

8. The Board shall have power on any election to adjourn the election for the purpose of considering the qualifications of

the persons whose names have been brought before them, or ascertaining whether some other person, whom the Board might prefer, is willing to take the office.

The Board shall also have power to regulate in general its own proceedings, but no election of a Librarian shall be made unless two-thirds at least of the number of the existing Board be present at the time of voting.

9. In the final voting no election shall be made unless a majority of the votes of the members present be given for some one person; and if no election be made within twelve weeks from the day for electing, the appointment of the Librarian for that turn shall be made by the Chancellor of the University. For the purposes of this section the Vice-Chancellor shall not exercise the power herein given to the Chancellor.

10. The Board shall have power to act notwithstanding one or more vacancies in the number of its members.

11. In the event of a vacancy in the office of Librarian occurring in the interval between the passing of this Statute and the twentieth day of February next after the first election of the Board, the election to the office of Librarian shall be made as if the Statute hereby repealed remained in force.][1]

SECTION 6. *Admission to Office.*

Every person elected to an office which is to be held for more than one year shall be duly admitted to the same, and upon admission shall make the prescribed declaration.

No one who has been duly elected to any office in the University shall refuse or delay to undertake it, unless for some cause approved as sufficient by the persons by whom he was elected.

No one, however, who has attained the age of sixty years shall be compelled to undertake any office.

[1] Grace 5 of 28 January 1909, and Grace 4 of 11 February 1909, confirming a Report of the Library Syndicate (*Reporter*, 24 December 1908, page 367). Sealed, 20 February 1909. Approved by the King in Council, 18 October 1909 (*Reporter*, 26 October 1909, page 127).

CHAPTER V

OFFICES.

[SECTION 1. *Offices of Chancellor and Vice-Chancellor.*

The Chancellor shall have power to call Congregations, to admit Candidates to degrees and to reject those who have not fulfilled the required conditions, to see that all officers of the University duly perform their duties and to punish members *in statu pupillari* for disobedience to the Statutes or Ordinances of the University by suspension of Degree or other lighter sentence at his discretion.

The Chancellor shall decide whether or not any person charged with any offence shall be prosecuted in his Court.

The Chancellor shall have the custody of the box in which the University Seal is kept. The box shall have two keys of different make, one of which shall be kept by the Chancellor and the other by the Registrary, and they shall not allow the seal to be affixed to any document without the authority of a Grace of the Senate.

Except where it is otherwise specially provided, in case of an equality of votes at an election under the Statutes of the University or on a question at a meeting where the Chancellor presides he shall have a second or casting vote.

Except where it is otherwise specially provided, whatsoever in the Statutes of the University is authorised to be done by the Chancellor may be done by the Vice-Chancellor in his absence or with his consent in his presence, or even when the office of Chancellor is vacant.

SECTION 2. *Office of Orator.*

It shall be the duty of the Orator to write letters in the name of the University whenever the Chancellor or the Council of the Senate think fit, the letters to be submitted to the Senate for approval by Grace. When the Chancellor or the Council of the Senate think fit the Orator shall carry to eminent persons the letters addressed to them after these have been duly approved and sealed. He shall whenever the Chancellor or the Council of the Senate think fit welcome persons of eminence visiting the University. He shall also present to the Chancellor and University persons on whom Degrees or titles of Degrees are conferred *honoris causâ*.

If the Orator has the status of a Master of Arts he shall have precedence in rank immediately after the Doctors. He shall walk by himself in processions and have a separate seat of honour assigned to him in all public proceedings.

The Orator shall as a general rule be resident in the University throughout full term time and he shall not be absent for more than seven days in succession during full term time without appointing a deputy approved by the Chancellor.

The Senate shall determine from time to time by Grace what is to be held to constitute residence for the Orator, and it shall be the duty of the Orator to make to the Chancellor all such returns with regard to his residence as the Senate shall by Grace from time to time direct.

If at any time whether during term or during vacation the Orator be prevented by illness, or by other reasonable cause approved by the Chancellor from performing the duties of his Office the Chancellor shall appoint a Deputy provided that no Deputy shall be so appointed for a longer period than three months unless his appointment is confirmed by a Grace of the Senate. Any Deputy appointed for a longer period than three months shall receive from the Orator such stipend as may be approved by Grace, being not less than one third or more than two thirds of the proportional part of the whole annual income of the office of the Orator for the time for which the Deputy is appointed.

The Chancellor and the *sex viri* appointed under the seventh chapter of this Statute shall have power to admonish the Orator or to remove him from his Office for serious neglect of duty or for other grave misconduct.

SECTION 3. *Office of Registrary.*

It shall be the duty of the Registrary to keep an accurate record of the proceedings of the University, to place in the Registry in due order of arrangement all letters, writings, and documents delivered to him by the Chancellor, to construct indexes of reference whereby easy access may be had by the

Chancellor and all concerned in the business of the University to the knowledge of past transactions.

The Registrary shall attend for this purpose all Congregations of the Senate, the courts of the Chancellor, the audits of University accounts, matriculations, and all public proceedings of the Chancellor or of the University. He shall preserve carefully all writings and documents delivered to him and shall not allow them to be taken away or be copied without leave of the Chancellor. He shall perform such other duties as the Senate shall from time to time prescribe by Grace.

The Registrary shall as a general rule be resident in the University throughout term time and he shall not at any time be absent from the University for more than seven days in succession without appointing a Deputy approved by the Chancellor.

The Senate shall determine from time to time by Grace what is to be held to constitute residence for the Registrary, and subject to the provision contained in the last preceding paragraph what period of residence is to be required of him, and it shall be the duty of the Registrary to make to the Chancellor all such returns with regard to his residence as the Senate shall by Grace from time to time direct, provided always that the amount of residence to be required of the Registrary shall not be increased during his tenure of the Office without his consent.

If at any time whether during term or during vacation the Registrary be prevented by illness or by other reasonable cause approved by the Chancellor from performing the duties of his Office the Chancellor shall appoint a Deputy provided that no Deputy shall be so appointed for a longer period than three months unless his appointment is confirmed by a Grace of the Senate. Any Deputy appointed for a longer period than three months shall receive from the Registrary such stipend as may be approved by Grace being not less than one third or more than two thirds of the proportional part of the whole annual income of the Office of the Registrary for the time for which the Deputy is appointed.

The Chancellor and the *sex viri* appointed under the seventh chapter of this Statute shall have power to admonish the

Registrary or to remove him from his Office for serious neglect of duty or for other grave misconduct.

SECTION 4. *Office of Librarian.*

A Syndicate of the Library shall be elected according to regulations made by the University and shall have the power of making rules for the management of the Library and such rules shall be binding upon the Librarian and all other persons provided that they be not inconsistent with any Grace of the Senate.

Subject to the orders of the Library Syndicate in all cases the Librarian shall have the custody of the books of the University and shall arrange them in order in classes. He shall place them on their proper shelves at stated times and shall enter in the catalogues from time to time all newly acquired books.

The Librarian shall as a general rule be resident in the University throughout term time and he shall not at any time be absent from the University for more than seven days in succession without appointing a Deputy approved by the Chancellor.

The Senate shall determine from time to time by Grace what is to be held to constitute residence for the Librarian and subject to the provision contained in the last preceding paragraph what period of residence is to be required of him, and it shall be the duty of the Librarian to make to the Chancellor all such returns with regard to his residence as the Senate shall by Grace from time to time direct. Provided always that the amount of residence to be required of the Librarian shall not be increased during his tenure of the Office without his consent.

If at any time whether during term or during vacation the Librarian be prevented by illness or by other reasonable cause approved by the Chancellor from performing the duties of his Office the Chancellor shall appoint a Deputy provided that no Deputy shall be so appointed for a longer period than three months unless his appointment is confirmed by a Grace of the Senate. Any Deputy appointed for a longer period than three months shall receive from the Librarian such stipend as may be approved by Grace being not less than one third or more than two thirds of the proportional part of the whole annual income of the Office of the Librarian for the time for which the Deputy is appointed.

The Chancellor and the *sex viri* appointed under the seventh chapter of this Statute shall have power to admonish the Librarian or to remove him from his Office for serious neglect of duty or for other grave misconduct.

SECTION 5. *Office of Esquire Bedell.*

There shall be two Esquire Bedells equal in rank.

The Esquire Bedells shall attend the Chancellor on all public occasions and perform such other duties as may be defined from time to time by Grace.

The Chancellor and the *sex viri* appointed under the seventh chapter of this Statute shall have power to admonish an Esquire Bedell or to remove him from his Office for serious neglect of duty or for other grave misconduct.

[SECTION 5 A. *Retirement of University Officers.*

The University shall have power to require any person elected after the approval by the King in Council of this Statute to any of the offices of Orator, Registrary, Librarian, or Esquire Bedell to retire from office at such time and under such conditions as may be prescribed in any scheme relating to the retirement of officers and the provision of pensions which shall have been established by Grace before the date of his election. The University shall also have power to make the provisions of any such scheme apply to any person elected before the approval by the King in Council of this Statute or before the establishment of such scheme to one of the said offices who shall signify in writing to the Vice-Chancellor his desire to be placed under the operation of such scheme.][1]

[1] Grace 16 of 23 May 1912 and Grace 15 of 25 April 1913, confirming a Report of the Council of the Senate (*Reporter*, 25 February 1913, page 701). Sealed, 5 May 1913. Approved by the King in Council, 14 May 1914 (*Reporter*, 26 May 1914, page 1007).

SECTION 6. *The Annual Audit and the Appointment of Bankers.*

The Accounts of all moneys received and expended on behalf of the University relating to funds administered for general purposes or in trust or otherwise shall be audited once in every year.

The time of such Audit, the number of Auditors, and the mode of their appointment shall be determined by Grace.

An abstract of the accounts shall be made after the Audit as nearly as practicable in the form contained in the Schedule attached to this Chapter. Such abstract shall be signed by the Auditors and published to the University by the Vice-Chancellor.

The accounts of receipt and expenditure of money raised under the borrowing powers of the University shall be annually audited and published to the University.

The University shall have power to appoint Bankers to the University and shall from time to time make provision for the safe custody of its title deeds muniments and other valuables which are the property of the University.

SECTION 7. *Temporary Provision.*

The conditions of residence and tenure and the duties of the persons who hold the Office of Orator or Registrary or Librarian at the time when this chapter of Statute A comes into operation shall be governed by the Statutes under which they held their respective offices at the date on which this chapter of Statute A came into operation. Provided that any one of these Officers may by notice in writing to the Chancellor put himself under the operation of this chapter so soon after the approval by the King in Council of this chapter as the Senate shall have made the regulations prescribed in this chapter with regard to the residence of the Officer concerned and from the date of such notice his conditions of residence and tenure and his duties shall be governed by this chapter of Statute A.][1]

[1] Graces 2 to 8 of 30 January 1902, and Grace 2 of 13 March 1902, confirming a Report of the Council of the Senate (*Reporter*, 19 November 1901, page 216). Sealed, 27 May 1902. Approved by the King in Council, 28 March 1903 (*Reporter*, 21 April 1903. page 614).

Schedule for the form of abstract of accounts to be published by the Vice-Chancellor.

Abstract of accounts of receipts and disbursements of the University for the year ended

The University Chest.

	£ s. d.
Receipts:	
Common rents and dividends	
Quarterly payments and capitation tax of Members	
Fees for Matriculations	
Fees for Examinations	
Fees for Degrees	
Fines from the Proctors	
Other receipts	

	£ s. d.
Disbursements:	
Stipends and Salaries:	
University officers	
University servants	
Public Examiners	
Professors	
Other stipends and salaries	
Burwell	
Sermons	
Gifts	
St Mary's Church	
Senate House, University schools and rooms ..	
Registrary's office	
Observatory	
Museums and Lecture rooms	
Rates and taxes	
Repairs, insurance, &c.	
Legal expenses	
Printing and stationery	
Miscellaneous	

	£ s. d.
Balance at commencement of account	
Total receipts	

	£ s. d.
Total expenditure	
Balance in hand	

The Common University Fund.

Receipts:	£ s. d.
Peterhouse	
Clare College	
Pembroke College	
Corpus Christi College	
Gonville and Caius College	
Trinity Hall	
King's College	
Queens' College	
St Catharine's College	
Jesus College	
Christ's College	
St John's College	
Magdalene College	
Trinity College	
Emmanuel College	
Sidney Sussex College	
Downing College	
Miscellaneous	

Disbursements:	£ s. d.
Professors' stipends	
Readers' stipends	
Lecturers' stipends	
Pensions	
Demonstrators, Curators, &c.	
Erection of buildings	
Maintenance and furniture of buildings ..	
Sites for buildings	
Interest and payments on account of borrowed money	
Miscellaneous	

	£ s. d.
Balance at commencement of account	
Total receipts	

	£ s. d.
Total expenditure	
Balance in hand	

Trust and other Funds.

Abstracts of accounts of the receipts and disbursements of the following Trust and other Funds shall be published annually in such a form as to shew the receipts and disbursements of each separately:

Professorships.
Scholarships.
Prizes.
University Library.
Fitzwilliam Museum.
Botanic Garden.
Local Examinations.
Local Lectures.
Board for non-Collegiate Students
Teachers' Training.
Miscellaneous.

CHAPTER VI

SERMONS AND COMMEMORATIONS.

SECTION 1. *Sermons.*

[Sermons shall be preached in the University Church every Sunday during Term; also on Christmas Day, Good Friday, Easter Day, and Ascension Day, and on such other days as may be appointed by the Chancellor or by Grace of the Senate.][1]

No one shall be allowed in any sermon before the University to impugn the doctrine or discipline of the Church of England as established by law.

The University may require Members of the Senate who are in Holy Orders to preach according to regulations made from time to time for that purpose, or to make such other provision for preachers as may seem expedient.

SECTION 2. *Commemoration of Benefactors.*

There shall be a Commemoration of Benefactors yearly in the University Church, at such time and in such manner as the University may prescribe by Grace.

[1] Grace 3 of 6 December 1894, and Grace 1 of 31 January 1895, confirming a Report of the Select Preachers Syndicate (*Reporter*, 20 November 1894, page 224). Sealed, 8 February 1895. Approved by the Queen in Council, 13 May 1896 (*Reporter*, 26 May 1896, page 801).

CHAPTER VII

DISCIPLINE.

For the due maintenance of good order and discipline within the University, the University shall from time to time prescribe such regulations as may be thought expedient in regard to the wearing of Academical dress, the rendering assistance and obedience to all persons in authority, the definition and determination of offences, the penalties on offenders, and the manner in which pecuniary penalties and fines shall be disposed of.

The Chancellor and six persons, called the *sex viri*, elected singly by Grace for two years, or four at least of the number, of whom one shall always be the Chancellor, shall adjudicate respecting all persons not *in statu pupillari* charged with offences against the Statutes or Ordinances of the University. They shall punish offenders, at their discretion, by deprivation or suspension of Degree, or any lighter sentence. Appeal may be made from their sentence to the University in the manner described in the eighth chapter of this Statute.

In the case of graver offences, the court of discipline for persons *in statu pupillari* shall consist of the Chancellor and six Heads of Colleges appointed by Grace to serve for three years in such manner that two of the six shall go out of office every year but be capable of re-election. No sentence involving deprivation of Degree, rustication, or expulsion shall be valid without the concurrence of the Chancellor and three at least of the other members of the Court.

If the Head of the College to which a person *in statu pupillari* charged with any offence belongs be not a member of the Court, notice shall be given to him to enable him to be present as an assessor, but he shall not be entitled to vote. Regulations for the procedure of the Court shall be made by the Court from time to time, subject to the approval of the Senate.

[If the Chancellor and the *sex viri* or four at least of their number, of whom the Chancellor shall be one, shall report to the Council of the Senate that it has been proved to their satisfaction that a graduate of the University has been convicted of a crime for which he has been sentenced to penal servitude or imprisonment and that such crime is one which renders him unfit to be a graduate of the University, then the Council of the Senate may propose to the Senate a Grace depriving him of his Degree or Degrees and of all privileges enjoyed by him as a graduate of the University, and in case the Grace is approved by the Senate he shall be deprived accordingly.][1]

CHAPTER VIII

Judicial Proceedings.

All causes and contentions which belong to the cognizance of the University shall be submitted to the judgment of the Chancellor or the Commissary, unless one of the litigants be a person having the Degree of Master of Arts, or some equal or higher Degree, in which case the Chancellor shall have jurisdiction. They shall be determined with as little delay as possible, and without the formalities of law.

Appeal from a judgment of the Commissary may be made to the Chancellor within twenty-four hours after judgment given.

Appeal from a judgment of the Chancellor, whether the cause was heard by him in the first instance or an appeal from the Commissary, may be made to the Senate within two days after judgment given; and the appeal shall be made known by the Appellant to one of the Proctors within three days after judgment given.

The Proctor shall give notice immediately to the Judge whose judgment is appealed against that he take no fresh

[1] Grace 4 of 9 May 1895, and Grace 1 of 13 June 1895, confirming a Report of the Council of the Senate (*Reporter*, 23 April 1895, page 713). Sealed, 23 July 1895. Approved by the Queen in Council, 13 May 1896 (*Reporter*, 26 May 1896, page 799).

steps during the appeal; the usual caution determined by Grace being first deposited with him, to be restored to the Appellant if his appeal be sustained, or to be applied to the use of the University, if his appeal be found to have been without sufficient cause, or if after the assignment of Judges Delegate he either fails to prosecute his appeal, or puts it off for more than ten days. If also, through fault of the Appellant, the hearing of the case be delayed for more than twenty days, the appeal shall be held to be abandoned and be dismissed.

A second appeal to the University shall on no account be admitted.

The Judges Delegate shall give judgment with as little delay as possible, and the judgment of a majority of them shall be binding.

Five Judges Delegate shall be assigned in every appeal. They shall be nominated by the Council of the Senate for election by Grace singly. If any of the persons nominated be not elected by the Senate, the Council shall nominate others in their places. If any of the persons so nominated in the second instance be not elected, the Council shall again nominate others in their places. If any of the persons so nominated in the third instance fail to be elected, the major part of the Council shall for that turn elect others in their places, so as to complete the whole number of five Judges.

CHAPTER IX

Ordinances of the University.

[The University shall have power to make Ordinances for the encouragement of learning and the maintenance of good order and discipline provided that they be not contrary to anything contained in the Statutes of the University.

The University shall have power to require contributions of money from any of its members for University purposes as also payments from candidates for matriculation or for Degrees or on account of services rendered by University Officers.

The University may accept from any of its members who have been admitted to their first Degree sums of money to be determined by Grace as compositions in lieu of future annual payments.][1]

CHAPTER X

Repeal of existing Statutes.

The Statutes of the University confirmed by Order of the Queen in Council, 31 July 1858, with the exception of the Statutes for the establishment and regulation of Hostels and the four Statutes relating to questions of a temporary nature framed 24 March 1858, by the Cambridge University Commissioners under 19 and 20 Vict. c. 88, are hereby repealed, yet not so as to revive the Royal Statutes which were repealed by the said Statutes of 31 July 1858. The Statute for the Degree of Master in Surgery confirmed by Order of the Queen in Council, 16 April 1861, is hereby repealed.

All Ordinances also of the University which are inconsistent with these Statutes are hereby repealed.

[CHAPTER XI

Status pupillaris.

The following persons shall be deemed to be *in statu pupillari*, namely:

Undergraduates, Bachelors of Music, Bachelors of Law, Bachelors of Arts, Bachelors of Surgery.

Bachelors of Medicine, Inceptors in Arts Law or Surgery, and Doctors Designate in Music shall be deemed to be not *in statu pupillari*.][2]

[1] Grace 3 of 27 February 1902, and Grace 3 of 13 March 1902, confirming a Report of the Council of the Senate (*Reporter*, 28 January 1902, page 481). Sealed, 27 May 1902. Approved by the King in Council, 28 March 1903 (*Reporter*, 21 April 1903, page 614).

[2] Grace 5 of 21 November 1889, and Grace 4 of 25 February 1892, confirming a Report of the Council of the Senate (*Reporter*, 15 October 1889, page 62). Sealed, 26 February 1892. Approved by the Queen in Council, 16 May 1893 (*Reporter*, 30 May 1893, page 876).

DECLARATIONS

In Admissione ad Officia

Cancellarii vel alius cujusvis officiarii.

Dabis fidem te bene et fideliter praestiturum omnia quae spectent ad officium cancellarii (vel alius cujusvis officiarii) academiae Cantabrigiensis.

Respondeat admittendus Ita do fidem.

Vicarii alicujus.

Dabis fidem te bene et fideliter praestiturum ea omnia, ad quae deputatus sis a procuratore (vel alio quovis officiario), quatenus ad ejus officium spectent, quoad absit.

Respondeat admittendus Ita do fidem.

Lectoris.

Dabis fidem te omnes et singulas ordinationes de lectura tua pro virili juxta vim, formam et effectum earundem observaturum.

Respondeat admittendus Ita do fidem.

CYCLE FOR THE NOMINATION OF PROCTORS

1914	Jesus College. St John's College.
1915	Queens' College. Trinity Hall.
1916	Gonville and Caius College. Sidney Sussex College.
1917	King's College. Emmanuel College.
1918	Trinity College. Peterhouse.
1919	St John's College. St Catharine's College.
1920	Pembroke College. Christ's College.
1921	Clare College. Corpus Christi College.
1922	Queens' College. Trinity College.
1923	Magdalene College. St John's College.
1924	King's College. Jesus College.
1925	Gonville and Caius College. Sidney Sussex College.

1926	Peterhouse. Emmanuel College.
1927	Trinity College. Pembroke College.
1928	St John's College. Christ's College.
1929	Clare College. St Catharine's College.
1930	Corpus Christi College. Queens' College.
1931	King's College. Trinity College.
1932	Trinity Hall. St John's College.
1933	Magdalene College. Downing College.
1934	Peterhouse. Gonville and Caius College.
1935	Pembroke College. Jesus College.
1936	Trinity College. Christ's College.
1937	St John's College. Sidney Sussex College.
1938	King's College. Emmanuel College.
1939	Clare College. St Catharine's College.
1940	Queens' College. Trinity College.
1941	Corpus Christi College. St John's College.
1942	Peterhouse. Gonville and Caius College.
1943	Pembroke College. Magdalene College.
1944	Jesus College. Christ's College.
1945	Trinity College. King's College.
1946	St John's College. Sidney Sussex College.
1947	Clare College. Emmanuel College.
1948	Queens' College. St Catharine's College.
1949	Gonville and Caius College. Trinity Hall.
1950	Corpus Christi College. Trinity College.
1951	St John's College. Peterhouse.
1952	Pembroke College. Christ's College.
1953	King's College. Magdalene College.
1954	Jesus College. Trinity College.
1955	Clare College. St John's College.
1956	Queens' College. Sidney Sussex College.
1957	Gonville and Caius College. Emmanuel College.
1958	Downing College. St Catharine's College.
1959	Trinity College. Peterhouse.
1960	St John's College. King's College.
1961	Christ's College. Corpus Christi College.
1962	Pembroke College. Clare College.
1963	Magdalene College. Trinity College.

STATUTE B

Approved by the Queen in Council, 29 *June* 1882.

This Statute is declared to be a Statute for the University of Cambridge.

CHAPTER I

For Contributions of Colleges for University Purposes.

1. Each of the Colleges shall pay to the University in every year for University purposes the sum determined by subsequent provisions of this Statute, according to a percentage on its income.

The income of a College shall, for the purposes of this Chapter, be taken to be the gross income, external and internal, including the profits, if any, derived from the hall, kitchen, buttery, sale of commodities, and supply of service, including also such parts of the income arising from the investment of sums received from members of the College as compositions for dues thereafter payable to the University or to the College or both as may be applied, either yearly or otherwise, to the general revenue of the College or to any purpose within the College; not including, however, the rents paid for rooms, but including instead thereof the amount at which the College buildings are from time to time assessed under the provisions of the Cambridge Award Act, 1856, or any other Act for the assessment of property in the town of Cambridge for the purposes of parochial or municipal rates, after deducting from such gross income any sums paid thereout under the several heads next following:

(*a*) Rates, taxes, and insurance on the College buildings.

(*b*) Rates, taxes, insurances, tithe or other rentcharge, fee farm rents, quit rents, fines on copyhold estates, fines on renewals of leases, if and when paid by the College.

(*c*) The University dues paid to the University in each year by the College for such of its members as have not made compositions for dues payable to the University or the College.

(*d*) The cost of maintenance and repairs of the College buildings.

(*e*) The cost of maintenance, repairs, and improvements on the College estates incurred by the College.

(*f*) Necessary repairs of chancels in all cases where the same are chargeable upon the College and paid by it.

(*g*) Compulsory charges on the College estates or general revenue for the augmentation of benefices, and stipends of perpetual curates in parishes where the College possesses tithe rentcharge or land given in lieu of tithe.

(*h*) The cost of management of the College estates including the stipends paid to College officers for the purpose.

(*i*) The interest on debts and loans and the repayment of principal money by instalments in all cases in which the debt has been incurred or the loan contracted for the extension of the College buildings or for the improvement of the College estates and such instalments are spread over a period of not less than twenty years.

(*k*) Such receipts from minerals or other sources as the College is by law required to treat as capital.

(*l*) Such portions of the income of trust funds as are applicable exclusively to purposes without the College.

(*m*) One half of the income derived from the tuition fees paid by students.

[2. Subject to the deductions mentioned in the clause next following the aggregate sum to be contributed by the Colleges in each of the years 1891, 1892, 1893, 1894, 1895, shall be not less than £20,000 nor more than £24,000; in each of the years 1896, 1897, 1898, 1899, 1900, 1901, 1902, not less than £25,000 nor more than £30,000; and in every subsequent year, £30,000 or such larger sum being not greater than £30,500 as may be found more convenient for the purpose of calculating the rate *per centum* in any year.

Provided that in case it appears at any time hereafter to the Financial Board hereinafter constituted that the aggregate income of the Colleges has fallen so low that the contribution required under this Chapter would be an excessive burden upon the Colleges, the Chancellor may, upon the application of the Financial Board, inquire into the matter and if he be satisfied that the fact is so he may at his discretion direct that the amount to be levied under this Chapter be diminished for any period not exceeding five years by any sum not exceeding one-fifth part of the minimum amount named in this Chapter for each year of such period. For the purposes of this proviso the Vice-Chancellor shall not exercise the power herein given to the Chancellor.

3. From the contributions so determined each College shall be entitled to deduct for each Professorial Fellowship in the College held by a Professor of the University :

In each of the years 1891, 1892, 1893, 1894, 1895, £160 ; and in every subsequent year, £200.][1]

CHAPTER II

For the Common University Fund.

The accounts of the receipt and expenditure of money paid by the Colleges for University purposes shall be kept distinct from the other accounts of the University. Such accounts shall be called the accounts of the Common University Fund.

Payments out of this Fund shall be made for the following purposes only, viz. :

The stipends of Professors, Readers, and University Lecturers ;

Retiring pensions[2] ;

[1] Grace 5 of 4 February 1892, and Grace 2 of 12 May 1892, confirming a Report of the Council of the Senate (*Reporter*, 15 December 1891, page 312). Sealed, 12 May 1892. Approved by the Queen in Council, 16 May 1893 (*Reporter*, 30 May 1893, page 877).

[2] The omission from this paragraph of the words "for *emeriti* Professors and Readers" was approved by the King in Council, 14 May 1914 (see *Reporter*, 26 May 1914, page 1007). For further references see Chapter VI, Section 10a.

The salaries of Demonstrators, Superintendents, and Curators, in the several departments of learning and science;

The erection of Museums, Laboratories, Libraries, Lecture-rooms, and other rooms for University business, together with the provision of sites for such buildings, and interest on money borrowed for such purposes, and sinking funds for the repayment thereof;

The maintenance and furniture of such buildings, including the payment of assistants, skilled workmen and servants, and the provision of books, maps, plans, models, instruments, and apparatus;

Grants of money for special work in the way of research, and for investigations conducted in any branch of learning or science connected with the studies of the University.

The amount of the sum paid in any year for the provision of sites and for the erection of buildings and for the maintenance and furniture of buildings, including interest and payments towards sinking funds for the repayment of money borrowed for such purposes, shall not exceed one-third of the income of the Fund for that year.

No payment out of the Fund shall be made without the authority of a Grace of the Senate.

CHAPTER III

For Professorial Fellowships.

1. Besides the Professorial Fellowships assigned in certain cases to particular Professorships in accordance with Schedule A of this Chapter, there shall be in the Colleges Professorial Fellowships not so assigned as enumerated in Schedule B of this Chapter.

2. So long as a Professorial Fellowship is vacant in any College, the College, in addition to the payment provided by

Chapter I for Contributions of Colleges for University Purposes, shall pay annually to the Common University Fund the excess (if any) of one Fellowship dividend over the sum which the said College would be entitled by the Chapter aforesaid to deduct from the contribution of the College in respect of such Fellowship if it had been full.

3. The electors to Fellowships in any College at which a Professorial Fellowship not assigned to any Professorship in accordance with Schedule A of this Chapter is vacant, shall be at liberty to elect thereto any Professor not already holding a Professorial Fellowship, or the Headship of a College counting as such as hereinafter provided.

4. If the Professor so elected be admitted to the Fellowship he shall thereby vacate any Headship or Fellowship he may hold at any other College.

5. If a Fellow of a College at which one of the Professorial Fellowships enumerated in Schedule B is vacant hold or be elected to any Professorship other than those mentioned in Schedule A of this Chapter, and be not already holding a Professorial Fellowship, he shall, so far as the University is concerned, be deemed to be transferred to the vacant Professorial Fellowship.

6. The holder of a Professorial Fellowship at any College shall not vacate his Fellowship by lapse of time so long as he remains Professor, nor by resigning his Professorship merely for admission into another Professorship in the University, nor by vacating a periodically terminable Professorship by expiration of the period provided he be forthwith re-elected; but if in any other way he cease to be Professor a Professorial Fellowship at the College shall be vacated thereby, subject to the provision next hereinafter contained.

If a Professor holding a Professorial Fellowship vacates his Professorship, but is entitled by reason of past service in the College, or otherwise, to retain his Fellowship, a Fellowship vacant at the same time, or the Fellowship next vacant, shall become a Professorial Fellowship in place of that held by him, and until such vacancy occurs the College shall pay to the Common University Fund the sum payable under Section 2 of this Chapter during the vacancy of a Professorial Fellowship in addition to its ordinary contribution.

7. If the Head of a College be elected to any Professorship other than those enumerated in Schedule A of this Chapter, or any Professor holding a Professorship other than those enumerated in Schedule A of this Chapter be elected to the Headship of a College, one vacant Professorial Fellowship (if any) in the College of which he is the Head shall remain vacant so long as he holds both offices, and the payments by the College to the University shall be the same as if the said Fellowship were held by a Professor.

8. So long as any of the Professors enumerated in Schedule C of Chapter VI holds any Fellowship or Headship the stipend of the Professorship in any year shall be reduced by £200. Provided, however, that if in any year the deduction of £200 would reduce the stipend of a Professor below the amount derived from the endowment, the stipend of the Professor for that year shall be the amount derived from the endowment.

9. In every College at which one Fellowship is required by this Statute to be a Professorial Fellowship, one of the two Fellowships which shall become vacant next after the approval of this Statute by the Queen in Council, or one of the Fellowships, if any, which shall be vacant at the time of such approval, shall be the Professorial Fellowship if there be then no Professor holding a Professorship other than those mentioned in Schedule A of this Chapter on the Foundation of the College, but if there be then one of the said Professors on the Foundation of the College, the Fellowship which he holds shall be the Professorial Fellowship.

In every College at which more than one Fellowship is required by this Statute to be a Professorial Fellowship, if at the time of the approval of this Statute there be on the Foundation of the College the full number required of such Professors as aforesaid, the Fellowships which they hold shall be the Professorial Fellowships; but if there be one, or more than one, less than the full number required, the Fellowship which shall become vacant next after the approval of this Statute by the Queen in Council, or one of the Fellowships, if any, which shall be vacant at the time of such approval, shall be a Professorial Fellowship, as shall also the first Fellowship which shall be or shall become vacant in each successive period of two years after the expiration of two years from the date of such approval, until either in this way or by the operation of Section 5 of this Chapter, or by the election to Fellowships of one or more Professors holding Professorships other than those mentioned in Schedule A of this Chapter, the required number of Professorial Fellowships is complete.

If at the time of the approval of this Statute there be more than the required number of such Professors holding Fellowships or the Headship at any College, the College shall determine, by College Order, which of the Fellowships held by such Professors shall be Professorial Fellowships.

No Professor shall be deemed to be a Professor of the University within the meaning of this Statute unless by the rules which govern his Professorship he be liable to residence and duties within the University.

Schedule A.

PROFESSORIAL FELLOWSHIPS ASSIGNED TO PARTICULAR PROFESSORSHIPS.

Trinity ..	Regius of Greek.
Emmanuel ..	Dixie of Ecclesiastical History.
Downing ..	Law. Medicine.

Schedule B.

PROFESSORIAL FELLOWSHIPS NOT ASSIGNED TO PARTICULAR PROFESSORSHIPS.

Colleges	Professorial Fellowships
Peterhouse	1
Clare	1
Pembroke	1
Gonville and Caius	2
Trinity Hall	1
Corpus Christi	1
King's	4
Queens'	1
St Catharine's	1
Jesus	1
Christ's	1
St John's	5
Magdalene	1
Trinity	5
Sidney Sussex	1
	27

CHAPTER IV

FOR THE FINANCIAL BOARD OF THE UNIVERSITY.

1. A Financial Board shall be appointed for the care and management of the property and income of the University, consisting of the Vice-Chancellor, two members of the General Board of Studies elected by that Board, four members of the Senate elected by the Colleges in common, and four members of the Senate elected by Grace on the nomination of the Council of the Senate.

2. For the purpose of the election of members of the Board by the Colleges in common, each College shall elect one representative. The Vice-Chancellor shall summon a meeting of the representatives of the Colleges for the election of members of the Senate to serve on the Board. Each representative shall have one vote, together with one additional vote for each complete £100 for which the College is assessed in the preceding year for University purposes. At the first election the representatives shall have the following number of votes respectively.

	Number of Votes
Peterhouse	2
Clare	3
Pembroke	3
Gonville and Caius	4
Trinity Hall	2
Corpus Christi	2
King's	7
Queens'	2
St Catharine's	2
Jesus	4
Christ's	4
St John's	9
Magdalene	2
Trinity	12
Emmanuel	3
Sidney Sussex	2
Downing	2

3. Of the members of the Board elected by the Colleges in common, not more than one shall belong to any one College.

4. In the elections first made after the approval of this Statute by the Queen in Council, one of the members elected by the General Board of Studies shall be elected for two years, and one for four years; two of the members elected by the Colleges shall be elected for two years, and two for

four years; and two of the members elected by Grace shall be elected for three years, and two for five years.

At every subsequent election, except as hereinafter provided, the member shall be elected for four years.

5. All members retiring from the Board shall be capable of re-election.

6. In case of a vacancy occurring from any other cause than the expiration of the time of tenure, a new member shall be elected in the same manner as the person whose substitute he is to fill the vacant place, and shall continue to be a member of the Board as long as the person whose substitute he is would have continued.

7. The Board shall be competent to regulate its own proceedings, but no business shall be transacted at any meeting unless five members at least be present.

8. The Board shall have power to employ a secretary, a land agent, and such other officers as they think necessary; the stipends and remuneration of all such officers being determined by Grace.

9. It shall be the duty of the Board to prepare and publish in every year a statement of the income and expenditure of the University during the preceding year, together with a report of its property and liabilities, and an estimate of its probable income and expenditure in the ensuing year.

10. It shall be the duty of the Board also to prepare in every year a statement of the sum within the limits prescribed by Chapter I, Section 2, which in their judgment ought to be raised in the ensuing year by contributions of the Colleges for University purposes. Such statement shall be submitted to the Senate for approval by Grace, and the sum if so approved shall be raised. When no sum is so approved, the minimum named in Chapter I, Section 2, shall be raised.

When the sum to be raised has been thus determined, the Board shall declare the respective incomes of the several Colleges subject to per-centage according to the returns of the previous year, shall fix the per-centage and assess the Colleges severally for their proportional payments, and collect the money.

11. The Board shall have power to require from any College explanations of the accounts of the College published by the Vice-Chancellor, and may thereupon for the purpose of the assessment correct and adjust such accounts, subject to appeal to the Chancellor as hereinafter provided.

If any question arises between the Financial Board and any College respecting the amount of income subject to per-centage in any year, the matter shall be referred to the judgment of the Chancellor, whose determination shall be final.

The Chancellor shall have power to require on such occasions from the College the production of all accounts and documents which he may wish to see.

For the purposes of this section the Vice-Chancellor shall not exercise the power herein given to the Chancellor.

12. The Board shall prepare and present to the Senate as occasion shall require reports as to prospective expenditure and the means of meeting the same, and shall lay before the Senate such recommendations as may be necessary for sanctioning and providing for future expenditure, and for the due administration of the finances of the University.

13. The Board shall undertake the care and management of all lands, houses, buildings, and other property belonging to the University or held in trust for University purposes, providing for ordinary repairs and insurances, arranging the conditions of letting property on lease or otherwise, and taking care that such provisions are duly fulfilled by the tenants; provided, however, that all leases, and all questions concerning repairs, improvements, alterations, allowances to tenants, and other matters which involve more than ordinary outlay, shall be referred to the judgment and decision of the Senate. Provided also that, subject to such general control as the Board may think fit from time to time to exercise, the detailed management of the University Press and other special departments, including the buildings belonging to them, may be committed by the Senate to Special Boards or Syndicates appointed for the purpose.

14. The Board shall pay out of the Common University Fund or other income of the University all stipends, pensions, and other outgoings authorised by the Statutes and Ordinances of the University, together with all sums voted by Grace for expenditure on the University library, museums, lecture rooms, laboratories, and other institutions, for the erection, establishment, and maintenance of new institutions, for the encouragement and aid of research, and for other objects.

15. The Board shall arrange for the consideration and decision of the Senate the terms and conditions of all loans which the University may desire to obtain on security of its property or income for University purposes, taking care, however, to provide in the case of every such loan for the repayment of the money borrowed by annual instalments extending over a period of not more than thirty years.

16. The Board shall perform all such other duties as may be committed to them from time to time by Grace.

CHAPTER V

For Boards of Studies.

1. The Statute for the appointment of Boards of Studies confirmed by Order of the Queen in Council, 27 August 1860, is hereby repealed.

Special Boards.

2. The University shall appoint Special Boards of Studies for all important departments of study recognised in the University, to consist of the Professors hereinafter assigned to such Boards severally, together with such Readers, University Lecturers, Examiners, and other persons as may be appointed from time to time by or under the authority of a Grace of the Senate.

3. The number of such Special Boards to be appointed as soon as may be after the approval of this Statute by the Queen in Council shall be twelve, viz., for

Divinity.
Law.
Medicine.
Classics.
Oriental Studies.
Medieval and Modern Languages.
Mathematics.
Physics and Chemistry.
Biology and Geology.
History and Archaeology.
Moral Science.
Music.

But the University shall have power to vary the number and designation of Special Boards from time to time hereafter on the recommendation of the General Board of Studies, provided that the whole number of such Boards shall never be less than eight[1].

4. The Professors assigned to the said twelve Boards shall be as follows:

Divinity	Lady Margaret's. Regius. Norrisian. Hulsean. Ely.
Law	Regius. Downing. Whewell.
Medicine	Regius. Anatomy. Downing. Pathology.
Classics	Regius of Greek. Latin.
Oriental Studies	Regius of Hebrew. Arabic (Sir Thomas Adams's). Arabic (Lord Almoner's). Sanskrit.
Medieval and Modern Languages	Anglo-Saxon.

[1] Under this clause there have been established by Ordinance a Special Board for Economics and Politics and a Special Board of Indian Civil Service Studies.

Mathematics	Lucasian. Plumian. Lowndean. Sadleirian.
Physics and Chemistry	Chemistry. Jacksonian. Mineralogy. Cavendish of Physics. Mechanism and Applied Mechanics.
Biology and Geology	Botany. Woodwardian. Zoology and Comparative Anatomy. Physiology.
History and Archaeology	Regius of Modern History. Disney. Slade. Dixie.
Moral Science	Knightbridge. Political Economy[1]. Mental Philosophy and Logic.
Music	Music.

But the University shall have power to vary by Grace from time to time hereafter on the recommendation of the General Board of Studies the assignment of Professors to the several Special Boards, and to appoint any Professors *ex officio* members of one or more Special Boards other than those to which they shall have been severally assigned.

5. One or more of the elected members of every Special Board shall retire after a definite term of service, but the length of such term of service, the times of election, and other details of the constitution of the Special Boards shall be determined from time to time by Grace.

6. It shall be the duty of every Special Board to consult together from time to time on all matters relating to the studies and examinations of the University in its department,

[1] The Professor of Political Economy is now assigned by Grace to the Special Board for Economics and Politics.

and to prepare, whenever it appears to them desirable, and present to the Vice-Chancellor, a report to be published by him to the University.

The Board shall also, after consultation with the Professors, Readers, and University Lecturers connected with its department, frame a scheme of lectures in every year: taking care to provide that the subject of the said lectures be determined with regard to the general objects of every particular Professorship, and so as to distribute the several branches of learning in the department among the said Professors, Readers, and University Lecturers; having regard also to the regulations and instructions which the General Board of Studies may have issued.

7. Every scheme so settled by any Special Board shall be submitted to the General Board of Studies; and no scheme shall be taken to be final until it has received the approval of the said General Board.

8. Two or more Special Boards may deliberate together and take such action in common as may appear to them desirable.

General Board.

9. The University shall appoint a General Board of Studies, consisting of the Vice-Chancellor, one member of each Special Board of Studies elected by that Special Board, and eight members of the Senate elected by Grace.

10. One or more of the members of the General Board shall retire after a definite term of service, but the length of such term of service, the times of election, and other details of the constitution of the General Board shall be determined from time to time by Grace.

11. In case of a vacancy occurring from any other cause than the expiration of the time of tenure, a new member shall be elected in the same manner as the person whose substitute he is to fill the vacant place, and he shall continue to be a member of the General Board as long as the person whose substitute he is would have continued.

12. It shall be the duty of the General Board to consult together from time to time on all matters relating to the studies and examinations of the University, including the maintenance and improvement of existing institutions, and the establishment and maintenance of new institutions. They shall prepare, whenever it appears to them desirable, and present to the Vice-Chancellor a report to be published by him to the University.

13. The General Board shall issue from time to time as they think fit, regulations and instructions in respect to the subjects and character of the lectures to be delivered, the superintendence of laboratory work, the subordination when necessary of the Readers and University Lecturers to the Professors, the extent to which in any cases discourses shall be supplemented by oral or written examinations, the times and places of lecturing, the arrangements to be made for the distribution of students among the different teachers, so as to secure classes of suitable size, and to group separately the more and less advanced students, and any other matters affecting the method of instruction to be pursued, with the view of providing suitable and efficient education in all subjects of University study for all students whether more or less advanced who may require it.

14. The General Board shall also consider the schemes for lectures in every year submitted to it by the several Special Boards, and shall approve the said schemes or remit them for further consideration with alterations and amendments, or, if necessary, frame schemes; provided that, in case the General Board of Studies and any of the Special Boards shall be unable to agree as to any scheme, the question shall be referred to a meeting of the Members of the General Board and of the Special Board deliberating together, whose decision shall be final. When such schemes have been finally determined, the General Board shall present them to the Vice-Chancellor for publication.

15. The General Board shall perform such other duties as may be committed to it from time to time by the Senate.

CHAPTER VI

For Professors.

1. The Statute for the additional endowment of existing Professorships, and for the establishment of additional Professorships, which was confirmed by Order of the Queen in Council, 16 April 1861, is hereby repealed.

2. Professorships shall be established in the University for the following subjects, viz.:

Physiology,
Pathology,
Mental Philosophy and Logic.

The Professors shall be appointed in such order as the University may think fit, as soon as sufficient funds can be provided conveniently for the purpose from the Common University Fund or from other sources.

The Professors of Physiology and of Pathology shall not be allowed to undertake the private practice of medicine or surgery.

3. The University shall have power to establish from time to time Professorships for other departments of learning or science; provided that in every case where it is proposed to establish a new Professorship, the Grace for establishing it be offered to the Senate not more than fourteen days before, nor more than fourteen days after, the division of any term, and that notice of such Grace be given to the Senate in the term preceding that in which the Grace is offered. Professorships so established may be limited to a definite term of years or to the tenure of office of one Professor only; and if not so limited, they may be suspended or discontinued on the occurrence of any vacancy.

4. The election to the Professorships established by or under the foregoing provisions of this Chapter shall be governed by Chapter IX, for Elections to certain Professorships, the Special Board of Studies in every case being the Board with which the Professorship is connected.

5. The Professorships shall be governed by Chapter IX, for the Residence and Duties of Professors and Readers, and the Professors shall comply with the provisions of the said Chapter.

6. The University shall have power to accept benefactions for the endowment of new Professorships, and to establish such Professorships; the regulations for the election, duties, residence, and government of the Professors, and the conditions and duration of tenure being determined by the Graces by which the Professorships are established severally. Such regulations may be altered from time to time by Grace, except so far as they may have been prescribed by any instrument of endowment which is still in force. The University shall make provision where necessary for the payment of suitable stipends to the persons holding such Professorships.

7. The University shall have power also to provide from time to time, by Grace, additional stipends for Professorships already established in the University.

8. Yearly stipends in accordance with Schedule C of this Chapter shall be paid to the Professors enumerated in that Schedule, subject to the provisions of Chapter III, Section 8, such stipends including the income, if any, arising from endowments.

Schedule C.

Professors with Stipends subject to deduction:

	£
Regius of Law	800
Regius of Physic	700
Arabic (Sir Thomas Adams's)	700
Lucasian	850
Knightbridge	700
Chemistry	850
Plumian	800
Anatomy	600
Regius of Modern History	800
Botany	700

	£
Woodwardian	700
Lowndean	800
Jacksonian	800
Mineralogy	600
Political Economy	700
Sadleirian	850
Zoology and Comparative Anatomy ..	700
Sanskrit	700
Latin	800
Cavendish of Physics	850
Mechanism and Applied Mechanics ..	700
Physiology..	800
Pathology	800
Mental Philosophy and Logic	700

The University shall have power to vary the said stipends from time to time on the recommendation of the General Board of Studies, provided that no such variation shall affect the interest of a Professor without his consent, or diminish the stipends of persons holding Professorships founded less than fifty years before the tenth day of August, 1877, below the sums derived from their several incomes of endowment.

Subject to the like power of variation, such addition shall be made in each year to the amounts received from Downing College by the Downing Professor of the Laws of England and the Downing Professor of Medicine as shall raise their whole yearly stipends, not including their lodges or any equivalent for them, to amounts greater by £500 and £300 respectively than the amount of a Fellowship dividend at Downing College for that year.

The yearly stipend of £360 shall be paid to the Regius Professor of Greek in addition to the stipend of £290 paid to the said Professor by Trinity College.

9. The preceding clause shall come into operation in the case of new Professorships, on the establishment of the Professorship, and in the case of existing Professorships upon the next vacancy of the Professorship, or at such earlier time as

the Professor may come under this Statute, in accordance with the provisions of Chapter XIX.

10. The University shall have power to give pensions to retiring Professors according to circumstances, as the Senate may think fit.

[10a. The University shall have power to require any Professor elected after the approval by the King in Council of this Statute to retire from office at such time and under such conditions as may be prescribed in any scheme relating to the retirement of Professors and the provision of pensions which shall have been established by Grace before the date of his election. The University shall also have power to make the provisions of any such scheme apply to any Professor elected before the approval by the King in Council of this Statute or before the establishment of such scheme who shall signify in writing to the Vice-Chancellor his desire to be placed under the operation of such scheme.][1]

11. The University shall have power to determine from time to time the application of the income of vacant or suspended Professorships.

[12. Except in cases in which the University shall by Grace determine otherwise, two Professorships in the University shall not be held at the same time by the same person; and upon a Professor's acceptance of a second Professorship, that already held by him shall become, *ipso facto*, vacant.

13. Except in cases in which the University shall by Grace determine otherwise, the office of Professor shall not be tenable together with that of Reader or that of University Lecturer in the University; and if a person holding any one of these three offices shall accept either of the others he shall thereby, *ipso facto*, vacate the one previously held by him.][2]

[1] Grace 16 of 23 May 1913, and Grace 15 of 25 April 1913, confirming a Report of the Council of the Senate (*Reporter*, 25 February 1913, page 701). Sealed, 5 May 1913. Approved by the King in Council, 14 May 1914 (*Reporter*, 26 May 1914, page 1007).

[2] Grace 2 of 7 March 1908, and Grace 2 of 12 March 1908, confirming a Report of the Council of the Senate (*Reporter*, 4 February 1908, page 532).

CHAPTER VII

FOR READERS.

1. In connexion with the departments of study for which Special Boards of Studies are appointed there shall be a body of teachers called Readers.

2. The number of Readers to be appointed, after the approval of this Statute by the Queen in Council, shall be not less than twenty, and the subjects to which Readerships are to be assigned shall be determined from time to time by Grace of the Senate on the recommendation of the General Board of Studies.

They shall be appointed as soon as sufficient funds can be provided conveniently for the purpose from the Common University Fund, or from other sources.

[On the occasion of a vacancy in any Readership, a Reader shall be appointed in the subject to which the Readership has been assigned to fill the vacancy, unless within twelve weeks of the vacancy, days of any vacation not being reckoned, on the recommendation of the General Board the Readership is by Grace transferred to another subject or is suppressed.][1]

3. The office of Reader shall be tenable ordinarily during good behaviour, and the stipend shall be ordinarily £400 a year; but the Senate shall have power, upon the recommendation of the General Board of Studies, to assign a different tenure or stipend in the case of any Readership. No variation at any time, however, in these respects shall affect the interest of a Reader without his consent.

4. The Readers shall be appointed by the General Board of Studies, subject to the confirmation of the appointment in

Sealed, 27 March 1908. Approved by the King in Council, 19 October 1908 (*Reporter*, 30 October 1908, page 154).

[1] Grace 1 of 7 March 1908, and Grace 1 of 12 March 1908, confirming a Report of the Council of the Senate (*Reporter*, 4 February 1908, page 532). Sealed, 27 March 1908. Approved by the King in Council, 19 October 1908 (*Reporter*, 30 October 1908, page 154).

every case by the Special Board with which the Readership is connected.

[If the General Board and the Special Board do not agree in any appointment within twelve weeks after the vacancy, or within twelve weeks after the transference of the Readership by Grace of the Senate, days of any vacation not being reckoned, the appointment shall be made for that turn by the Council of the Senate.][1]

5. If a member of the General Board or a member of the Special Board be a candidate for the office, he shall be thereby disqualified from acting in the matter of the appointment, and the other members of the Board shall have power to act without him.

6. The office of Reader shall be governed by Chapter XI, for the Residence and Duties of Professors and Readers; and the Readers shall comply with the provisions of that Chapter.

7. The University shall have power to give pensions to retiring Readers according to circumstances, as the Senate may think fit.

[8. Except in cases in which the University shall by Grace determine otherwise, two Readerships in the University shall not be held at the same time by the same person; and upon a Reader's acceptance of a second Readership, that already held by him shall become, *ipso facto*, vacant.

9. Except in cases in which the University shall by Grace determine otherwise, the office of Reader shall not be tenable together with that of Professor or that of University Lecturer in the University; and if a person holding any one of these three offices shall accept either of the others, he shall thereby, *ipso facto*, vacate the one previously held by him.][2]

[1] Grace 1 of 7 March 1908, and Grace 1 of 12 March 1908, confirming a Report of the Council of the Senate (*Reporter*, 4 February 1908, page 532). Sealed, 27 March 1908. Approved by the King in Council, 19 October 1908 (*Reporter*, 30 October 1908, page 154).

[2] Grace 3 of 7 March 1908, and Grace 3 of 12 March 1908, confirming a Report of the Council of the Senate (*Reporter*, 4 February 1908, page 532). Sealed, 27 March 1908. Approved by the King in Council, 19 October 1908 (*Reporter*, 30 October 1908, page 154).

[10. The University shall have power to require any Reader elected after the approval by the King in Council of this Statute to retire from office at such time and under such conditions as may be prescribed in any scheme relating to the retirement of Readers and the provision of pensions which shall have been established by Grace before the date of his election. The University shall also have power to make the provisions of any such scheme apply to any Reader elected before the approval by the King in Council of this Statute or before the establishment of such scheme who shall signify in writing to the Vice-Chancellor his desire to be placed under the operation of such scheme.][1]

CHAPTER VIII

FOR UNIVERSITY LECTURERS.

1. The General Board of Studies may choose as Lecturers in the department of study for which any Special Board is formed such College Lecturers or other persons as they may think fit, but the appointment in every case shall be subject to confirmation by the Special Board.

[If in any case in which it has been decided by a Grace of the Senate that a Lecturer in a specified subject shall be appointed, the General Board of Studies and the Special Board with which the Lecturer is to be connected do not agree in any appointment within four weeks after the General Board have communicated an appointment to the Special Board, days of any vacation not being reckoned, the appointment shall be made on that occasion by the Council of the Senate, unless the Grace establishing the Lectureship be rescinded by a Grace offered on the recommendation of the Council of the Senate notwithstanding the provision of Section 4.][2]

[1] Approved by the King in Council, 14 May 1914 (*Reporter*, 26 May 1914, page 1007). For further references see Chapter VI, Section 10a.

[2] Grace 6 of 10 May 1900, and Grace 15 of 7 June 1900, confirming a Report of the Council of the Senate (*Reporter*, 27 February 1900, page 549). Sealed, 13 October 1900. Approved by the King in Council, 13 May 1901 (*Reporter*, 28 May 1901, page 918).

2. The Lecturers so chosen shall be called University Lecturers, and each of them shall receive from the University an annual stipend of not less than £50.

3. The University Lecturers shall order the subjects and number of their lectures, together with the times and places of delivery, according to schemes approved by the General Board of Studies, and shall conform to all regulations and instructions issued by the said General Board. They shall also make such returns as the General Board of Studies, or the Special Boards with which they are connected, shall from time to time require.

4. The number of University Lecturers and their connexion with the Special Boards of Studies shall be determined from time to time by Grace upon the recommendation of the General Board.

5. The appointment of any University Lecturer may be cancelled at any time by the General Board of Studies with the concurrence of the Special Board with which he is connected.

6. The University shall have power to appoint Lecturers also on any subject not immediately connected with any Special Board of Studies for such time and on such conditions as may seem good.

CHAPTER IX

For Elections to certain Professorships.

1. In those cases in which the election to a Professorship is governed by this Statute the election shall be made by a Board consisting of the Vice-Chancellor and eight persons elected by the Senate, two of such persons being nominated by the Council of the Senate, three by the General Board of Studies, and three by the Special Board of Studies to which the Professorship is assigned.

2. With a view to the representation of opinion outside the University, one at least of the three persons nominated by the General Board, and one at least of the three persons nominated by the Special Board, shall be persons who are not resident in the University nor officially connected with it.

3. On the twentieth day of February in every year one of the eight elected members shall retire from the Board, and his place shall be supplied by a person nominated by the body which nominated him, and elected by the Senate; the retiring member being capable of re-election.

4. In order to establish such system of retirement, at the first election of each Electoral Board one of the members nominated by the Council of the Senate shall be elected for four years, and one for eight years; one of the members nominated by the General Board of Studies shall be elected for two years, one for five years, and one for seven years; one of the members nominated by the Special Board shall be elected for one year, one for three years, and one for six years.

At every subsequent election, except as herein-after provided, the member shall be elected for eight years.

5. In case of a vacancy occurring from any other cause than the expiration of the time of tenure, a new member shall be elected to fill the vacant place. He shall be nominated by the body which nominated the person whose substitute he is, and under the same conditions, and he shall continue a member of the Board as long as the person whose substitute he is would have continued.

6. If a member of the Board nominated and elected as being not resident and not officially connected with the University comes into residence or becomes officially connected with the University, the place of such member on the Board shall not thereby become vacant; but at the next election to the Board of a person nominated by the body which nominated the said member, such person shall be not resident and not officially connected with the University, unless there be a member of the Board nominated by the same body, who fulfils the required conditions.

7. If a member of the Board be a candidate for any Professorship to which the Board elects, he shall be thereby disqualified from acting in the matter of the appointment, and the other members of the Board shall have power to act without him.

8. If an election to the Board be made in the interval between the vacancy of a Professorship and the election of the new Professor, the member so elected shall not have any voice in the election of the Professor, but the person into whose place he was elected, if not a candidate for the Professorship, shall retain his right to vote in that election.

[9. In the event of a vacancy in any Professorship, the election to which is governed by this chapter, the Vice-Chancellor shall inform the Council of the Senate thereof at their next meeting after the vacancy is made known to him, and they may if they think fit delay the announcement of the vacancy for such period, not exceeding six months, as may be necessary for submitting a Grace to the Senate with a view to the suspension or to the discontinuance of the Professorship. If on or before the fourteenth day after the Council have been so informed the Vice-Chancellor shall receive from two members of the Council written notice of their intention to propose a motion delaying the announcement of the vacancy, he shall forthwith give notice to the Council of such motion, which shall be proposed at their next meeting held in full term and shall defer the announcement of the vacancy pending the result of such motion; but if the Vice-Chancellor shall receive no such notice of such motion, he shall forthwith, if it is term time, or on the first day of the following term; announce the vacancy by fixing a written or printed paper on the door of the Senate House, and shall at the same time and in like manner give notice of the day for electing a new Professor, such day to be not less than twenty-eight days nor more than forty-two days after the date of this announcement.][1]

[1] Grace 3 of 9 May 1912, and Grace 7 of 23 May 1912, confirming a Report of the Council of the Senate (*Reporter*, 27 February 1912, page 646). Sealed, 14 June 1912. Approved by the King in Council, 11 February 1913 (*Reporter*, 25 February 1913, page 686).

10. The Board shall have power on any election to adjourn the election for the purpose of considering the qualifications of the persons whose names have been brought before them, or ascertaining whether some other person, whom the Board might prefer, is willing to take the office.

The Board shall also have power to regulate in general its own proceedings, but no election of a Professor shall be made unless two-thirds at least of the number of the existing Board be present at the time of voting.

11. In the final voting no election shall be made unless a majority of the votes of the members present be given for some one person; and if no election be made within twelve weeks from the day for electing, the appointment of the Professor for that turn shall be made by the Chancellor of the University. For the purposes of this section the Vice-Chancellor shall not exercise the power herein given to the Chancellor.

12. The Board shall have power to act notwithstanding one or more vacancies in the number of its members.

CHAPTER X

For the Suspension of Elections to Professorships.

[The University may by Grace suspend the Election to a vacant Professorship for a period not exceeding twelve calendar months in cases where it seems expedient to apply to the King in Council or to the High Court of Justice for a new Statute to govern the Professorship or for power to discontinue the Professorship, and if within such period of suspension any such application shall be made by the University, the election shall be further suspended pending the result of the application.][1]

[1] Grace 3 of 9 May 1912, and Grace 7 of 23 May 1912, confirming a Report of the Council of the Senate (*Reporter*, 27 February 1912, page 646) Sealed, 14 June 1912. Approved by the King in Council, 11 February 1913 (*Reporter*, 25 February 1913, page 686).

CHAPTER XI

For the Residence and Duties of Professors and Readers.

1. The provisions in the Statutes for any Professorship which are inconsistent with the provisions of this Statute are hereby repealed, except so far as they regard the rights and duties of the Professors who may be holding office at the time of the approval of this Statute by the Queen in Council.

2. The University shall have power to determine from time to time by Grace for every Professorship and Readership the time during which the Professor or Reader shall be bound to reside in the University, care being taken that the Professors and Readers shall as a general rule be resident throughout full term time, provided that in the cases of the Regius Professor of Hebrew and the Ely Professor of Divinity due regard be had to their obligations of residence and other duties as Canons of the Cathedral Church of Ely.

3. The University shall have power to determine from time to time by Grace what is to be held to constitute residence.

4. The University shall have power to determine from time to time by Grace the minimum number of lectures to be delivered by each Professor and Reader during the year.

The University shall have power, upon the recommendation of the General Board of Studies, to prescribe from time to time by Grace the duties attached to any Readership.

5. It shall be the duty of every Professor and Reader as well to devote himself to research and the advancement of knowledge in his department as to give lectures in every year and to order the subjects and number of his lectures, together with the times and places of delivery according to schemes determined as in Chapter V, for Boards of Studies, and to conform to all the regulations and instructions issued by the General Board, and to make all such returns as the General Board may direct.

6. Every Professor and Reader shall deliver to the Special Board of Studies with which he is connected, before the end of the Easter Term in every year, a statement in writing of the number of lectures given by him during the preceding year, and of the times of delivery, together with the number of weeks in each of the three terms during which he has resided in the University.

7. If it shall be proved to the satisfaction of the Vice-Chancellor and the six persons elected and acting in accordance with Chapter VII of Statute A of the Statutes of the University that any Professor or Reader has been wilfully neglectful of his duties, or guilty of gross or habitual immorality, it shall be competent to the Vice-Chancellor and the said six persons to admonish the said Professor or Reader, or to deprive him of his office, as the case may seem to them to require; and if the sentence of deprivation be thus passed upon him, his office of Professor or Reader shall thereupon become *ipso facto* vacant; but in every case, whether of admonition or of deprivation, an appeal to the University shall be allowed in accordance with the provisions of Chapter VIII of Statute A of the Statutes of the University.

8. If by reason of sickness, necessary absence from the University, or other sufficient cause, any Professor or Reader desire to have a deputy to discharge the duties of his office, he shall be required to obtain the consent of the General Board of Studies, such consent to be given in writing and to specify the time for which the deputy is to be appointed.

The deputy shall be nominated by the General Board of Studies and approved by Grace, and shall receive from the Professor or Reader such stipend as may be approved by the General Board of Studies and by Grace, being not less than one-third nor more than two-thirds of the proportional part of the whole annual income of the office of the Professor or Reader (not including the dividend or emoluments of any Professorial Fellowship) for the time for which the deputy is appointed; provided that in the cases of the Regius Professor of Hebrew and the Ely Professor of Divinity, the portion of the whole annual income of the Professorship assigned to the deputy shall not exceed one-half.

9. If it be certified to the General Board of Studies that any Professor or Reader has become unable to discharge his duties by age, ill-health, or other serious impediment, and if the said General Board shall deem the inability to be sufficiently proved, they shall have the power of requiring a deputy to be appointed for any time not exceeding twelve calendar months and such appointment may be renewed if necessary, from time to time.

The deputy shall be nominated by the General Board of Studies and approved by Grace, and shall receive out of the stipend of the Professor or Reader such stipend as may be also approved by the General Board and by Grace, being not less than one-third nor more than two-thirds of the proportional part of the whole annual income of the office of the Professor or Reader (not including the dividend or other emoluments of any Professorial Fellowship) for the time for which the deputy is appointed; provided that in the cases of the Regius Professor of Hebrew and the Ely Professor of Divinity, the portion of the whole annual income of the Professorship assigned to the deputy shall not exceed one-half.

If the appointment of a deputy for a period of twelve months shall have been renewed twice in successive years, and at the end of the three years during which a deputy shall thus have acted for the Professor or Reader the occasion for appointing a deputy still continues, the General Board shall have power to declare the office of Professor or Reader vacant, and a new Professor or Reader shall be thereupon elected. The University shall have power to give a pension to the Professor or Reader according to circumstances, as the Senate may think fit.

CHAPTER XII

For Fees payable for University Tuition.

The University shall have power to determine from time to time by Grace upon the recommendation of the General Board of Studies, what fees, if any, shall be paid by Students to the several Professors, Readers, and University Lecturers: provided that the payment of such fees does not interfere with the provisions of the Statute or Instrument of Foundation by which any Professorship is governed.

CHAPTER XIII

For the Apportionment of Stipends.

Except in cases where it is otherwise provided, all stipends payable by the University shall be considered as accruing from day to day and shall be apportionable in respect of time accordingly.

CHAPTER XIV

For the Ely Professorship of Divinity.

Whereas it is provided by the Universities of Oxford and Cambridge Act, 1877, that the Commissioners appointed by the said Act may, in a Statute or Statutes made by them for the University of Cambridge, with the concurrence of the Ecclesiastical Commissioners for England, provide for the Canonry in the Chapter of the Cathedral Church of Ely, which is annexed and united to the Regius Professorship of Greek, being on a vacancy severed therefrom, and being thenceforth permanently annexed and united to a Professorship in the University of a theological or ecclesiastical character:

And whereas it has been provided in Statutes made by the said Commissioners pursuant to the provisions of the said Act that from and after the next vacancy in the Professorship the Regius Professor of Greek shall receive a yearly stipend of £650, and shall also be entitled to a Fellowship, or the income of a Fellowship, in Trinity College:

And whereas the Ecclesiastical Commissioners for England have expressed their concurrence in the provisions of this Statute by affixing their seal thereto:

It is hereby ordained that—

1. On the next vacancy of the said Canonry there shall be established in the University a Professorship, to be called the Ely Professorship of Divinity, and the said Canonry shall be thereupon severed from the said Regius Professorship of Greek, and be permanently annexed and united to the said Ely Professorship of Divinity.

2. The Professor shall be elected in accordance with the provisions of Chapter IX for Elections to certain Professorships; the Special Board of Studies referred to in that Statute being the Board of Studies in Divinity:

3. No person shall be eligible who is not at the time of the election in Priests' Orders.

4. If the Professor is admitted to a Bishopric, or Deanery, or any benefice with cure of souls, his Professorship shall thereupon become *ipso facto* vacant.

5. It shall be competent to the Vice-Chancellor at any time to require the Professor to make the subscription prescribed by the Statutes of the University for candidates for degrees in Divinity, and if after three requisitions the Professor shall refuse to make the required subscription, his Professorship shall thereupon become *ipso facto* vacant.

CHAPTER XV

For Certain Professorships.

The following Professors shall be elected hereafter in accordance with the provisions of Chapter IX, for Elections to certain Professorships, viz.:

The Arabic (Sir Thomas Adams's) Professor.
The Knightbridge Professor.
The Professor of Music.
The Professor of Chemistry.
The Plumian Professor.
The Professor of Anatomy.
The Professor of Botany.
The Woodwardian Professor of Geology.
The Jacksonian Professor.
The Professor of Mineralogy.
The Professor of Political Economy.
The Professor of Zoology and Comparative Anatomy.
The Professor of Sanskrit.
The Cavendish Professor of Experimental Physics.
The Professor of Mechanism and Applied Mechanics.

The Professorship founded by Dr John Knightbridge shall be designated henceforth as a Professorship of Moral Philosophy.

The Ely Professor of Divinity shall be added to the Board of Electors to the Hulsean Professorship.

[On the occasion of the first vacancy which shall occur in or after the year 1912 in the Plumian Professorship the Vice-Chancellor, if he think that the University should have an opportunity of considering the question of connecting the Professorship with the study of Solar Physics, may, notwithstanding any provision to the contrary contained in Chapter IX, delay giving notice of the day for electing a new Professor for any period not exceeding twelve calendar months from the date of the notice of the vacancy, and if within such twelve months a new Statute be submitted to the King in Council the Vice-Chancellor shall further delay giving such notice of the day of election pending the result of the application; the day for such election shall be not less than twenty-eight nor more than forty-two days after the date of the notice of such day of election.][1]

CHAPTER XVI

For the Smith's Prizes[2].

1. The University shall have power, the will of the Founder or any Deed of Trust notwithstanding, to make from time to time a scheme or schemes for the award of the Premiums or Prizes founded by Dr Smith, including in such scheme or schemes regulations for the appointment of adjudicators, standing of candidates, conditions of candidature, subjects wherein the proficiency of the candidates shall be tested, and mode of testing such proficiency; provided that the object shall be always to encourage the study of the more advanced branches of Mathematics and Natural Philosophy.

2. The preference given by the will of the Founder in case of equality to a candidate of Trinity College is hereby abolished.

3. A prize shall not be awarded more than once to the same person.

CHAPTER XVII

For the Botanic Garden.

The management and regulation of the Botanic Garden, together with the appointment and removal of the Curators, Superintendents, Officers, and servants employed therein, shall

[1] Grace 5 of 25 April 1912, and Grace 8 of 23 May 1912, confirming a Report of the Council of the Senate (*Reporter*, 13 February 1912 page 601). Sealed, 14 June 1912. Approved by the King in Council, 11 February 1913 (*Reporter*, 25 February 1913, page 686).

[2] See *Endowmen's of the University*, ed. 1904, pp. 93–95.

henceforth be vested in a Syndicate consisting of the five Governors and Visitors appointed by Dr Walker, that is to say, the Chancellor, or in his absence the Vice-Chancellor of the University, the Master of Trinity College, the Provost of King's College, the Master of St John's College, and the Regius Professor of Physic, together with such other persons as may be appointed from time to time by Grace of the Senate.

CHAPTER XVIII

For the Management of Trust Estates.

1. The management and administration of the property of the following Endowments shall be vested hereafter in the Chancellor, Masters, and Scholars of the University, viz.:

The Regius Professor of Physic;
The Lucasian Professorship;
The Lowndean Professorship;
The Endowments of Mr Worts[1];
The Foundation of Mr Hulse.

2. The Provisions of this Chapter shall come into force for each Professorship on the next vacancy or at such earlier time as the Professor may declare in writing to the Vice-Chancellor his acceptance of the same: and for each of the other Endowments at the time of confirmation of this Statute.

CHAPTER XIX

For the Commencement of this Statute.

Except where otherwise provided, this Statute shall come into operation immediately after its approval by the Queen in

[1] Application was made to the Chancery Division of the High Court of Justice, 26 February 1887, for obtaining the transfer to the Chancellor, Masters, and Scholars of the University of the legal estate in the property belonging to this trust; but on the hearing of the Petition the Judge declined to make the order prayed for on the ground that the Court had no power or jurisdiction in the matter. See Grace 1 of 6 November 1884 (*Reporter*, 11 November 1884, page 155), and a Notice by the Vice-Chancellor (*Reporter*, 15 March 1887, page 506).

Council. But the provisions relating to Professors hereinbefore contained except the provisions of the ninth section of Chapter III shall not apply to any Professorship until the next vacancy. Provided, however, that if a resolution be passed by the Council of the Senate that it is desirable that they shall sooner come into operation with regard to any Professorship, and such resolution be assented to by the Professor affected thereby, and confirmed by Grace, the provisions shall then come into operation accordingly.

STATUTE C

Approved by the Queen in Council, 10 *March* 1882.

THE REGIUS PROFESSORSHIP OF GREEK.

WHEREAS We, the University of Cambridge Commissioners, in pursuance of the powers vested in us by the twenty-sixth section of the Universities of Oxford and Cambridge Act, 1877, have, with the concurrence of the Ecclesiastical Commissioners for England, provided for the canonry in the Chapter of the Cathedral Church of Ely, heretofore annexed and united to the Regius Professorship of Greek, being on a vacancy severed therefrom:

And whereas it is provided in the Statutes of Trinity College made under the powers of the said Act, that the Regius Professor of Greek shall be entitled to be admitted to a Fellowship at the said College, and to hold and enjoy the benefits and advantages of the same, subject to the provisions contained in the said Statutes, and shall receive from the College the annual stipend of forty pounds (£40), and also an additional annual stipend of two hundred and fifty pounds (£250):

And whereas it is enacted in the twenty-seventh section of the said Act, that a Statute for altering or modifying the trusts, Statutes, or directions relating to the endowments held by the Regius Professor of Greek, if affecting any Statute of Trinity College touching the said Professor or his endowments, shall not be made by us unless and until it receives the assent of Trinity College under its Common Seal:

And whereas the following Statute has received the assent of Trinity College under its Common Seal:

We, the said University of Cambridge Commissioners, in pursuance of the powers vested in us by the said Act, do hereby make the following Statute for the Regius Professorship of Greek in the University of Cambridge and declare it to be a Statute for the said University.

1. The Regius Professor of Greek shall be elected as heretofore by the Council of the Senate.

2. He shall comply with the provisions of the Statutes of the University for the Residence and Duties of Professors and Readers.

3. He shall be entitled to be admitted to a Fellowship at Trinity College, and such Fellowship shall thenceforth be the Professorial Fellowship assigned to the Regius Professorship of Greek, and shall be held subject to the provisions for Professorial Fellowships contained in the Statutes of the University.

4. He shall receive from the University an annual stipend of three hundred and sixty pounds (£360), in addition to the annual stipends of forty pounds (£40) and two hundred and fifty pounds (£250) paid to him by Trinity College.

5. This Statute shall come into operation from and after the approval of it by the Queen in Council, or from and after the first vacancy of the said Regius Professorship which shall take place after the severance of the canonry in the Chapter of the Cathedral Church of Ely from the said Regius Professorship, whichever event shall last happen; and from and after the time when this Statute comes into operation all provisions of previously existing Statutes which are contrary to any of the provisions of this Statute shall be of no force or effect.

STATUTE D

Approved by the Queen in Council, 10 *March* 1882.

This Statute is declared to be a Statute for the University of Cambridge.

THE DOWNING PROFESSORSHIP OF THE LAWS OF ENGLAND.

1. The election to the Downing Professorship of the Laws of England shall be in accordance with the provisions of the Statutes of the University for Elections to certain Professorships made under the powers of the Universities of Oxford and Cambridge Act, 1877, the Electors being the Board of Electors defined in the said Statutes together with the Master of Downing College if he be not a candidate, or in the event of the Mastership being vacant, or the Master being a candidate for the Professorship, the senior member of the Governing Body of Downing College who is not himself a candidate; provided that if at the time of any election the Master of Downing College, or the senior member of the Governing Body as aforesaid, be in any other capacity a member of the said Board he shall not on that ground have two votes.

2. The Downing Professor of the Laws of England shall be deemed to be holding a Professorial Fellowship within the meaning of the Statutes of the University made under the powers of the said Act.

3. The Downing Professor of the Laws of England shall comply with the provisions of the Statutes of the University for the Residence and Duties of Professors and Readers made under the powers of the said Act.

4. The Downing Professor of the Laws of England shall be entitled to receive from the University in each year such stipend as will raise his whole yearly stipend not including his lodge or any equivalent for it to an amount greater by five hundred pounds (£500) than the share of the revenue of Downing College paid to each Fellow of the College for that year.

5. From the sum estimated as due from Downing College on account of University purposes under the provisions of the Statutes of the University for Contribution of Colleges for University Purposes made under the powers of the said Act, the College shall be entitled to deduct in each year the whole amount of the share of the revenue of the College paid in that year to the Downing Professor of the Laws of England instead of any deduction which the College is entitled to make under the provisions of the aforesaid Statutes for Contribution of Colleges for University Purposes on account of the Professorial Fellowship held by the Professor: Provided always that if in any year the sum estimated as due from Downing College as aforesaid be less than the amount of the shares of the revenue of the said College paid in that year to the Downing Professor of the Laws of England and the Downing Professor of Medicine, the College shall not be entitled to deduct the balance from the contribution to the University in any subsequent year.

STATUTE E

Approved by the Queen in Council, 10 *March* 1882.

This Statute is declared to be a Statute for the University of Cambridge.

The Downing Professorship of Medicine.

1. The election to the Downing Professorship of Medicine shall be in accordance with the provisions of the Statutes of the University for Elections to certain Professorships made under the powers of the Universities of Oxford and Cambridge Act, 1877, the Electors being the Board of Electors defined in the said Statutes together with the Master of Downing College if he be not a candidate or in the event of the Mastership being vacant or the Master being a candidate for the Professorship the senior member of the Governing Body of Downing College who is not himself a candidate; provided that if at the time of any election the Master of Downing College, or the senior member of the Governing Body as aforesaid, be in any other capacity a member of the said Board he shall not on that ground have two votes.

2. The Downing Professor of Medicine shall be deemed to be holding a Professorial Fellowship within the meaning of the Statutes of the University made under the powers of the said Act.

3. The Downing Professor of Medicine shall comply with the provisions of the Statutes of the University for the Residence and Duties of Professors and Readers made under the powers of the said Act.

4. The Downing Professor of Medicine shall be entitled to receive from the University in each year such stipend as will raise his whole yearly stipend not including his lodge or any equivalent for it to an amount greater by three hundred pounds (£300) than the share of the revenue of Downing College paid to each Fellow of the College for that year.

5. From the sum estimated as due from Downing College on account of University purposes under the provisions of the Statutes of the University for Contribution of Colleges for University Purposes made under the powers of the said Act, the College shall be entitled to deduct in each year the whole amount of the share of the revenue of the College paid in that year to the Downing Professor of Medicine instead of any deduction which the College is entitled to make under the provisions of the aforesaid Statutes for Contribution of Colleges for University Purposes on account of the Professorial Fellowship held by the Professor; provided always that if in any year the sum estimated as due from Downing College as aforesaid be less than the amount of the shares of the revenue of the said College paid in that year to the Downing Professor of the Laws of England and the Downing Professor of Medicine, the College shall not be entitled to deduct the balance from the contribution to the University in any subsequent year.

STATUTE FOR THE UNIVERSITY AND FOR EMMANUEL COLLEGE IN COMMON

Approved by the Queen in Council, 3 *May* 1882.

This Statute is declared to be a Statute wholly for the University of Cambridge and for Emmanuel College therein in common.

Of the Dixie Professorship.

1. There shall be established in the University of Cambridge a Professorship to be called the Dixie Professorship of Ecclesiastical History.

2. The Professor shall comply with the provisions of the Statutes of the University for the Residence and Duties of Professors and Readers.

3. The election to the Professorship shall be in accordance with the provisions of the Statutes of the University for Elections to certain Professorships the Master of Emmanuel College being added to the Board of Electors as therein defined provided that if the Mastership of Emmanuel College be vacant or if the Master be himself a candidate for the Professorship the senior of the Fellows of Emmanuel College who is not a candidate shall take the Master's place on the Board provided also that if the Master of Emmanuel College or the senior of the Fellows as aforesaid at any time be in any other capacity a member of the Board he shall not on that ground have two votes.

4. The Dixie Professor of Ecclesiastical History shall by virtue of his admission to the Professorship without need of any further election be entitled to admission to the Professorial Fellowship assigned to the Dixie Professorship at Emmanuel College upon his making the declaration statutably required of other Fellows of the College and to hold the said Fellowship so long as he shall continue to hold the office of Dixie Professor and no longer.

5. The Dixie Professor of Ecclesiastical History shall in addition to the dividend and allowances of his Fellowship receive from the College by way of stipend the sum of five hundred pounds (500£) a year out of the income of the Dixie Estate and if the income of the Dixie Estate be insufficient in any year for this purpose the deficiency shall be paid from the ordinary revenue of the College.

6. After the approval by the Queen in Council of this Statute and of the two University Statutes herein-before mentioned and the assignment of a Fellowship to be the Professorial Fellowship the first election to the Dixie Professorship shall take place so soon as shall seem convenient to the Vice-Chancellor.

7. From the sum determined to be due from Emmanuel College for University Purposes in accordance with the Statutes of the University made under the powers of the Universities of Oxford and Cambridge Act, 1877, the College shall be entitled to deduct annually the sum of two hundred and fifty pounds (250£) on account of the stipend paid by the College to the Dixie Professor besides the deductions which the College is entitled to make on account of the Fellowship held by the Dixie Professor in accordance with the provisions of the Statutes of the University for Contributions of Colleges for University Purposes; provided always that if in any year the sum estimated as due from Emmanuel College as aforesaid be less than two hundred and fifty pounds (250£) and the amount of the said deductions the College shall not be entitled to deduct the balance from the contributions to the University in any subsequent year.

STATUTE FOR THE CROSSE SCHOLARSHIPS[1]

Grace 15 *of* 24 *May* 1894, *and Grace* 7 *of* 8 *November* 1894, *confirming a Report of the Special Board for Divinity* (*Reporter*, 1 *May* 1894, *page* 692). *Sealed*, 8 *February* 1895. *Approved by the Queen in Council*, 8 *March* 1895 (*Reporter*, 19 *March* 1895, *page* 654).

1. The Scholarships shall be called the Crosse Scholarships.

2. The Scholarships shall be open for competition to Bachelors of Arts, and to such other persons under the standing of Master of Arts, as may from time to time be determined by the University by Grace of the Senate.

3. The Examination of Candidates for these Scholarships shall "turn upon a knowledge of the Holy Scriptures in their original tongues, Hebrew and Greek, of Ecclesiastical History, of the earlier and later heresies, and such other subjects of useful enquiry as may be thought most likely to assist in the formation of valuable characters fitted to sustain or adorn the cause of true Religion."

4. The University shall have power to determine and alter from time to time by Grace of the Senate the regulations respecting (1) the number of the Scholarships and the length of their tenure; (2) the disposal of the funds accruing from vacant Scholarships, whether by investments or by grants to deserving Candidates; (3) the persons who are to examine the Candidates and elect the Scholars; (4) the date of the annual examination.

5. The foundation deed shall be subject to further amendment and alteration from time to time by the University, with the approval of the Queen in Council.

[1] See *Endowments of the University*, ed. 1904, pp. 314–319.

STATUTE FOR PRIVATE HOSTELS[1]

Five Statutes for the establishment and regulation of Private Hostels made by the Commissioners under the Cambridge University Act, 1856, *and approved by the Queen in Council,* 31 *July* 1858, *such Statutes being intituled respectively* (*Statutes, ed.* 1882, *pp.* 77—79)

Stat. I. De Principalibus hospitiorum et de conditionibus quibus licentia illis concedenda sit

Stat. II. De officio Principalis hospitii

Stat. III. De Scholaribus hospitiorum

Stat. IV. De suspensione vel revocatione licentiae

Stat. V. De statu scholarium post suspensam vel revocatam licentiam et post decessum principalis,

were excepted from repeal in the Statutes approved by the Queen in Council, 27 *February* 1882 (*Stat. A. cap. X. p.* 32). *These Statutes are now repealed, and replaced by the following :*

1. Any member of the Senate who has attained the age of twenty-eight years may apply for a Grace of the Senate licensing him to open his residence, if situate within a mile and a half of Great St Mary's Church, for the reception of Students who shall be admitted to the privileges of members of the University.

2. Every person to whom such licence is granted shall be called the Principal of a Private Hostel, and his residence so opened as aforesaid shall be called a Private Hostel.

3. No licence to open a Private Hostel shall be granted except by a Grace of the Senate. Every proposed Grace for the establishment of a Private Hostel shall specify the house in respect of which the licence is applied for and the maximum number of the Students who may be received into the Hostel, and shall be accompanied by a Report to the Senate from the Council of the Senate recommending that the licence be

[1] Grace 2 of 17 January 1895, and Grace 2 of 31 January 1895, confirming a Report of the Council of the Senate (*Reporter*, 11 December 1894, page 301). Sealed, 8 February 1895. Approved by the Queen in Council, 8 March 1895 (*Reporter*, 19 March 1895, page 654).

granted and stating that the following conditions have been fulfilled, namely:

(1) that the house which is to be opened as a Private Hostel is a fit and proper place for the residence of the specified number of Students; and

(2) that sufficient provision has been made for the maintenance of good order and discipline among the Students, and in particular for the shutting of the gates of the Hostel at night, and for the keeping of a proper record of the residence of the Students.

4. The Principal of a Private Hostel to whom such licence as aforesaid is granted, shall forthwith make and subscribe the following declaration and deliver the same to the Vice-Chancellor:

I *A.B.* hereby promise that I will observe the Statute for Private Hostels and I will conform to the conditions specified in my licence:

I will open my Hostel for the inspection of the Vice-Chancellor, Proctors, or other Officers of the University when called upon to do so, and will conform to all regulations that may be laid down by the University for the maintenance of good order and discipline among the Students:

I will keep my Hostel shut during such hours at night as the University may prescribe, and will provide that no person shall come in or go out without my knowledge during those hours:

I will cause my servants to obey and execute these regulations under my orders. *A.B.*

5. Every Principal of a Private Hostel shall—

(1) maintain good order and discipline among the Students of his Hostel, and for this purpose shall aid and assist the Vice-Chancellor, Proctors, and other Officers of the University whenever he shall be called upon to do so:

(2) keep a proper record of the residence of all Students in his Hostel, and at the end of every term send to the Registrary of the University a return under his hand setting forth the names of all the Students resident in his Hostel and the number of days for which they have resided in the said term:

(3) keep a proper record of every case in which any Student of his Hostel shall have come into or gone out from the Hostel during the hours for which the Hostel is required to be shut, and produce such record for the inspection of the Vice-Chancellor, Proctors, and other Officers of the University whenever called upon to do so:

(4) pay to the University all fees and other moneys which shall become due to the University from or in respect of any Student of his Hostel:

(5) reside continuously in his Hostel so long as any Student is resident there unless he shall with the written permission of the Vice-Chancellor have appointed some member of the Senate as his deputy to reside in his stead for a period to be specified on each occasion.

6. If it shall at any time appear to the Vice-Chancellor that the Principal of any Private Hostel has contravened this Statute or any Statute or Ordinance of the University or has not conformed to the conditions specified in his licence, or that the buildings of the Hostel have become unsuitable for the residence of Students, or that sufficient provision has not been made for the maintenance of good order and discipline, the Vice-Chancellor may with the consent of the Council of the Senate refer the matter to the Sex Viri who with the Vice-Chancellor shall enquire into it, and if after such enquiry the Vice-Chancellor and three at least of the Sex Viri shall be of opinion that there is just cause of complaint, the Vice-Chancellor shall report the case to the Council of the Senate, and the Council of the Senate may thereupon withdraw the licence.

7. In case the Principal of any Private Hostel shall die or become incapable of performing his duties, or in case his licence shall be withdrawn, it shall be lawful for the Vice-Chancellor to commit to some member of the Senate the care and governance of the then existing Students of the Hostel or to place such Students under any regulations that may for the time being be in force concerning those Members of the University who are not Members of any College or Hostel.

8. Nothing herein contained shall affect any Hostel that has been established under the provisions of the Statutes hereby repealed or any Hostel that has been or shall be established under any Statute or Ordinance of the University relating to Public Hostels.

REPEALING STATUTE[1]

In the Matter of the Act of Parliament passed in the 19th and 20th years of the reign of Her present Majesty Queen Victoria Cap. 88 intituled "An Act to make further provision for the Good Government of the University of Cambridge and of the Colleges therein and of the College of King Henry VI at Eton."

We the Chancellor Masters and Scholars of the University of Cambridge in pursuance and exercise of the power conferred upon us by the 43rd Section of the above mentioned Act and of every other power us hereunto enabling do hereby repeal the Statutes and parts of Statutes specified in the Schedule hereto if and in so far as the same were not repealed by Section 1 of Cap. XI. "For the residence and duties of Professors and Readers" in Statute B made by the Commissioners acting under "The Universities of Oxford and Cambridge Act 1877" and approved by Her Majesty the Queen in Council on the 29th day of June 1882 but saving the rights and duties of any existing Professor who shall not have become or shall not become subject to the provisions of the said Statute B and saving also all other interests rights matters and things already created done or suffered under the Statutes or parts of Statutes hereby repealed.

And we the said Chancellor Masters and Scholars humbly beg to submit the foregoing for the approval of Her Majesty the Queen in Council.

Given under our Common Seal this ninth day of June 1896.

LS

[1] Grace 3 of 12 March 1896, and Grace 1 of 21 May 1896, confirming a Report of the Council of the Senate (*Reporter*, 4 February 1896, page 432). Sealed, 9 June 1896. Approved by the Queen in Council, 29 June 1896 (*Reporter*, 6 October 1896, page 18).

The SCHEDULE above referred to.

PART I.

Titles of Statutes	Extent of repeal
Statute for the Regius Professorship of Divinity Hebrew and Greek confirmed by Order of the Queen in Council dated 10th May 1860 . .	Sections 7, 8, 9, 10, 11 12, 13, and 15.

PART II.

STATUTES confirmed by Order of the Queen in Council dated 1st August 1860.

Titles of Statutes	Extent of repeal
Statute for the Lady Margaret's Professorship of Divinity	Sections 6, 7, 8, 9, 10, 11, 12, and 15.
Statute for the Norrisian Professorship of Divinity	Sections 6, 7, 8, 9, 10, 11, 12, and 15.
Statute for Mr Hulse's Foundations (Hulsean Professorship of Divinity and Hulsean Lecturer) .	Sections 4, 5, 6, 7, 8, 9 10, and 20.

PART III.

STATUTES confirmed by Order of the Queen in Council dated 7th March 1860.

Titles of Statutes	Extent of repeal
Statute for the Sadleirian Professorship . . .	Sections 1, 2, 5, 6, and 7.
Statute for the Lucasian Professor of Mathematics	The additional provisions enacted by this Statute.
Statute for the Plumian Professorship of Astronomy and Experimental Philosophy . . .	The additional provisions enacted by this Statute.
Statute for the Lowndean Professorship of Astronomy and Geometry	Sections 2 and 3.
Statute for the Lucasian, the Plumian, the Lowndean, and the Sadleirian Professorships in common	Sections 2, 3, 4, 5, 6, and 7.

Part IV.

Statutes confirmed by Order of the Queen in Council dated 16th April 1861.

Titles of Statutes	Extent of repeal
Statute for Sir Thomas Adams's Professorship of Arabic	The additional provisions enacted by this Statute.
Statute for the Knightbridge Professorship of Moral Theology Casuistical Divinity and Moral Philosophy	Sections 1, 3, 4, 5, and 6.
Statute for the Regius Professorship of Modern History	Sections 2, 3, and 4.
Statute for the Woodwardian Professorship of Geology	Sections 1, 3, 4, and 5 of the additional provisions enacted by this Statute.
Statute for the Jacksonian Professorship of Natural Philosophy	The additional provisions enacted by this Statute.
Statute for the Regius Professorship of Civil Law	The whole Statute.
Statute for the Regius Professorship of Physic	The whole Statute.
Statute for the Professorship of Chemistry .	The whole Statute.
Statute for the Professorship of Anatomy . .	The whole Statute.
Statute for the Professorship of Botany . .	The whole Statute.
Statute for the Professorship of Mineralogy .	The whole Statute.
Statute for Sir Thomas Adams's Professorship of Arabic and certain other Professorships in common	The whole Statute.

STATUTES PRIOR TO 1877

STATUTE FOR NON-COLLEGIATE STUDENTS

Approved by the Queen in Council, 13 *May* 1869.

1. Notwithstanding anything expressed or contained in the Statutes of the University framed and sanctioned in accordance with the provisions of the Act of Parliament, 19 and 20 Vict. c. 88, it shall be lawful for the University to admit as Students to matriculate and to confer degrees on persons who may not be members of any College or Hall or of any Hostel.

2. The functions assigned to the Head or Praelector of a College or to the Principal of a Hostel in Cap. I, sec. 3, and Cap. III, sec. 1, of the said Statutes so framed and sanctioned as aforesaid shall be exercised in respect of such Students by a Member or Members of the Senate who shall be specially appointed from time to time for that purpose, but the said Statute shall in all other respects be deemed to apply and extend to such Students as well as others.

3. In addition to the provisions of the said Statutes the University shall have power from time to time to frame and enforce such Rules as may be deemed expedient for the admission, government, discipline, and instruction of such Students and for the payment to be made by them.

4. The University shall have power to make special provision for the temporary or permanent removal from the University of any such Student if at any time such removal shall appear necessary or expedient anything contained in the said Statutes notwithstanding.

5. The University shall have power from time to time to appoint a Board or Syndicate, to consist of such persons as may be determined by Grace of the Senate, for the purpose of exercising and carrying into effect the powers and provisions of this Statute or any of them subject to such Rules and Regulations as the University may from time to time prescribe, and all the acts of the Board for such purposes shall be deemed to be acts of the University.

STATUTE FOR THE REGIUS PROFESSORSHIPS OF DIVINITY, HEBREW, AND GREEK

Approved by the Queen in Council, 10 *May* 1860.

1. There shall be three Professors in the University, to be called respectively the Regius Professor of Divinity, the Regius Professor of Hebrew, and the Regius Professor of Greek; they shall be from time to time chosen and appointed by the Council of the Senate.

[2. The Professor of Divinity shall be a Bachelor or Doctor of Divinity and a Clerk in Holy Orders of the Church of England.][1]

[3. In case of a vacancy of any one of the Professorships, the Vice-Chancellor shall inform the Council of the Senate thereof at their next meeting after the vacancy is made known to him, and they may if they think fit delay the announcement of the vacancy for such period, not exceeding six months, as may be necessary for submitting a Grace to the Senate with a view to the suspension of election to the Professorship. If on or before the fourteenth day after the Council have been so informed the Vice-Chancellor shall receive from two members of the Council written notice of their intention to propose a

[1] Grace 2 of 1 March 1913, and Grace 14 of 25 April 1913, confirming a Report of a Syndicate on the Statutes for the Lady Margaret's and Regius Professorships of Divinity (*Reporter*, 4 February 1913, page 597). Sealed 5 May 1913. Approved by the King in Council, 12 August 1913 (*Reporter*, 2 October 1913, page 30).

motion delaying the announcement of the vacancy, he shall forthwith give notice to the Council of such motion which shall be proposed at their next meeting held in full term and shall defer the announcement of the vacancy pending the result of such motion; but if the Vice-Chancellor shall receive no such notice of such motion, he shall forthwith, if it is term time, or on the first day of the following term, give public notice of the vacancy by fixing a written or printed paper on the door of the Senate-House, and shall at the same time and in like manner give public notice of the day when the candidates are to attend in person before the Electors, and the day of election shall be not sooner than fourteen days nor later than twenty-eight days after the date of the notice.][1]

4. Every candidate shall, on a day to be assigned by the Electors, expound openly in the Public Schools for the space of one hour, a part of Holy Scripture, or of a book written in the Hebrew or Greek language, according as the Professorship vacant is that of Divinity, Hebrew, or Greek; such part of Holy Scripture, or of a book written in the Hebrew or Greek language, being assigned to him by the Electors.

5. The Electors shall meet to elect the Professor on the day following that on which the last of the candidates has expounded as aforesaid. No one shall vote in the election who has not attended the expositions of all the candidates. The person who has a majority of the votes of the members of the Council present, and entitled to vote, shall be deemed to be elected; and if, after three scrutinies, no candidate has such a majority, the appointment of the Professor shall for that time be made by the Vice-Chancellor of the University and the Master of Trinity College, or, if the Master of Trinity College be Vice-Chancellor, by the Vice-Chancellor and the Provost of King's College. If, however, the Vice-Chancellor and the Master of Trinity College, or the Vice-Chancellor and the Provost of King's College, do not agree in appointing the same

[1] Grace 1 of 14 March 1914 and Grace 4 of 1 May 1914, confirming a Report of the Council of the Senate (*Reporter*, 9 December 1913, page 341). Sealed, 16 May 1914. Approved by the King in Council, 16 July 1914.

person, the appointment shall then be made by the Chancellor of the University.

6. The Professorship of Divinity shall not be tenable with a deanery or any ecclesiastical preferment with cure of souls except that which is annexed to the Professorship by the statute 10 Anne, c. 45[1].

7—13. *Repealed. See page* 85.

14. It shall be competent to the Vice-Chancellor, if at any time he shall see occasion to do so, to require[2] any one of the three Professors appointed under this Statute to subscribe to the three articles of the thirty-sixth canon, in the form prescribed by the Statutes of the University for Candidates for Degrees in Divinity; and if, after three requisitions, such Professor shall refuse so to subscribe, his Professorship shall thereupon become *ipso facto* void.

15. *Repealed. See page* 85.

STATUTE FOR THE LADY MARGARET'S PROFESSORSHIP OF DIVINITY

Approved by the Queen in Council, 1 *August* 1860.

1. The provisions of the foundation deed[3] of the Lady Margaret's Professorship of Divinity, dated the nativity of the Virgin Mary, in the eighteenth year of the reign of King Henry VII [8 September 1502], excepting so far as they are re-enacted by the present Statute, are hereby repealed.

[2. The Electors to this Professorship shall be the Vice-Chancellor, together with the Doctors and Bachelors of Divinity who are also members of the Senate.

[3. In case of a vacancy of the Professorship the Vice-Chancellor shall inform the Council of the Senate thereof at their next meeting after the vacancy is made known to him,

[1] The Rectory of Somersham in Huntingdonshire, disannexed from the Professorship by the Act 45 and 46 Vict. Ch. 81 (1882). This Act is printed in *Endowments of the University*, ed. 1904, pp. 50–54.

[2] See Sections 2, 3 of the University Tests Act 1871 (pages 187–189).

[3] See *Endowments of the University*, ed. 1904, pp. 58–65.

and they may if they think fit delay the announcement of the vacancy for such period, not exceeding six months, as may be necessary for submitting a Grace to the Senate with a view to the suspension of election to the Professorship. If on or before the fourteenth day after the Council have been so informed the Vice-Chancellor shall receive from two members of the Council written notice of their intention to propose a motion delaying the announcement of the vacancy, he shall forthwith give notice to the Council of such motion which shall be proposed at their next meeting held in full term and shall defer the announcement of the vacancy pending the result of such motion; but if the Vice-Chancellor shall receive no such notice of such motion, he shall forthwith, if it is term time, or on the first day of the following term, give public notice of the vacancy by fixing a written or printed paper on the door of the Senate-House, and he shall require that names of intending Candidates shall be sent to him within such time as the University by Grace of the Senate shall direct. If not more than four persons send in names as applicants, they shall be the Candidates. If there are more than four applications, the Vice-Chancellor, together with those members of the Special Board of Divinity who are Electors and are not themselves applicants for the Professorship, shall select four of the applicants, and the applicants thus selected shall be the Candidates for the Professorship. The Vice-Chancellor shall announce to the Electors the names of the Candidates.][1]

4. The Vice-Chancellor shall fix, and notify to each candidate a day on which he shall attend before the Electors, the day of attendance to be not less than twenty-one days after the date of the announcement of the names of the candidates. Each candidate, at the time and place assigned by the Vice-Chancellor shall deliver a prelection before the Electors on some branch of Theology and such prelection shall not exceed one hour in length. The Electors shall meet to elect the Professor on the day following that on which the last prelection

[1] Grace 1 of 14 March 1914 and Grace 4 of 1 May 1914, confirming a Report of the Council of the Senate (*Reporter*, 9 December 1913, page 341). Sealed, 16 May 1914. Approved by the King in Council, 16 July 1914.

was made and no Elector shall vote in the election who has not heard the prelections of all the candidates. Any Elector who is himself a candidate shall be disqualified from voting at any stage of the election. An election shall not be made until a candidate has obtained a majority of the votes of those present and voting. If, after six scrutinies no election has been made, the appointment of the Professor for that turn shall be made by the Chancellor of the University. For this purpose the Vice-Chancellor shall not exercise the power herein given to the Chancellor.][1]

[5. The Professor who may be holding office at the time of the approval by the King in Council of this amended Statute shall be entitled to hold the Professorship for life.][2]

6—12. *Repealed. See page* 85.

13. It shall be competent to the Vice-Chancellor, if at any time he shall see occasion to do so, to require the Professor to subscribe to the three articles of the thirty-sixth canon in the form prescribed by the Statutes of the University for candidates for Degrees in Divinity; and if, after three requisitions, the Professor shall refuse so to subscribe, his Professorship shall thereupon become *ipso facto* void.

14. The Professorship shall not be tenable with a deanery, or any ecclesiastical preferment with cure of souls.

15. *Repealed. See page* 85.

[16. The University shall have power from time to time to make Ordinances for carrying out the provisions of this Statute.][3]

[1] Grace 16 of 8 June 1905, confirming a Report of a Syndicate appointed to consider the mode of Election to certain Professorships (*Reporter*, 23 May 1905, page 918). Sealed, 3 July 1905. Approved by the King in Council, 7 August 1905 (*Reporter*, 17 October 1905, page 106).

[2] Grace 15 of 25 April 1913, confirming a Report of the Council of the Senate (*Reporter*, 25 February 1913, page 701). Sealed, 5 May 1913. Approved by the King in Council, 12 August 1913 (*Reporter*, 2 October 1913, page 30).

[3] Grace 17 of 8 June 1905, confirming a Report of a Syndicate appointed to consider the mode of Election to certain Professorships (*Reporter*, 23 May 1905, page 918). Sealed, 3 July 1905. Approved by the King in Council, 7 August 1905 (*Reporter*, 17 October 1905, page 106).

STATUTE FOR THE LADY MARGARET'S PROFESSORSHIP AND THE NORRISIAN PROFESSORSHIP OF DIVINITY IN COMMON

Approved by the Queen in Council, 1 *August* 1860.

The whole of the tithe rentcharge of the rectory of Terrington St John's, and so much of the tithe rentcharge of Terrington St Clement's as is apportioned over the following lands, viz.,

			A.	R.	P.
Smeath	numbered 1 to 37 in the tithe apportionment map	containing	205	0	8
Fen	38 to 94		338	0	16
East field	443 to 491		219	2	22
Part of Jankin field	492 to 503		99	2	32

amounting altogether to £799. 19*s.* 6*d.*, shall be appropriated as an additional endowment of the Norrisian Professorship either on the next vacancy of the Lady Margaret's Professorship, or as soon as the present Lady Margaret's Professor shall give his assent to this appropriation; provided that from the time of such appropriation, or as soon as the present Norrisian Professor shall give his assent to the acceptance of the same, the new Statute for the Norrisian Professorship shall come into operation[1].

STATUTE FOR THE NORRISIAN PROFESSORSHIP OF DIVINITY

Approved by the Queen in Council, 1 *August* 1860.

1. The provisions prescribed by Mr Norris[2], for the regulation of the Professorship founded by him, and subsequently

[1] The Rectory of Terrington in Norfolk was given to the Lady Margaret's Professor by James I in letters patent dated 26 August 1605. They are printed in *Endowments of the University*, ed. 1904, pp. 38, 39. For the history of the severance of the Rectory from the Professorship, and of Mr Norris's foundation in general, see *Endowments*, ut supra, pp. 104, 105.

[2] See *Endowments of the University*, ed. 1904, pp. 104–116.

adopted by Dr Chapman and Lord Wodehouse in their benefactions thereto[1], excepting so far as they are re-enacted by this Statute, are hereby repealed.

[2. The Professor who may be holding office at the time of the approval by the King in Council of this amended Statute shall be entitled to hold the Professorship for life.][2]

3. The Electors to this Professorship shall be the Heads of the several Colleges of the University.

[4. In case of a vacancy of the Professorship, the Vice-Chancellor shall inform the Council of the Senate thereof at their next meeting after the vacancy is made known to him, and they may if they think fit delay the announcement of the vacancy for such period, not exceeding six months, as may be necessary for submitting a Grace to the Senate with a view to the suspension of election to the Professorship. If on or before the fourteenth day after the Council have been so informed the Vice-Chancellor shall receive from two members of the Council written notice of their intention to propose a motion delaying the announcement of the vacancy, he shall forthwith give notice to the Council of such motion which shall be proposed at their next meeting held in full term and shall defer the announcement of the vacancy pending the result of such motion; but if the Vice-Chancellor shall receive no such notice of such motion, he shall forthwith, if it is term time, or on the first day of the following term, give public notice of the vacancy by fixing a written or printed paper on the door of the Senate-House, and shall at the same time and in like manner give public notice of the day for electing a new Professor, and the day of election shall be not sooner than fourteen days nor later than twenty-eight days after the date of this announcement.][3]

[1] See *Endowments of the University*, ed. 1904, pp. 116, 117.

[2] Grace 15 of 25 April 1913, confirming a Report of the Council of the Senate (*Reporter*, 25 February 1913, page 701). Sealed, 5 May 1913. Approved by the King in Council, 12 August 1913 (*Reporter*, 2 October 1913, page 30).

[3] Grace 1 of 14 March 1914 and Grace 4 of 1 May 1914, confirming a Report of the Council of the Senate (*Reporter*, 9 December 1913, page 341). Sealed, 16 May 1914. Approved by the King in Council, 16 July 1914.

5. No election of a Professor shall take place unless eleven at least of the Electors are present and vote, and that person shall be elected who has a majority of all the votes; and if after two scrutinies no person has such a majority of votes, a third scrutiny shall take place, when that person shall be elected who has the greatest number of votes; but if, in this last scrutiny, the same number of votes are given for two or more persons, which are also more than those given for any other candidate, that one of the two or more such persons shall be elected for whom the Master of Trinity, or in his absence the Provost of King's, or in the absence of both the Master of Gonville and Caius, shall give his casting vote.

6—12. *Repealed.* *See page* 85.

13. It shall be competent to the Vice-Chancellor, if at any time he shall see occasion to do so, to require the Professor to subscribe to the three articles of the thirty-sixth canon in the form prescribed by the Statutes of the University for candidates for degrees in Divinity; and if, after three requisitions, the Professor shall refuse so to subscribe, his Professorship shall thereupon become *ipso facto* void.

14. The Professorship shall not be tenable with a deanery, or with any ecclesiastical preferment with cure of souls.

15. *Repealed.* *See page* 85.

STATUTE FOR MR HULSE'S FOUNDATIONS (HULSEAN PROFESSORSHIP OF DIVINITY AND HULSEAN LECTURER)

Approved by the Queen in Council, 1 *August* 1860.

Whereas it is expedient, with the view of more effectually carrying out the purposes contemplated by the late Rev. John Hulse in his foundations[1], to make various changes in the provisions of his Will for regulating the same, more especially by

[1] See *Endowments of the University*, ed. 1904, pp. 117—121. By Stat. B. XVIII. (p. 69) the management and administration of the property of this endowment is vested in the Chancellor, Masters, and Scholars of the University.

converting the office of Christian Advocate into a Professorship of Theology, modifying the duties of the Lecturer, and altering the distribution of the funds assigned to the Christian Advocate or proposed Professor, the Lecturer, and the Dissertator, it is ordained as follows, that:

[*The Hulsean Professor.*]

1. Instead of the office of Christian Advocate, there shall on the next vacancy thereof be established a Professorship of the University[1], the holder of which shall have the title of the Hulsean Professor of Divinity.

2. The Electors to the Professorship shall be the Vice-Chancellor, the Master of Trinity College, the Master of St John's College, the Lady Margaret's, Regius, Norrisian, and Ely[2] Professors of Divinity; and if either the Master of Trinity College or the Master of St John's College be Vice-Chancellor, his place shall be supplied by the Regius Professor of Greek. In case the votes of the Electors should be equally divided, the Vice-Chancellor shall have a casting vote.

[3. In the event of a vacancy in the Hulsean Professorship as established by this Statute, the Vice-Chancellor shall inform the Council of the Senate thereof at their next meeting after the vacancy is made known to him, and they may if they think fit delay the announcement of the vacancy for such period, not exceeding six months, as may be necessary for submitting a Grace to the Senate with a view to the suspension of election to the Professorship. If on or before the fourteenth day after the Council have been so informed the Vice-Chancellor shall receive from two members of the Council written notice of their intention to propose a motion delaying the announcement of the vacancy, he shall forthwith give notice to the Council of such motion which shall be proposed at their next meeting held in full term and shall defer the announcement of

[1] The omission from this Section of the words "tenable for life" was approved by the King in Council, 12 August 1913 (*Reporter*, 2 October 1913, page 30). For further references see Section 12A of this Statute.

[2] The Ely Professor is added by Statute B, chapter XV (page 67).

the vacancy pending the result of such motion ; but if the Vice-Chancellor shall receive no such notice of such motion, he shall forthwith, if it is term time, or on the first day of the following term, give public notice of the vacancy by fixing a written or printed paper on the door of the Senate-House, and shall at the same time and in like manner give public notice of the day for electing a new Professor, and the day of election shall be not sooner than fourteen days nor later than twenty-eight days after the date of this announcement.][1]

4–10. *Repealed.* *See page* 85.

11. It shall be competent to the Vice-Chancellor, if at any time he shall see occasion to do so, to require the Professor to subscribe to the three articles of the thirty-sixth canon in the form prescribed by the Statutes of the University for candidates for Degrees in Divinity; and if, after three requisitions, the Professor shall refuse so to subscribe, his Professorship shall thereupon become *ipso facto* void.

12. The Professor shall print and publish at least six lectures in the course of every six years of his tenure of office, reckoning from one year after his appointment; and, in case he should fail to publish such six lectures within the time specified, he shall forfeit one-half of his stipend in the seventh and every succeeding year, until such publication shall have taken place.

[12A. The Professor who may be holding office at the time of the approval by the King in Council of this amended Statute shall be entitled to hold the Professorship for life.][2]

[1] Grace 1 of 14 March 1914 and Grace 4 of 1 May 1914, confirming a Report of the Council of the Senate (*Reporter*, 9 December 1913, page 341). Sealed, 16 May 1914. Approved by the King in Council, 16 July 1914.

[2] Grace 15 of 25 April 1913, confirming a Report of the Council of the Senate (*Reporter*, 25 February 1913, page 701). Sealed, 5 May 1913. Approved by the King in Council, 12 August 1913 (*Reporter*, 2 October 1913, page 30).

[*The Hulsean Lecturer.*]

13. The Hulsean Lecturer shall hold this office for one year only, but shall be capable of re-election after an interval of five years.

14. The Lecturer shall be chosen and appointed from time to time by the Vice-Chancellor, the Master of Trinity College, the Master of St John's College, and the Lady Margaret's, Regius, Norrisian, and Hulsean Professors of Divinity; and if either the Master of Trinity or the Master of St John's shall be Vice-Chancellor, his place shall be supplied by the Regius Professor of Greek. In case the votes of the Electors should be equally divided, the Vice-Chancellor shall have a casting vote. Public notice of the election shall be given as in the case of the Hulsean Professor, and the election shall take place not sooner than fourteen, not later than twenty-eight days, after such notice.

15. The University shall have power to alter and determine from time to time, by Grace of the Senate, the time when the Lecturer is to be appointed.

16. The Lecturer shall preach at least four sermons during his year of office, at such times as shall be prescribed by the authority of the University. He shall not be required to print or publish his sermons.

17. Any candidate shall be capable of being chosen Professor or Lecturer who is thirty years of age or upwards, and in Holy Orders, and a Master of Arts, or of some higher degree in the University of Cambridge.

18. The Professorship shall not be tenable with a deanery, or any ecclesiastical preferment with cure of souls.

19. The whole net income in every year arising from Mr Hulse's benefaction, and applicable to the offices of Christian Advocate, Lecturer, and Dissertator, shall be divided into ten equal parts, eight of which parts shall be assigned to the Professor for his stipend, one to the Lecturer, and one to the Dissertator.

20. *Repealed. See page* 85.

STATUTE FOR THE SADLEIRIAN PROFESSORSHIP[1]

Approved by the Queen in Council, 7 March 1860.

1, 2. *Repealed.* *See page* 85.

3. The Electors to the said Professorship shall be the Vice-Chancellor, three Heads of Colleges, to be elected by the persons whose names are on the Electoral Roll of the University, and to hold office as long as they continue to be Heads of Colleges, and the Lucasian, the Plumian, and the Lowndean Professors. That person shall be elected to the Professorship for whom the majority of those present shall vote; and in case of an equality of votes the Vice-Chancellor shall have a casting vote. If after the votes shall have been taken three times there is no such majority for any one person, then that person shall be held to be elected who shall have the greatest number of votes, if there be only one such person. If two or more persons obtain an equal number of votes, exceeding in each case the number given for any other person, the Vice-Chancellor shall have a casting vote.

4. It shall be the duty of the Professor to explain and teach the principles of Pure Mathematics, and to apply himself to the advancement of that science.

5–7. *Repealed.* *See page* 85.

8. The Three per cent. Consolidated Bank Annuities, now standing in the name of the Governors of the Trust, shall be deemed to be a part of the capital endowment of the foundation; and the balance remaining in every year, after the payment of all monies charged upon the fund, shall be invested in the purchase of like Three per cent. Consolidated Bank Annuities, and added to the said capital endowment.

9. When all the Lectureships shall have become vacant, the management and administration of the Trust Estate shall

[1] The history of the benefaction of Lady Sadleir is given at length in *Endowments of the University*, ed. 1904, pp. 268, 269. The conveyance of the endowment by her trustees to the University is printed in *Endowments*, etc., ed. 1876, p. 321.

be thenceforth vested in the Chancellor, Masters, and Scholars of the University; and the said Bank Annuities, or any part thereof, may be sold, and the proceeds thereof invested upon Government or real securities in England, as the said Chancellor, Masters, and Scholars shall from time to time think proper.

STATUTE FOR THE LUCASIAN PROFESSOR OF MATHEMATICS

Approved by the Queen in Council, 7 *March* 1860.

The following provisions of the foundation deed[1] (19 December 1663) are hereby repealed, viz.:

1. Those which prescribe the number and length of the lectures of the Professor, and the times and places of delivery, together with deductions from the stipend of the Professor for the omission of lectures.

2. Those which prescribe conditions for the employment of a deputy to give lectures and to discharge the other duties of the Professorship, instead of the Professor.

3. That which requires the Professor to deliver to the Vice-Chancellor written copies of his lectures in every year.

4. That which requires the Professor to give assistance to Students in private.

5. Those which commit to the Vice-Chancellor the power of admonishing the Professor for neglect of duty; and to the Vice-Chancellor and Heads of Colleges the power of depriving him of the Professorship for neglect of duty or misconduct.

6. Those which prescribe the length of residence of the Professor in the University for every year, and the conditions of obtaining leave of absence, and deductions from his salary for absence without leave.

[1] See *Endowments of the University*, ed. 1904, pp. 165–171. By Stat. B. XVIII (p. 69) the management and administration of the property of this endowment is vested in the Chancellor, Masters, and Scholars of the University.

7. Those which prescribe the time of election of a new Professor in case of a vacancy of the Professorship and the time and mode of publication of the notice of the vacancy and election.

8. Those which require the Electors[1] to take an oath before the election, and the Professor elect to take an oath previous to his admission.

9. Those which commit to the Vice-Chancellor and Heads of Colleges the power of depriving the Professor of his office in case of incompetency, and assign the stipend to be paid to him after deprivation.

The directions affecting the Professorship, contained in the two Royal Letters[2] of King Charles the Second, dated 18 January, 15 Chas. II [1664] and 20 April, 27 Chas. II [1675] respectively, are hereby repealed.

[*This Statute contained certain additional provisions which have been repealed. See page* 85.]

STATUTE FOR THE PLUMIAN PROFESSORSHIP OF ASTRONOMY AND EXPERIMENTAL PHILOSOPHY

Approved by the Queen in Council, 7 March 1860.

The following provisions of the foundation deed[3] (11 June, 6 Anne [1707]) are hereby repealed, viz.:

1. Those which require the Professor to elect a Scholar to assist him in making observations and experiments, and to provide such Scholar with lodging and a stipend, to purchase instruments, to hire an observatory and a house, and to keep them in repair at his own expense.

2. That which requires the Professor to deliver two Latin lectures in the Public Schools every year.

[1] The Vice-Chancellor and the Heads of all the Colleges.

[2] See *Endowments of the University*, ed. 1904, pp. 170, 171.

[3] See *Endowments*, ut supra, pp. 79–88. The conveyance to the University is printed in *Endowments*, ed. 1876, p. 112 (38).

3. Those which prescribe the instruments to be used in making astronomical observations.

4. That which prescribes the time when a copy of the observations made in every year should be presented to the Vice-Chancellor.

5. Those which commit to the Vice-Chancellor the power of admonishing the Professor for neglect of duty; and to the Electors the power of punishing him by fines or deprivation of the Professorship.

6. That which gives the Vice-Chancellor the power of determining the fees to be paid for lectures by Students.

7. Those which prescribe the time of electing a new Professor in case of a vacancy of the Professorship, and the time and mode of publication of the notice of vacancy and election.

8. Those which require the Electors[1] to take an oath before the election, and the Professor elect to take an oath previous to his admission.

9. That which declares the election of the candidate who obtains the votes of three Electors or of the Chancellor of the University and two Electors.

[*This Statute contained certain additional provisions which have been repealed. See page* 85.]

STATUTE FOR THE LOWNDEAN PROFESSORSHIP OF ASTRONOMY AND GEOMETRY

Approved by the Queen in Council, 7 March 1860.

1. The provision contained in Mr Lowndes' Will[2] (6 May 1748), which directs that the Professor shall be from time to time chosen and appointed by the Lord High Chancellor, Lord

[1] The Vice-Chancellor, the Masters of Trinity, Christ's, Gonville and Caius, and the Lucasian Professor; but if any of those Heads of Colleges should be Vice-Chancellor, the Master of St John's is to become an elector

[2] See *Endowments of the University*, ed. 1904, p. 202. By Stat. B. XVIII (p. 69) the management and administration of this property is vested in the Chancellor, Masters, and Scholars of the University.

Keeper of the Great Seal of Great Britain, the Lord President of the Privy Council, the Lord Privy Seal, the Lord High Treasurer or the first Lord Commissioner of the Treasury, the Lord Steward of the King's household for the time being, or the major part of them, is hereby repealed: and in lieu of the said provision it is hereby enacted, that the Professor shall be from time to time chosen and appointed by the Vice-Chancellor of the University, the President of the Royal Society of London, the Astronomer Royal, the Lucasian Professor of Mathematics, and the Plumian Professor of Astronomy and Experimental Philosophy; and when the Sadleirian Professorship of Pure Mathematics shall have been established, the Sadleirian Professor and the President of the Royal Astronomical Society of London shall also be Electors. The candidate who has the votes of a majority of the whole body of the Electors shall be deemed to be elected; and if after three scrutinies no such majority be obtained, then that person shall be deemed to be elected in whose favour the Chancellor of the University and any two of the Electors, or, subsequently to the establishment of the Sadleirian Professorship, the Chancellor and any three of the Electors, shall concur.

2, 3. *Repealed.* *See page* 85.

STATUTE FOR THE LUCASIAN, THE LOWNDEAN AND THE SADLEIRIAN PROFESSORSHIPS IN COMMON[1]

Grace 1 *of* 14 *March* 1914 *and Grace* 4 *of* 1 *May* 1914, *confirming a Report of the Council of the Senate* (*Reporter*, 9 *December* 1913, *page* 341). *Sealed*, 16 *May* 1914. *Approved by the King in Council*, 16 *July* 1914.

In case of a vacancy of the Lucasian, Lowndean, or Sadleirian Professorship, the Vice-Chancellor shall inform the Council of the Senate thereof at their next meeting after the vacancy is made known to him, and they may if they think fit delay

[1] The election to the Plumian Professorship, which was formerly governed by this Statute, is now (by Statute B, Chapter XV) governed by Statute B, Chapter IX.

the announcement of the vacancy for such period, not exceeding six months, as may be necessary for submitting a Grace to the Senate with a view to the suspension of election to the Professorship. If on or before the fourteenth day after the Council have been so informed the Vice-Chancellor shall receive from two members of the Council written notice of their intention to propose a motion delaying the announcement of the vacancy, he shall forthwith give notice to the Council of such motion which shall be proposed at their next meeting held in full term and shall defer the announcement of the vacancy pending the result of such motion; but if the Vice-Chancellor shall receive no such notice of such motion, he shall forthwith, if it is term time, or on the first day of the following term, give public notice of the vacancy by fixing a written or printed paper on the door of the Senate-House, and shall at the same time and in like manner give public notice of the day for electing a new Professor, and the day of election shall be not sooner than fourteen days nor later than twenty-eight days after the date of the notice.

STATUTES FOR SIR THOMAS ADAMS'S PROFESSORSHIP OF ARABIC

I. *Approved by the Queen in Council*, 16 *April* 1861.

The following provisions, contained in the Royal Letters Patent[1], 4 July, 18 Car. 2 [1666], are hereby repealed, viz.:

1. That which requires the Professor to lecture once in every week during term time through the year.

2. That which prescribes the times when the Professor is to be prepared to give assistance to Students in private.

3. Those which give power to the Vice-Chancellor to admonish the Professor for neglect of duty, and to the Vice-Chancellor and Heads of Colleges to deprive him of his Professorship for neglect of duty or misconduct.

4. That which gives a preference to the election of the Professor to Heads and Fellows of Colleges and Gremials.

[1] See *Endowments of the University*, ed. 1876, p. 26.

5. Those which prescribe the time of election of the Professor after every vacancy and the time and mode of publication of the notice of the vacancy and election.

6. Those which require the Electors to take an oath before the election, and the Professor elect to take an oath previous to admission.

7. Those which give power to the Vice-Chancellor and Heads of Colleges to deprive the Professor of his office in case of incompetency, and assign the stipend to be paid to him after deprivation.

8. That which prevents Sir Thomas Adams's Professor from holding any other Professorship, so far as to enable him to hold with his Professorship the Lord Almoner's Readership in Arabic, if duly appointed thereto.

The remaining provisions of the said Letters Patent, as far as they are consistent with the provisions of this Statute, are hereby re-enacted.

[*This Statute contained certain additional provisions which have been repealed. See page* 86.]

II. *Grace* 5 *of* 18 *June* 1894, *and Grace of* 27 *June* 1894, *confirming a Report of the Council of the Senate* (*Reporter*, 12 *June* 1894, *page* 902). *Sealed*, 4 *July* 1894. *Approved by the Queen in Council*, 18 *July* 1894.

In the Matter of the Act of Parliament passed in the 19th and 20th years of the Reign of Her present Majesty, chapter 88, intituled "An Act to make further provision for the good government and extension of the University of Cambridge and the Colleges therein and of the College of King Henry 6th at Eton."

We, the Chancellor, Masters, and Scholars of the University of Cambridge, in pursuance and exercise of the power conferred upon us by the 43rd section of the above-mentioned Act do hereby repeal such portion of the statute for Sir Thomas Adams's Professorship of Arabic made by the Commissioners under the said Act on the 23rd day of October, 1860, and confirmed by Her Majesty the Queen in Council on the 16th day of April, 1861, as by re-enactment requires that the Professor shall be *ad minimum Magister Artium*[1]. And we the said Chancellor, Masters, and Scholars humbly beg to submit the foregoing before Her Majesty in Council.

Given under our Common Seal this fourth day of July one thousand eight hundred and ninety-four.

(LS)

STATUTE FOR THE KNIGHTBRIDGE PROFESSORSHIP OF MORAL THEOLOGY, CASUISTICAL DIVINITY, AND MORAL PHILOSOPHY[2]

Approved by the Queen in Council, 16 *April* 1861.

The following provisions contained in the Will of Dr John Knightbridge[3], or in the decree of the Court of Chancery, 18 July 1682[4], are hereby repealed, viz.:

1. That which requires the Professor to be a Doctor or Bachelor of Divinity, and of the age of forty years or upwards.

2. That which requires the Professor to give four Latin lectures in each term, and to deliver such lectures in writing to the Vice-Chancellor.

The remaining provisions of the said Will and of the said decree of the Court of Chancery, as far as they are consistent

[1] These words occur in the deed of foundation dated 13 June 1666. and signed by Sir Thomas Adams. It is printed in *Endowments of the University*, ed. 1904, pp. 174–177. The letters patent of Charles the Second, dated 4 July, 18 Car. 2, in which it is repeated, will be found in *Endowments*, ed. 1876, p. 26.

[2] By Stat. B. xv (p. 67) the designation of the Professorship is altered to "Professorship of Moral Philosophy."

[3] Printed in *Endowments of the University*, ed. 1904, p. 178.

[4] The provisions of this Decree are mentioned in *Endowments*, ut supra, p. 179. It is quoted in a subsequent Decree of the same Court, dated 4 June 1847, printed in *Endowments*, ed. 1876, pp. 37–52.

with the provisions of this Statute, are hereby re-enacted, and the following additional provisions are hereby enacted, viz.:

1. *Repealed. See page* 86.

2. The Chancellor, Masters, and Scholars of the University of Cambridge shall henceforth have the management and administration of the estate and funds held in trust for the Professorship.

3–6. *Repealed. See page* 86.

STATUTE FOR THE REGIUS PROFESSORSHIP OF MODERN HISTORY

Approved by the Queen in Council, 16 *April* 1861.

1. The directions, affecting the Professorship, contained in the Royal Letters Patent[1], 28 Sep., 11 Geo. 1 [1724], and 11 April, 1 Geo. 2 [1728], are hereby repealed, except so far as relates to the appointment of the Professor by the Crown.

2–4. *Repealed. See page* 86.

STATUTE FOR THE WOODWARDIAN PROFESSORSHIP OF GEOLOGY

Approved by the Queen in Council, 16 *April* 1861.

The following provisions contained in the Will[2] of Dr Woodward are hereby repealed, viz.:

1. Those which prescribe the time of election of a Professor after each vacancy and the notice to be given.

2. That which requires the Professor to be a bachelor.

3. That which prohibits the Professor from holding any preferment that requires his attendance out of the University.

[1] See *Endowments of the University*, ed. 1904, pp. 188–192.

[2] See *Endowments*, ut supra, pp. 196–202.

4. That which requires the Professor never to be absent from the University above the space of two months in the year.

5. Those which require four lectures to be read in every year on some of the subjects treated of in Dr Woodward's works, and one at least of the said lectures to be published in print.

6. That which requires the Professor to reside in or near the room where the fossils are kept, and to attend in the same and shew them to all who desire to have a view of them.

The remaining provisions of the said Will, as far as they are consistent with the provisions of this Statute, are hereby re-enacted; and the following additional provisions are hereby enacted, viz.:

1. *Repealed. See page* 86.

2. The Professor shall hold no such office of preferment, requiring his attendance out of the University, as shall interfere with the duties of his Professorship.

3–5. *Repealed. See page* 86.

STATUTE FOR THE JACKSONIAN PROFESSORSHIP OF NATURAL PHILOSOPHY

Approved by the Queen in Council, 16 *April* 1861.

The following provisions, contained in the Will and directions[1] of Mr Jackson, are hereby repealed:

1. That which requires the Professor to produce in every year, before receiving his salary, a certificate signed by eight Scholars at least who have attended his lectures for twenty days.

2. That which empowers the Regent Masters of Arts only to elect the Professor.

[1] See *Endowments of the University*, ed. 1904, pp. 208–216.

3. That which gives a preference in the election of the Professor to the members of Trinity College, and to the natives of certain specified counties.

4. Those which prescribe the time and place of election of the Professor, and the notice to be given of the vacancy and of the election.

5. Those which prescribe the number and length of the lectures to be given in every year, and the number of lectures to be attended by the free pupils.

6. Those which require the Master, Fellows, and Scholars of Trinity College, or some of them, or the Bursar, to give public notice of the neglect or omission of the Professor to give lectures for the term of one whole year, and declare the Professorship to be vacant by reason of such neglect or omission.

7. That which gives power to the Provost of King's College, the Master of Trinity College, and the Master of St John's College, or the majority of them, or to the Vice-Chancellor, or to the Bishop of Ely, to determine any doubt or dispute about the due reading of the lecture, or the proper subject of it.

8. That which requires the Professor to deliver, or cause to be delivered, in every year to the Vice-Chancellor two copies, fairly written, of one of the lectures read within the course exhibited that year.

The remaining provisions of the said Will and directions, as far as they are consistent with the provisions of this Statute, are hereby re-enacted.

[*This Statute contained certain additional provisions which have been repealed. See page* 86.]

STATUTE FOR THE CRAVEN SCHOLARSHIPS[1], THE BATTIE SCHOLARSHIP[2], THE DAVIES SCHOLARSHIP[3], AND THE PITT SCHOLARSHIP[4] IN COMMON

Approved by the Queen in Council, 16 *April* 1861.

1. The University shall have power to alter and determine from time to time, by Grace of the Senate, the regulations respecting the persons who are to examine the candidates and elect the Scholars; and also the regulations respecting notice of the vacancy of any Scholarship, the academical standing of candidates, the notice to be given by candidates of their intention to present themselves for examination, the time, mode, and subjects of examination, and the time of election.

2. In the election to any Scholarship the Electors shall not be required to take into consideration the pecuniary circumstances of the candidates.

3. In the election to any Scholarship the Electors shall not be required to take into consideration the relation of the candidates to the founder in name or kindred.

[4. Each Scholar elected after the first day of October 1914, who shall have matriculated in the Michaelmas or Lent Term in any academic year, shall hold his Scholarship as from the first day of October preceding the date of his election until the end of the third academic year after the academic year in which he shall have matriculated if he shall continue a member of the University and no longer, and each Scholar elected after the first day of October 1914, who shall have matriculated in the Easter Term in any academic year, shall hold his Scholarship as from the first day of October preceding the date of his election until the end of the fourth academic year after the academic year in which he shall have matriculated if he shall continue a member of the University and no longer, Provided that any holder of a Battie, Davies, or Pitt Scholarship who is

[1] See *Endowments of the University*, ed. 1904. pp. 283–293.
[2] *Ibid.*, pp. 294–300. [3] *Ibid.*, p. 300. [4] *Ibid.*, pp. 301–307.

elected to a Craven or a Waddington Scholarship shall vacate his former Scholarship as on the thirtieth day of September preceding such last mentioned election.

5. No student shall hold more than one of the Scholarships governed by this Statute at the same time, and no holder of a Battie, Davies, or Pitt Scholarship shall be eligible for another of such last mentioned Scholarships or for Sir William Browne's Scholarship or for a Porson Scholarship.

6. The University shall have power to regulate from time to time by Grace of the Senate the conditions of residence of the Scholars; if any Scholar fail to comply with such conditions, he shall vacate his Scholarship.][1]

7. The University shall have power by Grace of the Senate to augment, out of any funds at their disposal, the stipends of the Davies and Battie Scholarships, respectively.

[8. With a view to equalising as far as possible the number and value of the Scholarships to be offered in different years, the University shall have power from time to time by Grace of the Senate to alter and determine the stipends of the said Scholarships (except the Craven Scholarships), and to make regulations for withholding them or any of them (including the Craven Scholarships) temporarily from competition and for providing additional Scholarships on any of the several foundations (except the Craven foundation) and for applying accumulations of income to the payment of Scholarships and for limiting or determining the number of such Scholarships (including the Craven Scholarships) or of such Scholarships together with any other University Scholarships to be offered in any year or years, Provided that no such Grace shall alter or affect the value of the Scholarship of any Scholar elected before the first day of October 1914 or before the date of such Grace.][1]

[1] Grace 1 of 31 January 1914, and Grace 1 of 13 February 1914, confirming a Report of the Council of the Senate (*Reporter*, 20 January 1914, page 510). Sealed, 28 February 1914. Confirmed by the King in Council, 14 May 1914 (*Reporter*, 19 May 1914, page 935).

STATUTE FOR SIR WILLIAM BROWNE'S SCHOLARSHIP

Approved by the Queen in Council, 6 *April* 1858.

1. The University shall have power to make regulations from time to time, by Grace of the Senate, respecting the academical standing of candidates for the Scholarship.

2. The Scholar shall not be required to admit himself at Peterhouse, nor to reside there during his Undergraduateship.

[3. The University shall have power to regulate from time to time by Grace of the Senate the conditions of residence of the Scholar. If any Scholar fail to comply with such conditions he shall vacate his Scholarship.][1]

4. The Scholar shall not be required to produce every Sunday a copy of Greek or Latin verses; nor to go to lectures with the Mathematic Professor for three years.

[5. No Scholar shall be eligible for a Battie, Davies, Pitt, or Porson Scholarship or shall hold his Scholarship together with any of the said Scholarships or with a Craven or a Waddington Scholarship.][1]

6. The rules prescribed by Sir William Browne[2] shall be subject to further amendment and alteration from time to time by the University, with the approval of the Queen in Council.

[7. Each Scholar elected after the first day of October 1914, who shall have matriculated in the Michaelmas or Lent Term in any academic year, shall hold his Scholarship as from the first day of October preceding the date of his election until the end of the third academic year after the academic year in which he shall have matriculated if he shall continue a member of the University and no longer, and each Scholar

[1] Grace 1 of 31 January 1914, and Grace 1 of 13 February 1914, confirming a Report of the Council of the Senate (*Reporter*, 20 January 1914, page 510). Sealed, 28 February 1914. Confirmed by the King in Council, 14 May 1914 (*Reporter*, 19 May 1914, page 935).

[2] See *Endowments of the University*, ed. 1904, pp. 98–101.

elected after the first day of October 1914, who shall have matriculated in the Easter Term in any academic year, shall hold his Scholarship as from the first day of October preceding the date of his election until the end of the fourth academic year after the academic year in which he shall have matriculated if he shall continue a member of the University and no longer, Provided that if he is elected to a Craven or a Waddington Scholarship he shall vacate Sir William Browne's Scholarship as on the thirtieth day of September preceding such last mentioned election.

8. With a view to equalising as far as possible the number and value of the Scholarships to be offered in different years, the University shall have power from time to time by Grace of the Senate to alter and determine the stipend of the Scholarship, and to make regulations for withholding it temporarily from competition and for providing additional Scholarships and for applying accumulations of income to the payment of the Scholarship or Scholarships, Provided that no such Grace shall alter or affect the value of the Scholarship of any Scholar elected before the first day of October 1914 or before the date of such Grace.][1]

STATUTE FOR THE BELL SCHOLARSHIPS

Approved by the Queen in Council, 6 *April* 1858.

1. The University shall have power to alter and determine from time to time by Grace of the Senate the regulations respecting the persons who are to examine the candidates and elect the Scholars.

2. The Electors shall be at liberty to choose candidates from King's College or Trinity Hall.

3. Undergraduates shall be deemed to be of the first year of standing if of not more than one year's standing from the time of their first residence; of the second year, if of more than

[1] See note 1 on the preceding page.

one and not more than two years' standing from the time of their first residence; and of the third year, if of more than two and not more than three years' standing from the time of their first residence.

4. When the Electors meet to elect the Scholars, the foundation deed shall not be required to be read aloud by one of the Electors to the rest.

5. The foundation deed[1] shall be subject to further amendment and alteration from time to time by the University, with the approval of the Queen in Council.

STATUTE FOR THE PORSON SCHOLARSHIP

Approved by the Queen in Council, 6 *April* 1858.

1. The University shall have power to alter and determine from time to time, by Grace of the Senate, the regulations respecting the persons who are to examine the candidates and elect the Scholar; and also the regulation respecting the time of declaring the vacancy of the Scholarship, the notice to be given by candidates of their intention to present themselves for examination, and the times of examination and election.

[2. Each Scholar elected after the first day of October 1914, who shall have matriculated in the Michaelmas or Lent Term in any academic year, shall hold his Scholarship as from the first day of October preceding the date of his election until the end of the third academic year after the academic year in which he shall have matriculated if he shall continue a member of the University and no longer, and each Scholar elected after the first day of October 1914, who shall have matriculated in the Easter Term in any academic year, shall hold his Scholarship as from the first day of October preceding the date of his election until the end of the fourth academic year after the academic year in which he shall have matriculated if he shall continue a member of the University and no longer, Provided that if he is elected to

[1] See *Endowments of the University*, ed. 1904, pp. 302–307

a Craven or a Waddington Scholarship he shall vacate his Porson Scholarship as on the thirtieth day of September preceding such last mentioned election.][1]

3. The foundation deed[2] shall be subject to further amendment and alteration from time to time by the University, with the approval of the Queen in Council.

[4. No Scholar shall be eligible for Sir William Browne's Scholarship or for a Battie, Davies, or Pitt Scholarship, or shall hold his Scholarship with any of the said Scholarships or with a Craven or a Waddington Scholarship.

5. The University shall have power from time to time by Grace of the Senate to alter the regulations respecting the academical standing of candidates for the Scholarships.

6. The University shall have power from time to time by Grace of the Senate to regulate the conditions of residence of the Scholars. If any Scholar fail to comply with such conditions he shall vacate his Scholarship.

7. With a view to equalising as far as possible the number and value of the Scholarships to be offered in different years, the University shall have power from time to time by Grace of the Senate to alter and determine the stipend of the Scholarship, and to make regulations for withholding it temporarily from competition and for providing additional Scholarships and for applying accumulations of income to the payment of the Scholarship or Scholarships, Provided that no such Grace shall alter or affect the value of the Scholarship of any Scholar elected before the first day of October 1914 or before the date of such Grace.][1]

[1] Grace 1 of 31 January 1914, and Grace 1 of 13 February 1914, confirming a Report of the Council of the Senate (*Reporter*, 20 January 1914, page 510). Sealed, 28 February 1914. Confirmed by the King in Council, 14 May 1914 (*Reporter*, 19 May 1914, page 935).

[2] See *Endowments of the University*, ed. 1904, pp. 127–130.

STATUTE FOR THE SEATONIAN PRIZE

Approved by the Queen in Council, 6 *April* 1858.

1. The University shall have power to alter and determine from time to time, by Grace of the Senate, the regulations respecting the persons by whom the subject of the poem shall be given out and the Prize adjudged.

2. The rules prescribed by Mr Seaton[1] shall be subject to further amendment and alteration from time to time by the University, with the approval of the Queen in Council.

STATUTE FOR SIR WILLIAM BROWNE'S MEDALS

Approved by the Queen in Council, 6 *April* 1858.

1. The University shall have power to alter and determine from time to time, by Grace of the Senate, the regulations respecting the persons by whom the subjects are to be appointed and the Medals adjudged; and also the regulations respecting the times when the subjects are to be appointed, the exercises delivered, and the Medals given.

2. No candidate shall be entitled to receive a Medal who has not commenced his residence in the University when the exercises are delivered.

3. The Adjudicators shall be at liberty to require candidates for the Medal to be given for Greek verse, to write their exercises in Hexameter, Elegiac, or Lyric metre, the metre being named in every year when the subject is appointed.

4. If in any year the best Greek epigram and the best Latin epigram shall not be produced by the same candidate, two Medals shall be given in that year, each of the value of two guineas and a half, one to the candidate who produces the best Greek epigram, and the other to the candidate who produces the best Latin epigram.

[1] See *Endowments of the University*, ed. 1904, pp. 369, 370.

5. The rules, prescribed by Sir William Browne[1], shall be subject to further amendment and alteration from time to time by the University, with the approval of the Queen in Council.

STATUTE FOR THE NORRISIAN PRIZE

Approved by the Queen in Council, 6 *April* 1858.

1. The University shall have power to alter and determine from time to time, by Grace of the Senate, the regulations respecting the persons by whom the subject of the Essays is to be given out and the Prize adjudged; and also the regulations respecting the time and mode of publication of the subject, and the times of sending in the Essays, of adjudging the Prize, and of printing and publishing the Essay for which the Prize is given.

[2. The prize shall be given once in five years only and shall be the sum of the annuities of the five years preceding the adjudication, subject to deduction for any expenses incurred in the award of the prize, including any remuneration that may be assigned by Grace of the Senate to the Examiners.][2]

3. The candidates shall be Graduates of the University of Cambridge, and of not more than thirteen years' standing from admission to their first degrees when the Essays are sent in. They shall not be required to be between the ages of twenty and thirty, nor to have attended the lectures of the Norrisian Professor.

4. The successful candidate shall receive the Gold Medal described by Mr Norris, together with Books, to be selected by himself and approved by the Norrisian Professor, not exceeding

[1] See *Endowments of the University*, ed. 1904, pp. 98–103.

[2] Grace 5 of 2 March 1912, and Grace 9 of 23 May 1912, confirming a Report of the Council of the Senate (*Reporter*, 6 February 1912, page 571). Sealed, 14 June 1912. Approved by the King in Council, 19 July 1912 (*Reporter* 30 July 1912, page 1422).

in value fifteen pounds, and the remainder of the Prize in money; or money instead of the Gold Medal or Books, according to his option: but in no case shall the Medal or Books be given or the money paid, till the Essay has been printed and published.

5. The rules prescribed by Mr Norris[1] shall be subject to further amendment and alteration from time to time by the University, with the approval of the Queen in Council.

STATUTE FOR THE HULSEAN PRIZE

Approved by the Queen in Council, 6 *April* 1858.

1. The University shall have power to alter and determine from time to time by Grace of the Senate the Regulations respecting the times when, and the persons by whom, the subject of the dissertations shall be given out and the Prize adjudged.

2. The rules, prescribed by Mr Hulse[2], shall be subject to further amendment and alteration from time to time by the University, with the approval of the Queen in Council.

STATUTE FOR THE PORSON UNIVERSITY PRIZE

Approved by the Queen in Council, 6 *April* 1858.

1. The University shall have power to alter and determine from time to time by Grace of the Senate the regulations respecting the persons by whom the passages for translation are to be selected and the Prize adjudged.

2. Passages for translation may be chosen from the works of any standard English poet.

[1] See *Endowments of the University*, ed. 1904, pp. 112, 113.
[2] *Ibid.*, p. 120.

3. No candidate shall be entitled to the Prize who has not commenced his residence in the University when the translations are sent in.

4. The foundation deed[1] shall be subject to further amendment and alteration from time to time by the University, with the approval of the Queen in Council.

STATUTE FOR SIR PEREGRINE MAITLAND'S PRIZE

Approved by the Queen in Council, 6 *April* 1858.

[1. The University shall have power to alter and determine from time to time by Grace of the Senate the regulations respecting the persons by whom the subject is to be given out and the Prize adjudged; and also the regulations respecting the times when the subject is to be given out and the exercises sent in. The University shall also have power by Grace of the Senate to assign a payment to the Examiners for the Prize other than the Vice-Chancellor, such payment to be deducted from the amount that would otherwise be payable to the winner of the Prize.][2]

2. The candidates for the Prize shall be Graduates of the University, who are not of more than ten years' standing from admission to their first degrees, when the exercises are sent in.

3. The rules, prescribed in the foundation of the Prize[3], shall be subject to further amendment and alteration from time to time by the University, with the approval of the Queen in Council.

[1] See *Endowments of the University*, ed. 1904, pp. 124–127

[2] Grace 5 of 2 March 1912, and Grace 10 of 23 May 1912, confirming a Report of the Council of the Senate (*Reporter*, 6 February 1912, page 571). Sealed, 14 June 1912. Approved by the King in Council, 19 July 1912 (*Reporter*, 30 July 1912, page 1422).

[3] See *Endowments of the University*, ed. 1904, p. 388.

STATUTE FOR THE BURNEY ENDOWMENT

Approved by the Queen in Council, 6 April 1858.

1 and 2. *Repealed*[1].

3. The Foundation Deed[2] shall be subject to further amendment and alteration from time to time by the University, with the approval of the Queen in Council.

REGULATIONS FOR THE BURNEY PRIZE AND STUDENTSHIP

Grace 2 of 11 May 1905, and Grace 24 of 25 May 1905, confirming a Report of a Syndicate on the Burney Prize (Reporter, 7 March 1905, page 633). Sealed, 25 May 1906. Approved by the King in Council, 30 June 1906.

1. In lieu of the Burney Prize, which has been offered annually since 1847 "for the best English Essay on some moral "or metaphysical subject, on the existence, nature, and attri- "butes of God, or on the truth and evidence of the Christian "religion," there shall be henceforth in the University a Burney Essay Prize and a Burney Studentship, and the dividend of the sum standing in the name of the Chancellor, Masters, and Scholars of the University for the purposes of the Burney Trust shall be applicable to the payment of such Prize and such Studentship and to the other purposes hereinafter described.

2. The subject for which the Burney Prize and the Burney Studentship shall be awarded shall be the Philosophy of Religion: these words being interpreted so as to include Christian Ethics and questions relating to the truth and evidence of the Christian Religion.

[1] These two Sections and also the Regulations for the Burney Prize appended to the Deed of Trust were repealed in the year 1906, and the Regulations for the Burney Prize and Studentship which follow were substituted for them. See *Reporter*, 9 October 1906, page 46.

[2] See *Endowments of the University*, ed. 1904, pp. 391–393.

3. The Electors to the Prize and to the Studentship shall be the Vice-Chancellor, the Master of Christ's College (unless he hold the office of Vice-Chancellor, in which case a Deputy Elector shall be appointed in his place for that turn by Grace of the Senate), the Norrisian Professor of Divinity, and two Members of the Senate who shall be appointed by Grace before the division of the Michaelmas Term, one on the nomination of the Special Board for Divinity and one on the nomination of the Special Board for Moral Science. At the first appointment the senior in standing of the two appointed Electors shall be appointed for three years and the junior for two years: all subsequent appointments shall be for two years. If either of the two appointed Electors die resign or become incapable of acting, another person shall be appointed in like manner in his place for the remainder of the time for which he was appointed. All the powers of the Electors may be exercised by a majority of those present at a meeting duly summoned, provided that three Electors at least be present.

4. The subject for the Essay shall be announced by the Electors and the Essays shall be sent in to the Vice-Chancellor at such dates as the Senate shall from time to time determine. The successful Candidate shall not be required either to print or to publish his Essay; but he shall deposit a copy of it in the University Library.

5. Any member of the University who has been admitted to the title of the degree of Bachelor of Arts shall be eligible for the Prize, provided that on the day appointed for sending in the exercises not more than three years shall have elapsed since the completion of his first degree.

6. The Electors shall have power, on any occasion on which they think it desirable, to appoint one or more Examiners not belonging to their own body to report on the Essays; and each Examiner so appointed shall be paid the sum of £5 out of the income of the Trust.

In the event of the Essays of two of the Candidates being deemed by the Electors to be of equal merit, if one of such

Candidates be a member of Christ's College the Prize shall be adjudged to him.

7. The value of the Prize shall be such sum not less than £50 and not more than £80 as may be determined from time to time by Grace of the Senate.

8. The Prize shall not be awarded a second time to the same person.

9. The election to the Studentship shall be made annually at such time as the University shall determine.

10. Any member of the University who has been admitted to the title of the degree of Bachelor of Arts shall be eligible to the Studentship, provided that on the day appointed for the election in any year not more than four years shall have elapsed since the completion of his first degree.

11. The Electors may take such steps as they think fit to enquire into the qualifications of the Candidates for the Studentship, provided that it shall not be awarded by competitive examination. If the qualifications of two Candidates appear to the Electors to be equal, and if one of the two be a member of Christ's College, he shall be elected to the Studentship.

12. The Studentship shall be tenable for one year. A Student shall be eligible for re-election provided that he is within the limits of standing defined in section 10 hereof, and provided also that no person shall be re-elected to the Studentship more than once.

13. It shall be the duty of the Student to devote himself to study or research in the Philosophy of Religion, according to a scheme proposed by himself and approved by the Electors, provided that such scheme may be modified with the consent of the Electors.

14. The value of the Studentship shall be £120 a year, or such larger sum as may be determined from time to time by Grace of the Senate, payable by equal half-yearly payments (each payment to be made in advance), provided as regards the second payment that the Electors be satisfied that the

Student is diligently carrying out the scheme approved by them: provided also that the Student shall not be in receipt at the time of his appointment, from University or College endowments together with the Studentship, of more than £300 a year, and that he do not undertake without the sanction of the Electors during the term of his tenure of the Studentship any other work to which remuneration is attached.

15. A Burney Prizeman shall be eligible for the Studentship, and a Burney Student shall be eligible for the Prize: provided that they are within the limits of University standing required for the Studentship and for the Prize respectively.

16. The Burney Student may be required by the Electors to publish a thesis embodying the results of his study or research. In the event of a Burney Prizeman being elected to the Studentship the subject of his study or research may be the same as the subject of his Prize Essay, and if so he shall be required to publish a thesis embodying the results of his further study.

A Burney Student who publishes his thesis in accordance with these regulations shall cause to be delivered a copy thereof to the respective libraries of the Universities of Cambridge, Oxford, Dublin, and Edinburgh, and to the library of Christ's College, Cambridge, and also to each of the Electors.

17. If in any year there shall, in the opinion of the Electors, be no Essay sent in worthy of the Prize or no suitable Candidate for the Studentship, no Prize shall be awarded or no election shall be made for that year. Any income not required in any year for the purposes of the Trust as above defined shall be paid to a Reserve Fund out of which the Electors may if they think fit in any year award a second Prize, or a second Studentship, of such amount as they think fit and the state of the Fund allows, or they may at their discretion employ the Fund for the promotion of the study of the Philosophy of Religion in other ways, or any part of the Reserve Fund may be invested by the Financial Board on the recommendation of the Electors, and added to the capital of the trust.

18. The University shall have power to alter and determine from time to time by Grace of the Senate the regulations respecting the persons who shall be the Electors to the Prize and the Studentship.

19. Subject to the foregoing regulations and to any additional regulations which may at any time be made by the University by Statute and approved by the King in Council it shall be lawful for the Electors from time to time to make and if they shall see fit to vary such rules as may seem to them expedient for regulating their own proceedings.

STATUTE FOR THE LE BAS PRIZE

Approved by the Queen in Council, 6 *April* 1858.

1. [The University shall have power to alter and determine from time to time by Grace of the Senate the regulations respecting the persons by whom the subject of the Essays shall be selected and the Prize adjudged; and also the regulations respecting the times when the subject shall be given out, and the Essays sent in. The University shall also have power by Grace of the Senate to assign a payment to the Adjudicators of the Prize other than the Vice-Chancellor, such payment to be made out of the income of the Prize Fund.][1]

2. The candidates for the Prize shall be Graduates of the University, who are not of more than three years' standing from their first degrees, when the Essays are sent in.

3. The rules, prescribed in the foundation[2] of the Prize, shall be subject to further amendment and alteration from time to time by the University, with the approval of the Queen in Council.

[1] Grace 5 of 2 March 1912, and Grace 11 of 23 May 1912, confirming a Report of the Council of the Senate (*Reporter*, 6 February 1912, page 571). Sealed, 14 June 1912. Approved by the King in Council, 19 July 1912 (*Reporter*, 30 July 1912, page 1422).

[2] See *Endowments of the University*, ed. 1904, pp. 395, 396.

STATUTE FOR THE LADY MARGARET'S PREACHERSHIP.

Approved by the Queen in Council, 6 *April* 1858.

1. The University shall have power to alter and determine from time to time by Grace of the Senate the regulations respecting the time of appointment of the Preacher, and the qualifications of the candidates.

2. The Preacher shall be appointed by the Vice-Chancellor and shall hold office for one year.

3. The Preacher shall not be required to take any oath, nor to read the ordinances of the foundation deed, on admission to his office.

4. Instead of preaching in every year the six sermons prescribed by the foundation deed, the Preacher shall be required to preach one sermon in the University church at the Commemoration of Benefactors on the Sunday before the third day of November.

5. The Preacher shall not be obliged to reside in the University, nor be prevented from holding a benefice together with his Preachership.

6. The foundation deed[1] shall be subject to further amendment and alteration from time to time by the University, with the approval of the Queen in Council.

[1] See *Endowments of the University*, ed. 1904, pp. 65–70.

STATUTE FOR SIR ROBERT REDE'S FOUNDATION OF PUBLIC LECTURES

Approved by the Queen in Council, 6 *April* 1858.

1. Instead of the three Readers named in the foundation deed, to be elected in every year, there shall be one Reader only, who shall receive the stipends directed to be paid to all the three Readers heretofore appointed.

2. It shall be the duty of the said Reader to deliver one lecture in term time in every year.

3. The University shall have power to make regulations from time to time, by Grace of the Senate, respecting the time and mode of appointment of the said Reader, the length of tenure of the office, the subjects of the lectures, and the times and places of delivery.

4. The foundation deed[1] shall be subject to further amendment and alteration from time to time by the University, with the approval of the Queen in Council.

STATUTE FOR MR RUSTAT'S DONATION TO THE LIBRARY

Approved by the Queen in Council, 6 *April* 1858.

1. The University shall have power to alter and determine from time to time, by Grace of the Senate, the regulations respecting the persons by whose advice and consent the books are to be bought, and respecting the audit of the accounts.

2. Every book bought with the money arising from Mr Rustat's benefaction shall have, as heretofore, the impression

[1] See *Endowments of the University*, ed. 1904, pp. 262–268.

of Mr Rustat's arms upon it; but the University shall have power to make regulations under which the books may be taken out of the Library, and it shall not be required that they be placed together by themselves in a place set apart for that purpose in the Library.

3. The rules, prescribed by Mr Rustat[1], shall be subject to further amendment and alteration from time to time by the University, with the approval of the Queen in Council.

STATUTE RESPECTING MR WORTS'S ENDOWMENT FOR TRAVELLING BACHELORS[2]

Approved by the Queen in Council, 16 *April* 1861.

The annual pensions charged by Mr Worts upon his estate of £100 a year each to two young Bachelors of Arts, to be sent into foreign countries and to continue there for the space of three years, shall cease to be so applied, and shall constitute a fund, from which the University may make grants from time to time, by Grace of the Senate, at its discretion, for the promotion or encouragement of investigations in foreign countries respecting the religion, learning, law, politics, customs, manners, and rarities, natural or artificial, of those countries, or for purposes of geographical discovery or of antiquarian or scientific research in foreign countries; the conditions as to publishing the result of such investigations to be determined in every case when any grant is made.

[1] See *Endowments of the University*, ed. 1904: "The University Library."

[2] *Ibid.*, p. 92.

INTERPRETATIONS

OF

STATUTES

INTERPRETATIONS OF STATUTES BY THE CHANCELLOR

I

STATUTA ACADEMIAE CANTABRIGIENSIS

Approved by the Queen in Council, 31 *July* 1858.

CAPUT II. DE GRADIBUS. SECT. I. DE STUDIOSIS ARTIUM.

Power of University to examine Women[1].

DEVONSHIRE HOUSE,
PICCADILLY, W.
14 *June* 1881.

DEAR MR VICE-CHANCELLOR,

I forward herewith my interpretation of the two statutes, the meaning of which, in accordance with the provisions of the 42nd Section of the Act 19 and 20 Victoria, Cap. 88[2], I have been called upon by the Council to declare.

It appeared to me to be due to the University that my interpretation should not depend on my own individual judgment, and I have accordingly availed myself of the kind consent of Lord Cairns, Chancellor of the University of Dublin, to give me his assistance. My decision is in conformity with his advice, and the following extract from a paper which he has been so good as to draw up upon the subject will be sufficient to shew the principles on which his opinion has been formed.

[1] *Reporter*, 21 June 1881, page 706.
[2] The Cambridge University Act, 1856. See below, page 158.

"The main object of the incorporation and existence of the University is the advancement of Learning. The regulations as to Matriculation, Admission to Membership, residence and other matters *ejusdem generis* are means leading to that which is the end and object of the University. They may be relaxed or varied from time to time, and anything which is done by the University (in good faith and without the diversion of funds specifically appropriated to a particular purpose) having for its object the advancement of learning and the testing of such advancement by means of examination is in my opinion within the powers of the University."

He goes on to say that in order to prevent misunderstanding he wishes to add that nothing he has said is intended to cover the question of granting degrees to women.

I remain,

Dear Mr Vice-Chancellor,

Yours faithfully,

DEVONSHIRE.

The Rev. the Vice-Chancellor.

To the REVEREND THE VICE-CHANCELLOR *and the Members of the* COUNCIL *of the* SENATE.

DEVONSHIRE HOUSE,
PICCADILLY, LONDON,
14 *June* 1881.

GENTLEMEN,

Having given due consideration to the application made to me on the 2nd of May by the Council of the Senate for a declaration in writing of the true intent and meaning of two of the Statutes of the University in respect of certain matters, and to the Statement prepared by the Council which accompanied the application, I declare the true intent and meaning of the Statutes to be as follows :

The intent and meaning of the words "examina subeant per ordinationes academiae in hanc rem instituta" in Cap. II, De Gradibus, Sect. 1, *De studiosis artium*, are not such as to preclude the University from using the Previous and Tripos Examinations for purposes other than that of testing the proficiency of candidates for degrees in Arts, and in particular for the purpose of testing the proficiency of women in the manner sanctioned by the Graces 1, 2, 3 of 24 February 1881[1].

The intent and meaning of the words "liceat autem academiae novas ordinationes, ad eruditionis amplificationem et decori atque honesti conservationem inter scholasticos spectantes, sancire, modo ne quid his statutis detrahant aut officiant" in Cap. IX are not such as to preclude the University from making "ordinationes ad eruditionis amplificationem spectantes" for the increase of learning among others than members of the University.

I have the honour to be,

Gentlemen,

Your obedient Servant,

DEVONSHIRE.

[1] *Reporter*, 1 March 1881, page 391.

II

STATUTE A

Approved by the Queen in Council, 27 February 1882.

STATUTE A. CHAPTER II. SECTION 16. TERMS NOT KEPT BY RESIDENCE TO BE COUNTED IN SPECIAL CASES.

Number of Terms that may be allowed as kept by Residence[1].

DEVONSHIRE HOUSE,
PICCADILLY, W.
13 *July* 1899

HAVING considered the matter submitted to me by the Council of the Senate of the University of Cambridge on the 18th May 1899, I, as Chancellor of the University of Cambridge, in pursuance of the 52nd Section of the Universities of Oxford and Cambridge Act 1877[2], hereby declare in writing that according to the true meaning of the 16th Section of Chapter II of Statute A the power of the University by Special Grace to allow a term to be counted as kept by residence by a candidate for a degree, though he may not have resided the whole or any portion of the prescribed part of it, is not exhausted when one term has been so allowed and that any number of terms may on sufficiently grave grounds be allowed by the University.

DEVONSHIRE.

STATUTE A. CHAPTER II. SECTION 18. DEGREES AND TITLES OF DEGREES CONFERRED WITHOUT THE FULFILMENT OF THE USUAL CONDITIONS.

Conditions under which a Degree honoris causâ *may be conferred upon the Dean of a Cathedral Church*[3].

I, JOHN WILLIAM BARON RAYLEIGH, Chancellor of the University of Cambridge, in answer to the application of the

[1] *Reporter*, 31 October 1899, page 138.
[2] See below, page 207.
[3] *Reporter*, 10 June 1913, page 1215.

Council of the Senate of the University of Cambridge for a declaration by me of the true meaning of a certain portion of Statute A of the University approved by her late MAJESTY QUEEN VICTORIA in Council on 16 May 1893 do declare that according to the true meaning of the said Statute the University has *not* the power to confer a degree *honoris causâ* upon a person who has received from the Sovereign a Nomination and Presentation to the Deanery of a Cathedral Church before his Institution by the Bishop and Admission by the Canons, and has only power to do so after such Institution and Admission.

RAYLEIGH.

2 *June* 1913.

STATUTE B

Approved by the Queen in Council, 29 *June* 1882.

STATUTE B. CHAPTER V. BOARDS OF STUDIES. SECTION 6.

Reports of Special Boards[1].

I THE MOST NOBLE SPENCER COMPTON DUKE OF DEVONSHIRE K.G. Chancellor of the University of Cambridge in pursuance of Section 52 of 40 and 41 Victoria Cap. 48 upon the application made to me by the Council of the Senate of The University in the document hereunto annexed marked A to declare the meaning of part of Section 6 of Statute B Cap. 5 and to give my decision on four points submitted to me Do hereby declare in writing the meaning of the Statute on the matters submitted to me and give my decision as follows:

1. A Special Board has a right to present to the Vice-Chancellor for publication to the University a Report which is passed by a majority of those present at a meeting of the Board and which is signed by the Chairman only on behalf of the Board, and it is the duty of the Vice-Chancellor to publish such Report to the University in this form.

[1] *Reporter*, 9 May 1905, pages 827–832.

2. The Vice-Chancellor is not empowered to withhold a Report from publication to the University on the ground that it has not been signed in the form which has been generally adopted.

3. The Vice-Chancellor is not empowered to withhold a Report from publication to the University on the ground that it has not been signed in the form which is in the Vice-Chancellor's opinion convenient for the information of the University.

4. The University has not power to prescribe by Ordinance the mode in which Reports of Special Boards to be published to the Senate shall be signed.

WITNESS my hand this 14th day of April 1905.

DEVONSHIRE.

STATUTE B. CHAPTER XI. FOR THE RESIDENCE AND DUTIES OF PROFESSORS AND READERS. SECTION 2.

Residence of Professors[1].

Having considered the matter submitted to me by the Council of the Senate of the University of Cambridge on the 27th April 1908, I, as Chancellor of the University of Cambridge, in pursuance of the 52nd Section of the Universities of Oxford and Cambridge Act 1877, hereby declare in writing that according to the true meaning of Statute B, Chapter XI, Section 2, the University has power in exceptional cases to make for particular Professorships a permanent provision that the Professor shall not be bound to reside in the University throughout full term time.

RAYLEIGH.

19 *May* 1908.

[1] *Reporter*, 26 May 1908, page 951.

STATUTE B. CHAPTER XI. FOR THE RESIDENCE AND DUTIES OF PROFESSORS AND READERS. SECTIONS 8, 9.

The position of a Professor's Deputy[1].

AN application having been made to me by the Council of the Senate of the University of Cambridge in the Document hereunto annexed marked A to declare the true meaning of certain portions of Statute B for the University approved by Her Majesty the Queen in Council on the 29th June 1882, I as Chancellor of the said University do by virtue of Section 22 of the Universities of Oxford and Cambridge Act 1877 hereby declare the meaning of the Statute on the matters submitted to me in the said Document to be as follows:

1. If a Deputy is appointed in the manner prescribed in Statute B, Chapter XI, Sections 8 and 9, he *ipso facto* becomes competent and bound to exercise and perform all the duties and functions of the Professor.

2. It is not possible for the University by inserting any words in the Grace approving the Deputy to limit his duties so as for example to allow the Professor to remain an *ex officio* member of the Special Board or to retain the power of appointing and removing demonstrators.

3. If a Deputy is appointed for a definite time it is not competent for the Professor to resume his duties or some of them, should he wish to do so, before the expiration of that time.

Dated this eighth day of February 1900.

DEVONSHIRE,

Chancellor.

[1] *Reporter*, 20 February 1900, pages 514–517.

STATUTE B. CHAPTER XI. FOR THE RESIDENCE AND DUTIES OF PROFESSORS AND READERS. SECTIONS 4, 5. CHAPTER XII. FOR FEES PAYABLE FOR UNIVERSITY TUITION.

The University cannot prevent a Reader from taking private pupils[1].

AN application having been made to me by the Council of the Senate of the University of Cambridge in the Document hereunto annexed marked B to declare the true meaning of certain portions of Statute B for the University approved by Her Majesty the Queen in Council on the 29th June 1882, I as Chancellor of the said University do hereby declare the meaning of the Statute on the matters submitted to me in the said document to be as follows:

1. The University has no power under Statute B Chapter XII to preclude a Reader from taking private pupils.

2. The University cannot under Chapter XI, Section 4, Paragraph 2, prescribe as a duty attached to Readerships that the Readers shall not take private pupils.

3. The General Board cannot under Chapter XI, Section 5, issue any binding regulations or instructions to the effect that the Reader shall not take private pupils.

Dated this eighth day of February, 1900.

DEVONSHIRE,

Chancellor.

[1] *Reporter*, 20 February 1900, pages 517–520.

STATUTE B. CHAPTERS V, VI, XV.

Professorship of Mechanism and Applied Mechanics[1].

DEVONSHIRE HOUSE,
PICCADILLY,
17 *June* 1890.

I am of opinion that the Professorship of Mechanism and Applied Mechanics will not terminate on the resignation of Professor Stuart.

I do not think that the provisions of Statute B respecting this Professorship are actually inconsistent with the continuance in force of the Ordinance of October 28th, 1875, as they may be read as applicable to this particular Professorship in case the University may decide to continue it, but I agree with Mr Wright in what I understand to be his opinion that the fair result of the several parts of Statute B to which he refers is that this Professorship was intended to be and was made part of the Permanent Professorial Staff of the University, and this provision having been made by Statute overrides and supersedes the Ordinance of 1875, or (in other words) the Statute has in fact decided that this Professorship shall continue.

DEVONSHIRE.

[1] *Reporter*, 24 June 1890, pages 995–6.

ACTS

OF

PARLIAMENT

CERTAIN ACTS OF PARLIAMENT

RELATING TO

THE UNIVERSITY OF CAMBRIDGE

[NOTE.—The repealed portions of the Acts of Parliament are printed in smaller, the unrepealed portions in larger type. The letters *S. L. R. A.* stand for *Statute Law Revision Act.*]

THE CAMBRIDGE UNIVERSITY ACT, 1856.

19 & 20 VICT. CAP. 88.

An Act to make further Provision for the good Government and Extension of the University of Cambridge, of the Colleges therein, and of the College of King Henry the Sixth at Eton. [29th July 1856.]

WHEREAS it is expedient, for the Advancement of Religion and Learning, to enlarge the Powers of making and altering Statutes, Ordinances, and Regulations now possessed by the University of Cambridge and the Colleges thereof, and to make and enable to be made further Provision for the Government and for the Extension of the said University, and for the Abrogation of Oaths now taken therein, and otherwise for maintaining and improving the Discipline and Studies and the good Government of the said University of Cambridge and the Colleges thereof: Be it enacted by the Queen's most Excellent Majesty, by and with the Advice and Consent of the Lords Spiritual and Temporal, and Commons, in this present Parliament assembled, and by the Authority of the same, as follows: (*Repealed, S. L. R. A.*, 1892 *and* 1893.)

Appointment of Commissioners.

1. The several Persons herein-after named, (that is to say,) the Right Reverend John Lord Bishop of Lichfield, the Right Reverend John Lord Bishop of Chester, the Right Honourable Edward Henry

Stanley commonly called Lord Stanley, the Right Honourable Matthew Talbot Baines, Vice-Chancellor Sir William Page Wood Knight, the Right Honourable Sir Laurence Peel Knight, the Very Reverend George Peacock Dean of Ely, and the Reverend Charles John Vaughan Doctor in Divinity, shall be Commissioners for the Purposes of this Act, and shall have a Common Seal, and Three of the said Commissioners shall be a Quorum, and the Commissioner appointed or acting as Chairman shall have a Second or Casting Vote when the Votes of the said Commissioners shall be equally divided. (*Repealed, S. L. R. A.*, 1875.)

Duration of Powers of Commissioners.

2. The Powers hereby conferred on the Commissioners shall be in force until the First Day of January One thousand eight hundred and fifty-nine, and it shall be lawful for Her Majesty, if She shall think fit, by and with the Advice of Her Privy Council, to continue the same until the First Day of January One thousand eight hundred and sixty, and no longer. (*Repealed, S. L. R. A.*, 1875.)

Vacancy in Number of Commissioners.

3. If any Vacancy occurs in the Number of such Commissioners, by means of Death, Resignation, or Incapacity to act, Her Majesty may fill up such Vacancy. (*Repealed, S. L. R. A.*, 1875.)

Commissioners empowered to require Production of Documents, etc.

4. In the Exercise of the Authorities hereby vested in the Commissioners they shall have Power to require from any Officer of the University of Cambridge or of any College therein the Production of any Documents or Accounts relating to such University or College, and any Information relating to the Revenues, Statutes, Usages, or Practice thereof respectively; and no Oath which may have been taken by any such Officer shall be a Bar to any Authorities of the Commissioners. (*Repealed, S. L. R. A.*, 1875.)

Constitution of the University.

Establishment of Council of the Senate.

5. Upon the Sixth Day of November One thousand eight hundred and fifty-six, all Powers, Privileges, and Functions now possessed or exercised by the Caput Senatus of the said University shall cease and (*Repealed, S. L. R. A.*, 1892 *and* 1893), upon the Seventh Day of the said Month of November One thousand eight hundred and fifty-six there shall be elected in manner herein-after mentioned a Council, which shall be called the Council of the Senate, and which shall consider and prepare all Graces to be offered to the Senate, whether proceeding from individual Members of the Senate or from Syndicates, and no Grace shall be offered to the Senate without the Sanction of the major part of those voting upon it in the Council

6. The Council of the Senate shall consist of the Chancellor, the Vice-Chancellor, Four Heads of Colleges, Four Professors of the University, and Eight other Members of the Senate, such Eight Members to be chosen from the Electoral Roll herein-after mentioned, and such Heads of Colleges, Professors, and Members of the Senate to be elected by the Persons whose Names shall be on such Electoral Roll: Provided always, that there shall never be more than Two Members of the same College among such Eight elected Members. Composition of Council.

7. The Vice-Chancellor shall on or before Monday the Thirteenth Day of October One thousand eight hundred and fifty-six, and also (*Repealed, S. L. R. A.*, 1892 *and* 1893) on or before the Second Monday in October in every Year, cause to be promulgated, in such Way as may to him seem expedient for the Purpose of giving Publicity thereto, a List of the Members of the Senate, whom he shall ascertain to have resided within One Mile and a Half of Great Saint Mary's Church for Fourteen Weeks at the least between the First Day of the preceding Michaelmas Term and the First Day of the said Month of October; and such List, together with the following Persons, (that is to say,) all Officers of the University, being Members of the Senate, the Heads of Houses, the Professors, and the Public Examiners, shall be the Electoral Roll of the University for the Purposes of this Act. Vice-Chancellor to promulgate Lists of Members of Senate.

8. The Vice-Chancellor shall at the same Time fix some convenient Time and Place, not more than Fourteen nor less than Seven Days from the Time of such Promulgation, for publicly hearing Objections to the said List, which any Member of the Senate may make on the Ground of any Person being improperly placed on or omitted from the said List; and if any such Objections shall appear to the Vice-Chancellor to be well founded, he shall correct the said List accordingly, and he shall thereupon sign and promulgate the said List, which shall thenceforth be the Electoral Roll for the Year thence next ensuing, and until a new Roll shall in like Manner have been promulgated. Lists may be objected to and amended.

As to vacating of seats of Members of Council.

9. Two of the Heads of Colleges, Two of the Professors, and Four of the other Members of the Council to be elected on the Seventh Day of November One thousand eight hundred and fifty-six, shall be elected to hold Office for Two Years only, and shall vacate their Seats at the End of Two Years, and the other Members of the Council to be then elected shall hold Office for Four Years, and shall vacate their Seats at the End of Four Years; and the Election of the Two Heads of Colleges, Two Professors, and Four other Members of the Council, who are to hold Office for Two Years only, shall be made separately from the Election of the other Heads of Colleges and Professors and other Members of the Council. (*Repealed, S. L. R. A.*, 1875.)

For Supply of periodical Vacancies in Council.

10. The Places of the Members of the Council vacating their Seats shall be supplied by a new Election, to be made on the Seventh of November, or in case the Seventh of November should be Sunday, on the Eighth of November in every other Year, in the same Manner as is herein-before prescribed as to the Election to take place on the Seventh Day of November One thousand eight hundred and fifty-six, save only that all Members of the Council to be then elected shall be elected to hold office for Four Years; and all Members so vacating their Seats shall (if otherwise eligible) be capable of Re-election.

Members vacating may be re-elected.

As to filling up of casual Vacancies.

11. Any casual Vacancy occurring by Death, Resignation, or otherwise among the Members of the Council shall be filled by the Election of a qualified Person, according to the Directions of this Act, upon a Day not later than Twenty-one Days or sooner than Seven Days after such Occurrence, to be fixed by the Vice-Chancellor and publicly notified by him; but if such Vacancy shall occur during Vacation the Occurrence shall be deemed for the Purpose of such Notice to have taken place on the First Day of the ensuing Term; and the Person so elected shall be subject to the same Rules and Conditions as to the Tenure of Office, and in all other respects, as the Person to whose Place he succeeds would have been subject to if no such Vacancy had taken place.

Votes of Electors.

12. In all Elections of Members of the Council every Elector may vote for any Number of Persons, being Heads of Colleges, Professors, or Members of the Senate as aforesaid

respectively, not exceeding the Number of Heads of Colleges, Professors, or Members of the Senate respectively to be then chosen; and in case of an Equality of Votes for any Two or more of such Heads of Colleges, Professors, or Members of the Senate respectively, the Vice-Chancellor shall name from amongst those Persons for whom the Number of Votes shall be equal as many as shall be requisite to complete the Number of Heads of Colleges, Professors, or Members of the Senate to be then chosen.

Casting-vote of Vice-Chancellor.

13. If any Member of the Council, other than the Chancellor or the Vice-Chancellor, shall have been absent from all the Meetings of the Council during the whole of One Term, his Seat shall at the Close of such Term become and shall be declared by the Vice-Chancellor to be vacant.

Absence from Meetings for a certain Time to create a Vacancy.

14. If any Member of the Council shall become Vice-Chancellor his Seat shall not thereby become vacant, nor shall the Seat of any Member of the Council become vacant by reason that after his Election he may have become or may have ceased to be a Professor or a Head of a College: Provided always, that if any of the Eight Members of the Senate chosen from the Electoral Roll as aforesaid shall afterwards cease to be on the Electoral Roll, his Seat shall thereupon become and be declared to be vacant.

Member of Council becoming Vice-Chancellor, Professor, or Head, not to vacate Seat.

15. No Professor shall be ineligible for the Council by reason of anything contained in the Statutes of his Foundation.

Professors eligible.

16. The Vice-Chancellor shall, before the Tenth Day of October One thousand eight hundred and fifty-six; make and promulgate all such Regulations as to the Voting for, Election, Resignation, and Return of Members of the Council, as may be necessary for the Election and assembling of the Council according to this Act, and for keeping the Number of such Council complete, and shall appoint the Time and Place at which they shall assemble; and if the Vice-Chancellor fails to comply with the Provisions of this Section, the Commissioners shall thereupon make such Regulations in respect of the Matters aforesaid as they may think fit. (*Repealed, S. L. R. A.*, 1875.)

Vice-Chancellor to make Regulations respecting Council.

17. Subject to the Provisions of this Act, and without Prejudice to the Rights of the Senate in the making of Statutes, Regulations, and Ordinances for the University of

Power to Council to make Rules

for Regulation of its own Proceedings.

Cambridge, the Council shall have Power from Time to Time to make Rules for the Regulation of its own Proceedings, and to revise or alter the Regulations herein-before directed to be made by the Vice-Chancellor, or, in the Case of his failing to do so, by the Commissioners, and also to appoint Committees for the Purpose of examining all Questions referred to them by the said Council.

Date of Meeting.

18. The Council shall meet for the Despatch of Business on the Eighth Day of November One thousand eight hundred and fifty-six. (*Repealed, S. L. R. A.*, 1875.)

Who shall be President of the Council.

19. The President of the Council shall be the Chancellor, or in his Absence the Vice-Chancellor, or a Member of the Council appointed by the Vice-Chancellor to act as his Deputy, or if at any Council duly convened and assembled neither the Chancellor nor the Vice-Chancellor nor any Deputy so appointed shall be present, then some Member to be chosen by the Members of the Council then assembled.

Quorum of Council.

Questions in the Council to be decided by the Majority.

20. No business shall be transacted in the Council unless Five Members at least be present; and all Questions in the Council shall be decided by the Majority of the Votes of the Members present, and the President shall have a Second or Casting Vote when the Votes are equally divided: Provided always, that in case of a Difference of Opinion between the Chancellor, or the Vice-Chancellor or his Deputy, and the Majority of the Members present at any Meeting of the Council, the Question as to which such Difference may exist shall not be deemed to be carried by such Majority unless the same shall constitute a Majority of the whole Council, but in such Case the Question shall be adjourned to the next Meeting of the Council, and such adjourned Question shall be finally decided by the Majority of the Members of Council then present.

Council to nominate to Offices.

21. The Council shall nominate Two qualified Persons to the Senate, of whom the Senate shall choose One, in the Manner heretofore accustomed, to fill every vacant Office in the University to which the Heads of Colleges have heretofore nominated Two Persons to the Senate; provided

always, that the Persons nominated as aforesaid to the Office of Vice-Chancellor shall be Heads of Colleges.

22. Every Oath directly or indirectly binding the Juror— Certain Oaths deemed illegal, and not to be administered.

Not to disclose any Matter or Thing relating to his College, although required so to do by lawful Authority ;

To resist or not concur in any Change in the Statutes of the University or College ;

To do or forbear from doing anything the doing or the not doing of which would tend to any such Concealment, Resistance, or Non-concurrence,

shall from the Time of the passing of this Act be an illegal Oath in the said University and the Colleges thereof, and no such Oath shall here-after be administered or taken.

23. Any Member of the University, of such Standing and Qualifications as may be provided by any Statute hereafter to be made, may obtain a Licence from the Vice-Chancellor to open his Residence, if situate within One Mile and a Half of Great St Mary's Church, for the Reception of Students, who shall be matriculated and admitted to all the Privileges of the University, without being of necessity entered as Members of any College (*Repealed by University Statute*, see above, p. 80) ; but no such Licence as aforesaid shall be granted by the Vice-Chancellor until such Regulations as are herein-after mentioned have come into operation. (*Repealed, S. L. R. A.*, 1875.) Power to Vice-Chancellor to License Members of the University to open their Residences for Reception of Students.

24. Every Person to whom such Licence is granted shall be called a Principal, and his Residence so opened as aforesaid shall be called a Hostel. (*Repealed by University Statute*, see above, p. 80.) Hostels.

25. The University, before the First Day of January One thousand eight hundred and fifty-eight, may proceed to frame Statutes— Power of University to make Statutes as to Hostels.

For regulating the Terms and Conditions of granting Licences to Principals, and the Qualifications of such Principals :

For the Government of Hostels, the Discipline of the Students therein, and their Status in the event of the Death or Removal of any such Principal, or of the Withdrawal or Suspension of his Licence :

For punishing Neglect or Breach of Regulation on the Part of a Principal by the Withdrawal or Suspension of his Licence, and on the Part of any Student by such reasonable Penalties or other Punishments as the University may think fit :

But no such Statute shall be of any Force or Effect unless and until it shall have been approved in the Manner herein-after mentioned. (*Repealed, S. L. R. A.*, 1875.)

If University omit to frame Statutes, etc., it shall be incumbent on Commissioners to do so.

26. If the said University shall not, on or before the First Day of January One thousand eight hundred and fifty-eight, have framed, and submitted for the Approval of the Commissioners, such Statutes as may in the Opinion of the Commissioners be sufficient for carrying into effect the Objects of this Act with respect to the Establishment and Regulation of Hostels, the Commissioners shall forthwith proceed to frame Statutes in that Behalf. (*Repealed, S. L. R. A.*, 1875.)

Power to Colleges to frame Statutes for certain Purposes.

27. In order to promote useful Learning and Religious Education in the Colleges and University, and the main Designs of the Founders and Donors so far as is consistent with these Purposes, it shall be lawful for the Governing Body of any College or the major Part thereof, at any Time before the First Day of January One thousand eight hundred and fifty-eight, without Prejudice to any existing Interest of any Member of such College, and notwithstanding anything contained in the Statutes, Charters, Deeds of Composition, or other Instruments of Foundation or Endowment either of such College or of any Emolument therein, to make Statutes for the Purposes following; (that is to say,)

1. For repealing, altering, and amending the College Statutes, and for making fresh Provision respecting the Eligibility of Persons to the Headship or the Fellowships or other College Emoluments, respecting the Right and Mode of appointing, nominating, or electing to such Headship, Fellowships, and Emoluments, and respecting the Duration and Conditions of the Tenure of such Fellowships and Emoluments, so as to ensure such Fellowships and Emoluments being conferred according to personal Merits and Fitness, and being retained for such Periods as are likely to conduce to the better Advancement of the Interests of Religion and Learning, and for the said Objects to modify or abolish any Right of Preference:
2. For altering or abolishing the Oaths or any of them required to be taken by the Statutes of the College:
3. For re-distributing or apportioning the divisible Revenues of the College:
4. For rendering Portions of the College Property or Income available to Purposes for the Benefit of the University at large:
5. For the Consolidation, Division, or Conversion of Emoluments, including therein the Conversion of Fellowships or Scholarships attached to Schools into Scholarships or Exhibitions so attached, or either partly so attached and partly open, or altogether open, and of Fellowships otherwise limited into Scholarships or Exhibitions either subject or not subject to any similar or modified Limitation:

6. For the Creation of a sufficient Number of Open Scholarships either by Conversion of Fellowships or otherwise:
7. For incorporating Bye-Fellowships with the original Foundation either in reduced Number or otherwise:
8. For transferring to the College in its corporate Capacity any Trusts now vested in any One or more of the Master and Fellows:
9. And generally for making further Provision for maintaining and improving the Discipline, Studies, and good Government of such College, and for amending the Statutes thereof from Time to Time:

But all Statutes so made by the Governing Body of such College, or the major Part thereof, shall be of no Force or Effect until they shall have been approved in the Manner herein-after mentioned: Provided that nothing herein contained with respect to the Right of nominating or appointing to the Headship of a College shall be deemed to apply to the Headship of Mary Magdalen College, unless the Consent by Deed of the Person or Persons entitled to such Right shall be first had and obtained. (*Repealed, S. L. R. A.*, 1875.)

Power to sever Benefices from Headships.

28. And whereas it is expedient, where certain Benefices with or without Cure of Souls are annexed to the Headship of a College, or may at the Option of the Head for the Time being be had with his Headship, to enable the Colleges to put an end to such Annexation or Option: Be it enacted, That it shall be lawful for the Governing Body of any College or the major Part thereof, at any time before the First Day of January One thousand eight hundred and fifty-eight, without Prejudice to any existing Interest of any Member thereof, and notwithstanding anything contained in any Act of Parliament or in any Deed or Instrument whatever, to make Statutes for putting an end to such Annexation or Option, and either for selling such Benefices or for adding them to the Number of those already in the Patronage of the College, and for making adequate Compensation out of its revenues to the Head of the College for the consequent Diminution of his Income: Provided always, that all such Statutes, and also all Statutes made by any College under the Powers of the Twenty-seventh Section of this Act, shall be laid before the Commissioners, who shall have Power, by Writing under their Common Seal, to approve of or reject the same, and to remit the same from Time to Time for further Consideration or Revision, with Amendments or Alterations therein. (*Repealed, S. L. R. A.*, 1875.)

When Colleges omit to make Statutes Commissioners may frame them.

29. If the Powers granted in the Twenty-seventh Section shall not be exercised by any College, or shall not be exercised to such Extent as the Commissioners may deem expedient, and no Statute for effecting the Objects of such Powers, or no Statute which the Commissioners may deem sufficient for that Purpose, shall be submitted by the Governing Body of such College, or the major Part thereof, to the Commissioners, and approved of by them, before the First Day of

January One thousand eight hundred and fifty-eight, it shall be lawful for the Commissioners to frame such Statutes or such further Statutes as shall appear to them to be expedient for the Purpose of effecting or promoting the Objects which the College is herein-before empowered to effect or promote; and all such Statutes, if sanctioned and confirmed as herein-after required, shall take effect as Statutes of such College, notwithstanding anything contained in the Statutes, Charters, Deeds of Composition, or other Instruments of Foundation or Endowment thereof: Provided always, that all such Statutes, when properly settled by the Commissioners, shall be laid before the College to which the same relate, and the Visitor thereof, Two Calendar Months at least before the same are submitted to Her Majesty in Council, as herein-after directed; and if within the next Two Calendar Months, or where the Statutes shall have been laid before the College and Visitor in Vacation then within Two Months after the First Day of the following Term, Two Thirds of the Governing Body of the said College shall by Writing under their Hands declare that in their Opinion any One or more of such Statutes will be prejudicial to the said College as a Place of Learning and Education, then such Statute or Statutes shall not take effect, but it shall be lawful for the Commissioners to frame and submit another Statute or other Statutes for the like Purpose to the said College, and so on as often as Occasion shall require. (*Repealed, S. L. R. A.*, 1875.)

University may frame new Statutes.

30. The Council of the Senate may prepare or cause to be prepared new Statutes,—

1. For repealing, altering, or adding to any of the existing Royal Statutes of the University:

2. Or, in order to promote useful Learning and Religious Education, and the main Designs of the Founders and Donors so far as is consistent with these Purposes, for altering or modifying the Trusts, Statutes, or Directions affecting any Gift or Endowment held or enjoyed by the University, or by any Professor, Lecturer, Reader, Preacher, or Scholar therein, or the Endowment of Lady Sadleir for Lecturers in the Several Colleges, or the Endowment of the Offices of Christian Preacher and Christian Advocate, or the Endowment of William Worts for Bachelors of Arts:

And all such Statutes shall be submitted to the Senate by way of Grace for their Adoption or Rejection; but no such Statute shall be of any Force or Effect until it shall have been assented to by the Commissioners under their Seal, and shall have been approved by Her Majesty by an Order in Council, as herein-after mentioned; but no Statute framed by the Council for altering or modifying the Trusts, Statutes, or Directions affecting the Endowments held by the Regius Professors of Greek, Hebrew, or Divinity, and which affect or alter any Statute of Trinity College touching such Professors or their Endowments, shall be submitted to the Senate until it shall have received the

Assent of the said College under its Common Seal. (*Repealed, S. L. R. A.*, 1875.)

31. If no new Statute for any of the Purposes in the next preceding Section of this Act mentioned shall be submitted to the Commissioners for their Assent as aforesaid, or if any such new Statute for such Purpose shall not be approved by the Commissioners, and shall not be assented to by them, the Commissioners, after the First Day of January One thousand eight hundred and fifty-eight, may frame Statutes for such Purpose, and such Statutes shall be laid before Her Majesty in Council in the Manner herein-after directed: Provided always, that any such Statutes framed by the Commissioners shall be laid before the Council of the Senate Two Calendar Months before the same are submitted to Her Majesty in Council as herein-after directed; and if within the next Two Calendar Months, or if such Statutes shall be laid before the Council in Vacation, then within Two Calendar Months from the First Day of the following Term, Two Thirds of the whole Council shall, by Writing under their Hands and Seals, declare that in their Opinion any One or more of such Statutes will be prejudicial to the University as a Place of Learning and Education, then such Statute or Statutes shall not take effect, but it shall be lawful for the Commissioners to frame and submit another Statute or other Statutes for the like Purpose, and so on as often as Occasion shall require. (*Repealed, S. L. R. A.*, 1875.)

Commissioners may frame University Statutes.

32. The University may provide by Statute that Members of the Senate may vote at any Election of a Chancellor or High Steward of the University by Proxy, such Proxy being a Member of the Senate authorised by an Instrument in Writing signed by the Member nominating such Proxy; but no Member shall be entitled to vote as a Proxy unless the Instrument appointing him has been transmitted to the Vice-Chancellor not less than Forty-eight Hours before the Time appointed for holding such Election of a Chancellor or High Steward, as the Case may be; and such Instrument may be in the Form contained in the Schedule to this Act annexed.

Votes may be given by Proxy.

33. If in the Execution of the Powers of this Act it shall be proposed by the Governing Body of any College, or the major Part thereof, or by the Commissioners, to make any Statute for the Abolition of any Right of Preference in Elections to any Emolument within any College, now lawfully belonging to any School or other Place of Education beyond the Precincts of the University, individually named or designated in any Statute, Deed of Composition, or other Instrument of Foundation or Endowment, and which Right has been exercised or enjoyed by such School or Place of Education on the Occurrence of any One of the Three Occasions next before the passing hereof on which

Right of Preference belonging to Schools not to be abolished in certain Cases if Governors of Schools or Charity Commissioners dissent therefrom.

such Right might have been exercised or enjoyed, or for the Conversion of any Fellowship or Scholarship attached to such School or other Place of Education into One or more Scholarships or Exhibitions, either partly so attached and partly open, or altogether open, where any Appointment or Election to any such Fellowship or Scholarship of a Person educated in such School or Place has taken place on the Occurrence of any One of the Three Vacancies of such Fellowship or Scholarship next before the passing of this Act, Notice thereof shall be given in Writing to the Governing Body of every such School or Place of Education, and also to the Commissioners appointed under "The Charitable Trusts Act, 1853," at least Two Calendar Months before any final Resolution for that Purpose shall be adopted by such College or by the Commissioners; and in Cases where it is proposed by such Statute to abolish any Right of Preference in Elections to any Emolument other than a Fellowship, or to convert any Fellowship or Scholarship attached to any School or other Place of Education into One or more Scholarships or Exhibitions, either partly so attached and partly open, or altogether open, no such Statute shall be made if within Two Calendar Months after receiving such Notice Two Thirds of the said Governing Body, or if there shall be several Schools interested in such Right of Preference then Two Thirds of the aggregate Body composed of the several Governing Bodies of such Schools, or the said Commissioners appointed under "The Charitable Trusts Act, 1853," shall by Writing under their Hands and Seals declare their Opinion that such Statute would be prejudicial to such School or Place of Education as a Place of Learning and Education: Provided always, that every such Right of Preference, when retained, shall be subject to all such Statutes as may be made by the Governing Body of any College, or by the Commissioners, under the Powers given by this Act, for the Purpose of making such Emolument more conducive to the mutual Benefit of such College and such School or Place of Education as aforesaid, or of throwing the same open to general or extended Competition upon any Vacancy for which no Candidate or Claimant of sufficient Merit may offer himself from any School or Place of Education so entitled as aforesaid; provided also, that where the Governing Body of any such School as aforesaid shall be a Corporate Body the Governing Body of the Corporation shall be deemed the Governing Body of the School; and when any Right of Preference shall belong to any School contingently only upon the Failure of fit Objects from some other School or Schools entitled to and in the Enjoyment of a prior Right of Preference, then and in such Case the Power of Dissent hereby given shall only belong to the Governing Body or Governing Bodies of the School or Schools entitled to and in the Enjoyment of the First Right of Preference; and if in any College where Fellowships are tenable by Undergraduates either the College or the Commissioners acting in respect thereof shall divide its Fellowships into Elder and Younger, the Elder only shall be taken to be Fellowships within the Meaning of this Section. (*Repealed, S. L. R. A.*, 1875.)

34. Where any such Notice in Writing as aforesaid is required to be given to the Governing Body of any School or Place of Education, such Notice, if served on the Master or Principal of any such School or Place of Education shall be deemed and taken to be a sufficient Notice to the Governing Body of the same School or Place of Education for all the Purposes of this Act. (*Repealed, S. L. R. A.*, 1875.)

Notice served on the Principal to be sufficient Notice to the Governing Body.

35. All Statutes framed by the Commissioners, and objected to by Two Thirds of the Governing Body or Bodies of the College, School or Schools, to which the same respectively relate, or by the said Commissioners appointed under the Charitable Trusts Act, 1853, shall, in all Cases where new Statutes shall not have been substituted under the Provisions of this Act for such as shall have been so objected to, be embodied in a Report to be transmitted forthwith to One of Her Majesty's Principal Secretaries of State, and laid before the Two Houses of Parliament. (*Repealed, S. L. R. A.*, 1875.)

Statutes objected to by Governing Body of College, etc., to be laid before Parliament.

36. And whereas by the Statutes of Trinity College and the Laws and Practice of Westminster School certain Scholarships in the said College have been annually appropriated to Scholars of the said School elected therefrom: Be it enacted, That the Governing Body of the said College, or the major Part thereof, with the Sanction of the Dean and Chapter of Westminster, signified by Writing under their Common Seal, may make and lay before the Commissioners any Statutes which to such College may seem fit for abolishing the said Preference of the said School, and for converting the said Scholarships into open Scholarships, and for enabling the said College to receive annually from the said School any Number of Exhibitioners not exceeding Three in any One Year, and may charge the Revenues of the said College with an annual Sum of Forty Pounds for each of such Exhibitioners, for or towards his Maintenance, from the Time of his commencing his Residence in the said College and during such Residence until by the Statutes of the University he shall be qualified to apply for the Degree of Bachelor of Arts, and the said Dean and Chapter may frame Statutes, with the Consent of Trinity College and of Christ Church College, Oxford, as to the Studies to be prosecuted in the said School, and the Mode of electing the Head Master and Under Master thereof, and may frame Statutes, with the Consent of Trinity College, as to the Persons by whom and the Mode in which the Election of such Exhibitioners shall be made, and generally as to the Conditions on which such Exhibitions shall be held and enjoyed; and the Commissioners shall have full Power, by Writing under their Common Seal, to approve of such Statutes (*Repealed, S. L. R. A.*, 1875): Provided always, that no such Exhibition shall be held for more than Three Years and a Quarter, and no such Exhibitioner shall by holding such Exhibition be disqualified from being elected a Scholar of the said College.

Statutes as to Scholarships in Trinity College appropriated to Scholars of Westminster School.

Statutes as to the Grindal Fellowship and Grindal Scholarships at Pembroke College.

37. And whereas certain Scholarships at Pembroke College, called the Grindal Scholarships, have heretofore been appropriated to Scholars educated at the Free Grammar School of Saint Beghes or Saint Bees in the County of Cumberland, and a certain Fellowship at the said College, called the Grindal Fellowship, has heretofore been appropriated to Scholars educated at the said School, and subsequently elected to the said Scholarships, and the Fellow and Scholars holding such Fellowship and Scholarships respectively have been from Time to Time maintained by the said College out of the general Revenues thereof, pursuant to a Covenant entered into by the Master, Fellows, and Scholars of the said College with the Keepers or Wardens and Governors of the said School, and contained in a certain Indenture of Demise, bearing Date the First Day of June in the Fourth Year of the Reign of His late Majesty King James the First, and made between the said Keeper and Governors of the one Part, and the said Master, Fellows, and Scholars of the other Part, by which Indenture, in consideration of the aforesaid Covenant on the Part of the said College, certain Lands situate at Croydon in the County of Surrey, called "Palmer's Fields," were demised by the Keepers or Wardens and Governors of the said School to the Master, Fellows, and Scholars of the said College, for the Term of One thousand Years from the Date of the said Indenture, at the yearly Rent of a Red Rose: Be it enacted, That it shall be lawful for the Governing Body of the said College or the major Part thereof, with the Consent of the Governing Body of the said School, to make and lay before the Commissioners Statutes for abolishing the aforesaid Preference of the said School, and for converting the said Grindal Fellowship and Grindal Scholarships partly into open Scholarships and partly into Exhibitions, and for that Purpose to charge the Revenues of the said College with the Payment to the said School of an annual Sum, to be applied in providing such Exhibitions for meritorious Scholars educated at the said School, and proceeding to any College in the University of Cambridge; and it shall be lawful for the Governing Body of the said School to convey the Reversion in Fee Simple expectant upon the Determination of the aforesaid Term of One thousand Years in the aforesaid Lands called "Palmer's Fields" to the said College, to be held by the said College as Part of the general Property thereof; and the Commissioners shall have full Power, by Writing under their Common Seal, to approve of such Statutes. (*Repealed, S. L. R. A.*, 1875.)

College of King Henry the Sixth at Eton to be subject to this Act with respect to Colleges.

38. The College of King Henry the Sixth at Eton shall, for the Purposes of this Act, be subject to the Provisions herein contained with respect to Colleges, and shall have the same or the like powers as are hereby given to the Colleges of the University, and be subject to the Authorities hereby conferred on the Commissioners for the Alteration and Amendment of Statutes, in like Manner as is hereby provided with respect to the Colleges of the University. (*Repealed, S. L. R. A.*, 1875.)

39. All Statutes which, under the Power herein contained, shall be made by the Governing Body of any College or the major Part thereof, and be approved of by the Commissioners, and all Statutes which shall be framed by the Commissioners, and not objected to in manner aforesaid, and every Statute passed by the University or framed by the Commissioners, under the Powers herein-before contained, for the Regulation of Hostels, or for altering or modifying the Trusts, Statutes, or Directions affecting any Gift or Endowment, or for repealing, altering, or adding to any of the existing Royal Statutes of the University, shall, as to Statutes made by the Commissioners, and liable to be objected to in manner aforesaid, after the Expiration of the Period within which the same may be objected to, and as to all other Statutes without any unnecessary Delay, be laid before Her Majesty in Council, and be forthwith published in the London Gazette; and it shall be lawful for every College, and for the Visitor thereof, and for the Trustees, Governors, and Patron of any University or College Emolument, and for the University, and for any other Person directly affected by such new Statutes, within One Month after the Publication as aforesaid in the London Gazette, to petition Her Majesty in Council praying Her Majesty to withhold Her Approbation of the whole or of any Part thereof; and every such Petition shall be referred by Her Majesty by Order in Council for the Consideration and Advice of Five Members of Her Privy Council, of whom Two, not including the Lord President, shall be Members of the Judicial Committee, who shall be named in such Order, and such Five Members may, if they think fit, admit any Petitioner or Petitioners to be heard by Council[1] in support of his or their Petition. (*Repealed, S. L. R. A.*, 1875.)

Statutes to be laid before the Queen in Council.

Power to Colleges, etc., to petition Her Majesty against Approbation thereof, etc.

40. All Statutes which shall be so published in the London Gazette as aforesaid shall be at the same Time laid before both Houses of Parliament, if Parliament be sitting, or if not then within Three Weeks after the Commencement of the next ensuing Session of Parliament; and, unless an Address is within Forty Days presented by One or other of the said Houses, praying Her Majesty to withhold Her Consent from such Statutes or any Parts thereof, or unless the Approbation of Her Majesty shall be withheld on such Petition as aforesaid, it shall be lawful for Her Majesty, by Order in Council, to declare Her Approbation of such Statutes respectively, or any Parts thereof, to which such Address shall not relate, or of which She shall not withhold Her Approbation on such Petition, and the same shall thereupon become Statutes of the University of Cambridge, or of the College therein to which the same respectively relate; and if any such Statutes, or any Part thereof, shall not be so approved by Her Majesty, it shall be lawful for Her Majesty to signify Her Disapproval of such Statutes or such Part thereof by Order in Council, and then the Commissioners may thereupon proceed to frame other Statutes in that Behalf, subject to the same Conditions and Provisions as to the Approbation of Her Majesty

Statutes to be laid before Parliament.

[1] Sic.

in Council, and all other Conditions and Provisions, as are imposed by this Act in relation to the making of original Statutes by the Commissioners, and so on from Time to Time as often as Occasion shall require. (*Repealed, S. L. R. A.*, 1875.)

Statutes made by Queen Elizabeth in 1570 for Regulation of University repealed.

41. After the First Day of January One thousand eight hundred and sixty, the Statutes made by Queen Elizabeth in the Year of our Lord One thousand five hundred and seventy for the Government and Regulation of the University, or such and so much of them or of any of them as shall be then unrepealed by any Statute made under the Authority of this Act, shall be repealed, but not so as to revive any Statute of the University thereby repealed. (*Repealed, S. L. R. A.*, 1875.)

Power to the Chancellor to settle Doubts as to Meaning of University Statutes.

42. If any Doubt shall arise with respect to the true Intent and Meaning of any of the new Statutes of the University framed and approved as aforesaid, or of any Statute which may hereafter be approved in the Manner herein-after mentioned for amending or altering the same, the Council may apply to the Chancellor of the University for the Time being, and it shall be lawful for him to declare in Writing the Intent and Meaning of the Statute on the Matter submitted to him, and such Declaration shall be registered by the Registry of the University, and the Intent and Meaning of the Statute as therein declared shall be deemed the true Intent and Meaning thereof. (*Repealed, S. L. R. A.*, 1892; *but this repeal was repealed by S. L. R. A.*, 1893.)

Statutes to be subject to Repeal, etc.

43. Every Statute made in pursuance of the Provisions of this Act by the University, or by any College, or by the Commissioners, and likewise all Provisions herein-before contained respecting the Election, Constitution, Powers, and Proceedings of the Council of the Senate, or respecting Hostels, shall be subject to Repeal, Amendment, and Alteration from Time to Time by the University or College, as the Case may be, with the Approval of Her Majesty in Council. (*Repealed, S. L. R. A.*, 1892; *but this repeal was repealed by S. L. R. A.*, 1893.)

Persons becoming Members not to possess vested Interests.

44. No Person who after the passing of this Act shall become a Member of any College, or shall be elected or become eligible to any University or College Emolument, shall be deemed or taken to have acquired or to possess an existing Interest within the Meaning of this Act. (*Repealed, S. L. R. A.*, 1875.)

45. From the First Day of Michaelmas Term One thousand eight hundred and fifty-six (*Repealed, S. L. R. A.*, 1892 *and* 1893), no Person shall be required, upon matriculating, or upon taking, or to enable him to take, any Degree in Arts, Law, Medicine, or Music (*Repealed, S. L. R. A.*, 1875), in the said University, to take any Oath or to make any Declaration or Subscription whatever; but such Degree shall not, until the Person obtaining the same shall, in such Manner as the University may from Time to Time prescribe, have subscribed a Declaration stating that he is *bonâ fide* a Member of the Church of England, entitle him to be or to become a Member of the Senate, or constitute a Qualification for the holding of any Office, either in the University or elsewhere, which has been heretofore always held by a Member of the United Church of England and Ireland, and for which such Degree has heretofore constituted One of the Qualifications. (*Repealed by the Universities Tests Act*, 1871, 34 *&* 35 *Vic. c.* 26, *sec.* 8.)

Not necessary to make Declaration or take an Oath on matriculating, nor on taking a Degree;

46. From and after the First Day of Michaelmas Term One thousand eight hundred and fifty-six (*Repealed, S. L. R. A.*, 1892 *and* 1893), it shall not be necessary for any Person, on obtaining any Exhibition, Scholarship, or other College Emolument available for the Assistance of an Undergraduate Student in his Academical Education, to make or subscribe any Declaration of his Religious Opinion or Belief, or to take any Oath, any Law or Statute to the contrary notwithstanding.

nor on obtaining any Exhibition, Scholarship, or other College Emolument.

47. The Stamp Duties now payable on Matriculations and Degrees shall be abolished so soon as Provision shall have been made by the University, to the Satisfaction of the Commissioners of Her Majesty's Treasury, in lieu of the Monies heretofore voted annually by Parliament. (*Repealed, S. L. R. A.*, 1875.)

Stamp Duties on Matriculations, etc., abolished.

48. It shall be lawful for any College, with the Consent of the Church Estates Commissioners, to sell any Estate in Lands or Hereditaments vested in such College, or to exchange any Estate in Lands or Hereditaments for any other Lands or Hereditaments, or either of them, and upon any such Exchange to receive or pay any Money by way of Equality of Exchange; and all Monies which on any such Sale or Exchange shall be received by or become payable to or for the Benefit of such College shall be paid into the Bank of England, for the Benefit of such College, to such Account as the said Church Estates Commissioners shall appoint in that Behalf; and the Receipt of the said Church Estates Commissioners shall be an effectual Discharge to any Purchaser for any Money therein expressed to be received, and shall be Evidence of their Consent as aforesaid; and all Monies so paid into the Bank of England shall be applied in Payment for Equality of Exchange as aforesaid, or shall be laid out by such College, with such Consent as aforesaid, in the Purchase of the absolute Estate

Colleges, with Consent of Church Estate Commissioners, may sell Estates, etc.

of Freehold in other Lands and Hereditaments, or either of them, to be conveyed to the Use or for the Benefit of such College; and such Lands and Hereditaments, and any Lands and Hereditaments received in Exchange by such College, shall be held by the College upon the like Trusts and for the like Purposes as the Lands and Hereditaments sold or given in Exchange by such College respectively; and the Monies from Time to Time remaining unapplied for the Purposes aforesaid shall be invested, by and in the Names of the said Church Estates Commissioners, in the Purchase of Government Stocks, Funds, or Securities, which the said Church Estates Commissioners shall hold in trust for such College, and the said Church Estates Commissioners may sell and dispose of the same for the Purpose of effecting any such Purchase of Lands and Hereditaments, or either of them, as aforesaid, or of paying Money for Equality of Exchange as aforesaid, as Occasion may require; and in the meantime the Interest, Dividends, and annual Proceeds of such Monies, Stocks, Funds, and Securities shall be paid to such College, to be applied to the same Purposes as the annual Income was applicable which arose out of those Lands and Hereditaments from the Sale or Exchange of which the Money invested in such Stocks, Funds, and Securities was produced: Provided that nothing in this Section contained shall apply to any Estate of the College in reversion in Lands or Hereditaments expectant upon any Lease for Lives, or for a Term of Years determinable upon any Life or Lives, or for a Term of Years whereof more than Seven shall be unexpired, on which a Rent less than Three Fourths of the clear yearly Value of such Lands or Hereditaments shall have been reserved. (*Repealed by the Universities and Colleges Estates Act*, 1858, 21 *&* 22 *Vic. c.* 44, *sec.* 5.)

Powers of University to continue in force, except as altered.

49. Except in so far as they are expressly altered or taken away by the Provisions of this Act, the Powers and Privileges of the University and its Officers, and of the Colleges and their Officers, shall continue in full Force.

Interpretation of Terms.

50. In the Construction of this Act the Expression "University or College Emolument" shall include all Headships, Downing Professorships, Fellowships, Bye-Fellowships, Scholarships, Exhibitions, Bible Clerkships, Sizarships, Subsizarships, and every other such Place of Emolument payable out of the Revenues of the University or of any College, or to be held and enjoyed by the Members of any College as such within the University; and the Word "Professor" shall be taken to include the Three Royal Professors of Hebrew, Greek, and Divinity, and Public Readers or Lecturers in the University, except the Barnaby Lecturers; and the Governing

Body of any College shall mean the Head and all actual Fellows thereof, Bye-Fellows excepted, being Graduates, and in Downing College shall mean the Head, Professors, and all actual Fellows thereof, Bye-Fellows excepted, being Graduates; and the Word "Statutes" shall be taken to include all Ordinances and Regulations of the University, and all Ordinances and Regulations contained in any Charter, Deed of Composition, or other Instrument of Foundation or Endowment of a College, and all Bye-laws, Ordinances, and Regulations; and the Word "Vacation" shall be taken to include that Part of Easter Term which falls after the Division of Term.

51. The Lands Clauses Consolidation Act, 1845, except the Parts and Enactments of that Act with respect to the Purchase and taking of Lands otherwise than by Agreement, and with respect to the Recovery of Forfeitures, Penalties, and Costs, and with respect to Lands required by the Promoters of the Undertaking, but which shall not be wanted for the Purposes thereof, shall be incorporated with and form Part of this Act, so far as relates to Land within the Town of Cambridge required for the Erection of any Buildings for the Extension of the Buildings of the said University, or of any College therein, and as if the Corporate Name of the University or College, as the Case may be, had been inserted therein instead of the Expression "the Promoters of the Undertaking."

Parts of Lands Clauses Act, 1845, incorporated herewith.

52. The several Powers given by Section Twenty-seven, Twenty-eight, Twenty-nine, Thirty, and Thirty-one of this Act may be exercised, notwithstanding anything contained in any Act of Parliament, Decree, or Order constituting, either wholly or in part, an Instrument of Foundation or Endowment, or confirming or varying any Foundation or Endowment, or otherwise regulating any Foundation or Endowment. (*Repealed, S. L. R. A.*, 1875.)

Powers given by Sections 27, 28, 29, 30, and 31, may be exercised, notwithstanding any Act, Decree, or Order.

53. Where, upon an Application of the University as to any University Emolument, or upon the Application of any College as to any Emolument within such College, it may appear to the Commissioners that it would be advisable for the Purposes of this Act to suspend for a limited Period the Election to such Emolument (not being the Headship of a College or Hall), it shall be lawful for the Commissioners, by Instrument under their Common Seal, to authorise

Elections to Emoluments may be suspended by Commissioners.

the University or such College, as the Case may be, to suspend such Election accordingly for such a Time as may appear to the Commissioners sufficient for the Purposes aforesaid. (*Repealed, S. L. R. A.*, 1875.)

SCHEDULE

A. B., a Member of the Senate, doth hereby appoint *C. D.*, a Member of the Senate, to be the Proxy of the said *A. B.* in his Absence, and to vote in his Name at the Election of a Chancellor, or High Steward, as the Case may be, for the University of Cambridge, on the Day of next, in such Manner as he the said *C. D.* may think proper. In witness whereof the said *A. B.* hath hereunto set his Hand, the Day of

(Signature) *A. B.*

THE CAMBRIDGE AWARD ACT, 1856.

19 VICT. CAP. XVII.

An Act to confirm an Award for the Settlement of Matters in difference between the University and Borough of Cambridge, and for other Purposes connected therewith. [5th June 1856.]

WHEREAS by a Letter bearing Date the Twenty-seventh Day of December One thousand eight hundred and fifty-four, addressed to the Right Honourable Sir John Patteson, Knight, One of Her Majesty's most Honourable Privy Council, by the Chancellor, Masters, and Scholars of the University of Cambridge, and the Masters, Fellows, and Scholars, Masters and Fellows, Provost and Scholars, President and Fellows, and Master, Professors, and Fellows respectively of the several Colleges and Halls in the said University, and the Mayor, Aldermen, and Burgesses of the Borough of Cambridge, and sealed with their respective Seals, after reciting, amongst other things, that Differences had arisen and were still pending between them, they requested the said Sir John Patteson to hear them by their respective Counsel, Attorneys, Agents, or Witnesses, and to determine all the matters in difference between them ; and they further respectively agreed with each other respectively to abide by and keep such Award as the said Sir John Patteson might make in Writing concerning the Premises. and to apply to the Legislature for an Act or Acts of Parliament, and to take all such Steps as might be necessary for the Purpose of making his Award valid and binding on each of them, or which he in his Award might think fit to direct to be taken by them or any of them respectively ; whereupon the said Sir John Patteson accepted the Reference thereby made to him, and was attended by the Counsel,

Attorneys, and Agents of the respective Parties, and heard such Arguments and perused and examined such Documents, Papers, and Evidences as they thought proper to lay before him respecting the Matters in difference, and having maturely considered the same, made his Award in Writing concerning the Premises, on the Thirty-first Day of August One thousand eight hundred and fifty-five: And whereas it is expedient to confirm the said Award, with certain Variations made with the Approbation of the said Arbitrator; but the Purposes aforesaid cannot be effected without the Authority of Parliament: May it therefore please Your Majesty that it may be enacted; and be it enacted and declared by the Queen's most Excellent Majesty, by and with the Advice and Consent of the Lords Spiritual and Temporal, and Commons, in this present Parliament assembled, and by the Authority of the same, as follows; (that is to say,)

Preliminary.

Short Title.

1. This Act may be cited for all Purposes as "The Cambridge Award Act, 1856."

Commencement of Act.

2. This Act shall, except in Cases where it is otherwise expressly provided, come into operation immediately after the passing thereof.

Interpretation of Terms.

3. In the Construction of this Act (if not inconsistent with the Context) the following Terms shall have the respective Meanings herein-after assigned to them; (that is to say,)

"University," "Chancellor, Masters, and Scholars," "Senate," "Vice Chancellor," "Proctors," "Proproctors," "Registrary," shall respectively be understood to refer to the University of Cambridge:

"Borough," "Mayor, Aldermen, and Burgesses," "Council," "Borough Fund," "Mayor," "Bailiffs," "Aldermen," "Justices of the Peace," "Town Clerk," "Treasurer," "Clerk to the Justices," "Councillor," "Watch Committee," "Burgess," "Inhabitant," "Inspector of Weights and Measures," shall respectively be understood to refer to the Borough of Cambridge:

"Alehouse Licences" shall mean Licences for keeping Inns, Alehouses, and Victualling Houses within the Borough:

"College" shall include every Collegiate Foundation and every public Academical Hall now established or hereafter to be established within the University, or within the Limits and Bounds of the Borough, and when applied to a Place and not to a Body Corporate shall mean every Building, Room, and Chamber within the University or Borough occupied or used by any Collegiate Corporation or Society, and the official Residence of the Head or any other Member thereof, and all Walks, Grounds, Gardens, and Groves appertaining thereto:

"Municipal Corporation Act" shall mean the Act Fifth and Sixth William the Fourth, Chapter Seventy-six, and the respective Acts passed to amend the same:

"Improvement Acts" shall mean the Cambridge Improvement Acts, Twenty-eighth George the Third, Chapter Sixty-four, Thirty-fourth George the Third, Chapter One hundred and four, and Ninth and Tenth Victoria, Chapter Three hundred and forty-five:

"Improvement Commissioners" shall mean the Commissioners acting in execution of the said last-mentioned Acts, or any one or more of them:

"Rates" shall mean all Local and Parochial Rates, but shall not include the Land Tax or any other Tax payable or to be payable to the Crown:

"Constabulary Force" shall mean the High and Chief Constables, and the Police Constables of the Borough, and the Constables of the respective Parishes therein, but shall not include the Proctors or Pro-proctors, or their Servants respectively, or Constables appointed under the Act Sixth George the Fourth, Chapter Ninety-seven.

Oaths.

Oaths of Mayor and Bailiffs.

4. The Mayor and Bailiffs shall not be required to take any Oath, or to make any Declaration for the Conservation of the Liberties and Privileges of the University.

Oaths of Aldermen, etc.

5. The Oaths required of certain Aldermen, Burgesses, and Inhabitants by the Letters Patent of King Henry the Third, dated the Twentieth Day of February in the Fifty-second Year of His Reign, shall be abolished and not taken henceforth.

Proctors.

Continuance of Power of the Proctors.

6. The Power of the University exercised by the Proctors shall be continued as it now by Law exists.

Exemption of Proctors from summary Jurisdiction of Justices.

7. And whereas it is expedient that the Acts of the Proctors, Pro-proctors, and their Men, in the Exercise of such Power, should not be subject to any summary Jurisdiction of Justices of the Peace : Be it further declared and enacted, That the Proctors, Pro-proctors, and their Men are and shall be exempt from and not subject to the summary Jurisdiction of Justices of the Peace under the Statute Ninth George the Fourth, Chapter Thirty-one, or any other Statute, in respect of any Act done or purporting to be done in the Exercise of the Authority of the Proctor, but without Prejudice to the Right of any person to proceed against the Proctors, Pro-proctors, or their Men, civilly or criminally, in any of Her Majesty's Courts.

Alehouse Licences.

Exclusive Privilege of Vice-Chancellor abrogated.

8. The Power of the Vice-Chancellor to grant Alehouse Licences within the Borough is hereby abrogated, subject to the Provision herein-after contained with respect to certain of such Licences, and saving to the Vice-Chancellor the same power as other Justices of the Peace may lawfully exercise.

Power to revoke Licences.

9. The Justices of the Peace may at any Time revoke any Alehouse Licence within the Borough, on the Complaint in Writing of the Vice-Chancellor, sent to the Clerk to the Justices, who shall forthwith upon the Receipt of such Complaint summon a special Session of the Justices of the Peace to consider the same, and give written Notice of the Complaint to the Person complained of, in order that he may make his Answer or Defence at such special Session.

10. Every Alehouse Licence granted by any Vice-Chancellor, and now in force, shall so continue till the next general annual licensing Meeting, unless such Licence shall previously be revoked, on the Complaint of the Vice-Chancellor, by the Justices of the Peace.

Existing Licences to continue in force for a limited Period.

11. The Power of granting Wine Licences within the Borough shall continue in and be exercised by the Chancellor, Masters, and Scholars of the University in the same Manner as it is now exercised under ancient Usage, and the Provisions of the Statutes Tenth George the Second, Chapter Nineteen, and Seventeenth George the Second, Chapter Forty, but no sum whatever shall be taken by the University from the Persons to whom Wine Licences are granted for or in respect of the Grant of the same.

Wine Licences.

No money to be taken for Licences.

12. The Chancellor, Masters, and Scholars lawfully can and may from Time to Time delegate to the Vice-Chancellor the power to grant Wine Licences, and it is not and shall not be necessary that they should be under the Common Seal of the University.

Power may be delegated to Vice-Chancellor.

13. All Powers and Authorities with respect to the Supervision of Weights and Measures in the Borough (except Powers and Authorities incidental to the Office of Inspector) shall be transferred from the University and its Officers to the Justices of the Peace of the Borough.

Weights and Measures.

Certain Powers of University to be exercised by Justices.

14. The Vice-Chancellor shall have Authority from Time to Time to appoint an Inspector or Inspectors of Weights and Measures, and the Council shall have the like Authority, provided that the Inspectors appointed by the Vice-Chancellor and the Council respectively have only concurrent Power, and the University shall provide from its own Funds for the Remuneration of every Inspector appointed by the Vice-Chancellor.

Appointment of Inspectors.

15. The Privileges, Powers, and Authorities heretofore exercised by the University and its Officers with respect to the Markets and Fairs of and within the Borough shall be abolished.

Markets and Fairs.

Abolition of Privileges of University.

Public Exhibitions.

Occasional public Exhibitions.

16. No occasional public Exhibition or Performance, whether strictly theatrical or not, other than Performances in Theatres which are regulated by the Act Sixth and Seventh Victoria, Chapter Sixty-eight, shall take place within the Borough (except during the period of Midsummer Fair, or in the Long Vacation), unless with the Consent in Writing of the Vice-Chancellor and the Mayor, and every Person who shall offend against this Enactment shall be liable to forfeit a Sum not exceeding Twenty Pounds, recoverable in like Manner as Penalties imposed by the said Act. (*See the Cambridge University and Corporation Act*, 1894, *sec.* 11, *infra, page* 231.)

Discommuning.

Continuance of discommuning Power, with certain Limitation.

17. The Power of discommuning, by which Members of the University *in statu pupillari* are prohibited from dealing with such Persons as have or shall have infringed or not complied with Rules or Decrees made from Time to Time by the Authorities of the University, and publicly proclaimed, shall be continued: Provided nevertheless, that Notice shall be given to the Person in respect to whom the Power is proposed to be exercised in order that he may attend, if he think fit, to shew that the Rules have not been infringed, or to explain the Circumstances under which they have been infringed; and provided further, that the said Power shall not extend to discommune any Person for adopting legal Remedies for the Recovery of a Debt without having given previous Notice to the University or College Authorities, or to the Deprivation or Suspension of a Wine Licence.

Conusance of Pleas, etc.

Abolition of Conusance of Pleas in certain Cases.

18. The Right of the University or any Officer thereof to claim Conusance of any Action or criminal Proceeding wherein any Person who is not a Member of the University shall be a Party, shall cease and determine.

Convictions of Members of the University.

Notice to Vice-Chan-

19. As often as any Member of the University shall be convicted by any Justice of the Peace of any Offence, a Duplicate or Copy of his Conviction shall be forthwith sent by the Clerk to the Justices to the Vice-Chancellor, and in such Case, and also in the Case of any Dismissal by any Justice of the Peace of any Charge against any Member of

the University, the Clerk to the Justices shall forthwith, after Application made to him by the Vice-Chancellor for a Copy of the Depositions, furnish the same to the Vice-Chancellor without making any Charge for the same. cellor of certain Convictions, etc.

University Constables.

Copies of Certificates to be sent to Town Clerk.

20. The Vice-Chancellor shall send to the Town Clerk a Duplicate or Copy of every Certificate of the Appointment of a Constable under the Act Sixth George the Fourth, Chapter Ninety-seven, as soon as practicable after such Certificate shall be made.

Rates on University and College Property.

University Property.

21. The Property of the University herein-after specified is situate within the Parishes in the Borough herein-after respectively mentioned; (that is to say,)

The Senate House in the Parish of Saint Mary the Great;

The Senate House Yard in the Parishes of Saint Mary the Great and Saint Edward;

The University Library, with the Lecture Rooms, Schools, and Museums thereunder, in the Parishes of Saint Mary the Great and Saint Edward, what was lately King's College Old Court in the Parish of Saint John;

The Pitt Press in the Parish of Saint Botolph;

The Fitzwilliam Museum in the Parish of Saint Mary the Less;

The Old Botanic Garden in the Parishes of Saint Edward and Saint Benedict;

The Theatre of Anatomy and the Lecture Rooms adjacent in the Parish of Saint Benedict;

The New Botanic Garden in the Parish of Saint Andrew the Less;

The Spinning House in the Parish of Saint Andrew the Great;

The Observatory in the Parish of Saint Giles:

and so much of the said Property as shall not be exempt from Rates under the subsequent Provisions of this Act, shall be assessed to Rates (Rates made under the Improvement Acts excepted) in the said Parishes respectively.

College Property.

22. The Property occupied by the several Colleges, and herein-after specified, is situate within the Parishes in the Borough herein-after respectively mentioned; (that is to say,)

Saint Peter's College in the Parish of Saint Mary the Less;
Clare College in the Parish of Saint John;
Pembroke College in the Parishes of Saint Mary the Less and Saint Botolph;
Gonville and Caius College in the Parish of Saint Michael;
Trinity Hall in the Parish of St John;
Corpus Christi College in the Parishes of Saint Benedict and Saint Botolph;
King's College in the Parishes of Saint John, Saint Benedict, Saint Edward, Saint Giles, and Saint Mary the Great;
Queens' College in the Parish of Saint Botolph;
Saint Catharine's College in the Parishes of Saint Benedict, Saint Botolph, and Saint Edward;
Jesus College in the Parishes of Saint Rhadegund and All Saints;
Christ's College in the Parishes of Saint Andrew the Great and Saint Andrew the Less;
Saint John's College in the Parishes of All Saints, Saint Giles, and Saint Peter;
Magdalen College in the Parishes of Saint Giles and Saint Peter;
Trinity College in the Parishes of All Saints, Saint Giles, and Saint Michael;
Emmanuel College in the Parish of Saint Andrew the Great;
Sidney Sussex College in the Parish of All Saints;
Downing College in the Parishes of Saint Benedict, Saint Botolph, and Saint Mary the Less;

and so much of the Property of the said several Colleges as shall not be exempt from Rates under the subsequent Provisions of this Act shall be assessed to Rates (Rates made under the Improvement Acts excepted) in the said Parishes respectively.

Exemptions from Rates.

23. No Rate whatever shall be assessed or imposed upon or in respect of the Senate House, the University Library, the Schools or the Museums of Science, Laboratories, or Lecture Rooms for the Time being of the University, nor upon or in respect of the Chapels or Libraries, for the Time being of any College; provided that the Buildings, Rooms, or Places respectively hereby exempted from Rates be used for the Purposes aforesaid at the Time of making the Valuation for Assessment then in force. (*Repealed*, *see page* 222.)

Colleges to be assessed for Property occupied by individual Members.

24. As respects College Property, the whole thereof shall be deemed to be in the Occupation of the College, although Parts may be exclusively occupied by individual Members thereof or Students; and the College, if a Corporation, shall be assessed for the same in its Corporate Name; and for the Property of any College not incorporated the Head thereof shall be assessed, and shall be liable to pay all Rates, although he himself may not occupy the whole or any Part of the Property rated.

Valuation of University and College Property.

25. The Amount at which Property occupied by the University or any College shall be assessed shall, as soon as practicable, be determined by Two Valuers, or their Umpire, One of such Valuers to be appointed by the Vice-Chancellor, and the other by the Mayor; and such Two Valuers shall appoint an Umpire before entering upon their Valuation, or in case they cannot agree in the Choice of an Umpire such Umpire shall be chosen by the Poor Law Board. (*Repealed*, *see page* 222.)

Ground Plans to define Parochial Boundaries.

26. As respects Property occupied by the University, or any College situate in more than One Parish (whether such Property be rateable or exempt from Rates), the said Valuers or Umpire shall make duplicate Ground Plans thereof, whereupon the Parochial Boundaries shall be marked, and such Ground Plans shall be signed by the Valuers or Umpire, and shall be deemed conclusive Evidence of such Boundaries, and One Duplicate of the Valuation and Ground Plans aforesaid shall be deposited in the Registrary's Office, and the other in the Town Clerk's Office, for the free Inspection at all reasonable Times of all Parties interested. (*Repealed*, *see page* 222.)

Provision for fresh Valuations of University and College Property.

27. At any Time after Three Years from the Completion of the First or any subsequent Valuation of Property occupied by the University or any College, the Vice-Chancellor or Mayor respectively may by Notice in Writing to the other of them require a fresh Valuation to be made, and the same shall be made accordingly, in like Manner in all respects as the First Valuation. (*Repealed*, *see page* 222.)

Powers of Valuers.

28. The said Valuers and Umpire respectively shall have free Access to the Rate Books of every Parish, and also the same Powers which by the Act to regulate Parochial Assessments (Sixth and Seventh William the Fourth, Chapter Ninety-six, Section Four), are given to Surveyors acting thereunder. (*Repealed, see page* 222.)

Valuations to be conclusive.

29. Every Valuation of Property occupied by the University or any College during the Time it continues in force shall be final and conclusive on all Parties interested, nor shall any Rate be subject to Objection, on Appeal or otherwise, in respect of the Amount at which any Property comprised in the Valuation in force for the Time being shall be assessed, provided such Amount be in conformity with such Valuation. (*Repealed, see page* 222.)

As to Costs of Valuations.

30. The Costs of and incidental to the making of the Ground Plans herein-before directed, and also the Costs of and incidental to the First Valuation of Property occupied by the University or any College, shall be paid in equal proportions by the Vice-Chancellor (on behalf of the University and Colleges), and by the Mayor, Aldermen, and Burgesses; and the Vice-Chancellor shall have Power to demand and collect from the several Colleges their respective Shares of such Proportion, according to the Amount of their respective Assessments; and in default of any special Agreement as to the Costs of and incidental to any subsequent Valuation which shall be required by the Vice-Chancellor, such Costs shall be paid by the Chancellor, Masters, and Scholars, and in default of any special Agreement as to the Costs of and incidental to any subsequent Valuation which shall be required by the Mayor, such Costs shall be paid by the Mayor, Aldermen, and Burgesses. (*Repealed, see page* 222.)

As to University and College Property acquired after Valuation.

31. Any Property occupied by the University or by any College which may be acquired by the University, or by any College after any Valuation shall have been made, or which may be accidentally omitted therefrom, shall (if not exempt from Rates under the Provisions of this Act or otherwise) be rated in the ordinary Manner until a new Valuation be made, when such Property shall be included in such new Valuation, if not exempt as aforesaid. (*Repealed, see page* 222.)

As to certain Rates on Magdalen College.

32. Magdalen College shall be exonerated from the Payment of all Rates imposed before the passing of this Act in the several Parishes of Saint Giles and Saint Peter in respect of any Property for which such College had not previously paid Rates, and the Council may make such Orders as may appear equitable for Payment out of the Borough Fund to the said Parishes, or either of them, of Compensation for the Loss sustained by such Parishes, or either of them, by reason of this Enactment.

33. The Liability of the University and Colleges to pay any Money under a certain Agreement made in October One thousand six hundred and fifty, or under any previous or subsequent Agreement on the same Subject, shall cease from the Time when by the Operation of this Act the Property occupied by the University and Colleges shall be actually assessed to the Poor Rate of any Parish.

For Cessation of Payments under Agreement of October 1650.

34. As respects any Vestry to be holden in any Parish wherein the University or any College shall be charged to the Rate for the Relief of the Poor, the Vice-Chancellor, or some Member of the Senate deputed by him, shall be deemed the duly authorised Agent of the University, and the Head of such College, or some Member of the College deputed by him, shall be deemed the duly authorised Agent of such College, within the Intent and Meaning of the Act Fifty-ninth George the Third, Chapter Eighty-five, Section two.

Vestry Meetings.

35. No Member of the University or of any College shall, by reason of any Rate on the Property occupied by the University or by such College, be entitled to be registered as an Elector of the Borough, or to be enrolled as a Burgess thereof, or be compellable to serve any Municipal or Parochial Office, or to serve or to be empannelled on any Jury or Inquest, or to perform any Service imposed on Ratepayers. (*See below, page* 222.)

Exemption from Municipal and Parochial Offices, etc.

36. So much of the Twenty-sixth Section of the Seventy-sixth Chapter of the Fourth and Fifth William the Fourth as provides that in any Union each of the Parishes shall be separately chargeable with and liable to defray the Expense of its own Poor, whether relieved in or out of the Workhouse, and so much of the Twenty-eighth Section of that Act as provides for the Mode of calculating the Average according to which the Contribution of Parishes in Unions shall be calculated, shall, in respect of the Cambridge Union, from and after the Twenty-ninth Day of September One thousand eight hundred and fifty-six, be of none Effect; and thenceforth all the Costs and Charges for the Relief of the Poor in the several Parishes

Union of Parishes, etc.

Relief in Cambridge Union to be borne by Common Fund.

in the said Union shall be borne by One Common Fund, to which such Parishes shall contribute in proportion to the annual rateable Value of the Lands, Tenements, and Hereditaments therein assessable by Law to the Relief of the Poor; and the Guardians of the said Union shall make their Orders for Contribution upon the Churchwardens and Overseers of such Parishes respectively according to such Proportion.

Guardians may obtain Valuation of Rateable Property.

37. The said Guardians may at any Time cause a Survey and Valuation of the Rateable Property, or any Part thereof, in any of such Parishes, to be made for the Purpose of ascertaining the true annual rateable Value thereof; and when such Survey and Valuation shall have been made and completed, the Guardians shall cause a Notice thereof to be published in some Newspaper circulating in the said Union; and the Valuation shall be deposited at the Office of the Clerk of the Guardians for the Inspection of all Persons interested therein without Fee or Reward for the Space of Seven Days next following the date of such Publication; and the said Guardians, after the expiration of such Period, may reject such Valuation, or adopt it as the Basis upon which to calculate the future Contributions of such Parish or Parishes to the said Common Fund, until the same be set aside or altered as herein-after provided or a fresh valuation be made: Provided, that as regards any property occupied by the University or any College, the same shall be valued as in this Act provided. (*Repealed, see page* 222.)

Provision for Appeal against such Valuation.

38. If any Person assessed to the Poor Rate in any Parish in the said Union, or liable to be assessed thereto, shall think himself aggrieved by such Valuation, he may appeal to the next practicable Quarter Sessions for the Borough, giving Notice in Writing of such Appeal to the Clerk of the said Guardians, and such Court shall hear and determine such Appeal by setting aside, confirming, or amending such Valuation, and make such Order as to the Costs attending such Appeal as in the Judgment of the Court shall be proper. (*Repealed, see page* 222.)

Until Valuation be made, Contributions to be calculated according to Poor Rate.

39. Until such Valuation shall be made and completed, the Guardians, in making their Orders for Contribution on the Churchwardens and Overseers of the several Parishes, shall take the annual rateable Value of such Property in every Parish from the Assessment made for the Relief of the Poor next preceding the making of such Orders.

Saving as to Error in Contribution Orders.

40. No Order for Contribution shall be deemed invalid by reason of Error in the Estimate of the rateable Value of Property upon which such Order shall have been calculated.

41. Every Churchwarden, Overseer, or Collector of any Parish in the said Union shall, when required so to do, produce to the Guardians as they shall direct any Rate Book, Assessment, or Valuation of rateable Property in his Possession or under his Control, for the Purposes of enabling the Guardians to ascertain the rateable Value of the Property in such Parish; and any such Churchwarden, Overseer, or Collector wilfully neglecting or refusing to produce the same shall for every such Offence pay to the Treasurer of the said Guardians such Sum, not exceeding Five Pounds, as any Two Justices shall order and direct, which Sum shall be recoverable, with Costs, in the Manner provided by the Eleventh and Twelfth Victoria, Chapter Forty-three, and such Penalties shall be placed to the Account of the Common Fund of the Union.

Rate Books, etc. to be produced to Guardians by Parish Officers.

42. The Guardians shall pay out of the Funds raised by the Contributions to be made according to the Provisions herein contained all the Costs and Charges of and for the Relief of the Poor in the several Parishes comprised in the said Union, together with all other Expenses attending the carrying into effect the Provisions herein-before contained relating to the Relief of the Poor, or set forth in the Seventy-sixth Chapter of the Fourth and Fifth William the Fourth, and of the several Acts for amending and extending the same, and the Orders of the Poor Law Commissioners and the Poor Law Board already or hereafter to be issued and directed to the said Guardians, so far as such Acts and Orders are applicable to such Union and the several Parishes comprising the same, or the Poor thereof, and all other Charges and Expenses payable by such Guardians by virtue of their Office.

All Payments to be made by Guardians out of the Common Fund.

43. The Guardians shall, as soon as may be after the passing of this Act, pay out of the Moneys in their Hands the outstanding Debts and Charges heretofore incurred for the building or enlarging of the Union Workhouse, and the Purchase of the Industrial Training Ground, and charged upon the Poor Rates of the said Union or of the said

Outstanding Debts to be paid off.

Parishes, or either of them, so far as they may be able to do so, and having due Regard to the respective Liabilities of the several Parishes towards those Debts.

Orders for Removal of Paupers and for Maintenance of Lunatics.

44. The Guardians may from Time to Time obtain Orders of Justices, upon their Complaint (in like Manner and with the same Powers, Incidents, and Authorities, and subject to the like Liabilities, as the Churchwardens and Overseers of the Poor of any Parish are by Law now empowered, entitled, or subject to), for the Removal of any poor Person, who, not being settled in any Parish in the said Union nor exempt from Removal, shall be or become chargeable to the said Common Fund (the Chargeability to such Fund being in all Cases deemed for the Purpose of such Order a Chargeability to the Parish wherein such poor Person shall inhabit), and the said Guardians shall receive every poor Person removed by Order to any Parish in such Union, and may appeal against any such Order, or any Order for the Maintenance of a pauper Lunatic, in like Manner and with the like Liabilities and subject to the same Provisions as such Churchwardens and Overseers.

Act not to affect Removability of Poor.

45. No poor Person who would be removeable if this Act had not passed shall be or become irremoveable by reason of anything in this Act contained.

Union of certain Parishes.

46. From the said Twenty-ninth Day of September One thousand eight hundred and fifty-six, the Parish of Saint Rhadegund shall for all Purposes be united to and form Part of the Parish of All Saints, and the Parish of Saint John the Baptist shall for all purposes be united to and form Part of the Parish of Saint Edward.

Guardians may make and revoke Orders under small Tenements Rating Act.

47. From and after the Twenty-ninth Day of September One thousand eight hundred and fifty-six, the Powers of the Vestries of the several Parishes in the Cambridge Union to make or rescind Orders for putting in force the Provisions of the Thirteenth and Fourteenth Victoria, Chapter Ninety-nine, may be exercised by the Guardians of the said Union exclusively of such Vestries.

48. The Lands, Tenements, and Hereditaments in any of the said Parishes which may, on or after the said Twenty-ninth Day of September One thousand eight hundred and fifty-six, be occupied by the Mayor, Aldermen, and Burgesses, or by the Guardians of the Poor of the said Union shall whilst so occupied respectively be exempt from Poor Rates.

Property occupied by Corporation and Guardians exempt from Poor Rates.

49. The Guardians of the said Union may pay all the Costs and Charges incurred by them in and about the procuring of this Act, when duly taxed by the Proper Officer, out of the Moneys in their Possession.

Costs of Guardians in procuring this Act.

Improvement Quota.

Reduction of University Quota under Improvement Acts.

50. So much of the Improvement Acts as enacts that Two Fifths of the annual Sum or Sums to be ascertained and raised under those Acts shall be paid by or on account of the University shall be repealed, and for the future One Fourth only of the annual Sum or Sums which the Improvement Commissioners shall from Time to Time ascertain and direct to be raised shall be paid by or on account of the University in the Manner provided and under the Powers given by the Improvement Acts, which Quota shall be in lieu and instead of any Assessment or Rate on the University or Colleges; and no other Assessment or Rate shall be made on them under the Improvement Acts, and the remaining Part of such annual Sum or Sums shall be paid in the Manner provided by those Acts. (*Repealed, see page* 222.)

Watch Committee.

Constitution of Watch Committee.

51. From and after the Ninth Day of November One thousand eight hundred and fifty-six the Watch Committee of the Borough shall consist of—

The Mayor for the Time being;

Nine other Members of the Council, appointed by the Council;

Five Members of the University, being Members of the Senate, appointed by the Senate;

and at any Meeting of such Committee the Mayor, if present, shall be the Chairman; and in the Absence of the Mayor a Chairman shall be chosen by the Members of the Committee then present; and in all Cases where the Votes are equal the Chairman shall have a Second or Casting Vote.

52. The Appointment of Members of the Watch Committee by the Council and Senate respectively shall be made on or before the Ninth Day of November in each Year, unless in any Year in which that Day shall be Sunday, and in such

Watch Committee to be appointed annually.

Year the said Appointment may be made on the Day following; and the Members of the Watch Committee shall continue in Office from the Tenth Day of November in the Year of their Appointment until and including the Ninth Day of November in the following Year.

For Supply of Occasional Vacancies.

53. Occasional Vacancies in the Watch Committee may be filled up by the Council or Senate respectively as the same may occur; and the Persons appointed to supply such Vacancies shall continue in Office for the Residue of the current Year.

Notice of Appointment of Members of Watch Committee.

54. The Town Clerk shall from Time to Time, with all practicable Despatch, notify in Writing to the Vice-Chancellor all Appointments of Members of the Watch Committee made by the Council, and the Registrary shall in like Manner notify in Writing to the Town Clerk all Appointments of Members of the Watch Committee made by the Senate.

Powers of Watch Committee.

55. The Determination of the Number, the Appointment, Dismissal, and entire Management and Direction of the Constabulary Force shall be vested in such Watch Committee, but the said Watch Committee shall not have the Power of making Orders for the Payment of Money out of the Borough Fund.

Borough Fund.

Senate to appoint Three Auditors to join in auditing Borough Fund.

56. And whereas it is expedient to provide Means for giving to the University and Colleges a Knowledge of any intended Expenditure from or out of the Borough Fund, and for urging any Objections they may have to it, as well as for giving the Right of removing Orders for Payment of Money into the Court of Queen's Bench, under the Statute Seventh William the Fourth and First Victoria, Chapter Seventy-eight, or other Statutes: Be it enacted, That the Senate shall annually appoint Three Members of the Senate to audit the Accounts of the Treasurer of the Borough conjointly with the Three Auditors elected and appointed under the Municipal Corporation Act; but it shall not be necessary that the Auditors so appointed by the Senate (hereinafter termed University Auditors) should take any oath or make any Declaration. (*Repealed, see page* 222.)

Duration of Office of University Auditors

57. The University Auditors shall continue in Office from the First Day of March in the Year of their Appointment, until and including the last Day of February in the following Year. (*Repealed, see page* 222.)

58. Occasional Vacancies in the Office of University Auditor may be filled up by the Senate as the same may occur, and the Persons appointed to supply such Vacancies shall continue in Office for the Residue of the current Year. (*Repealed, see page* 222.)

For Supply of occasional Vacancies.

59. The Registrary shall from Time to Time notify in Writing to the Town Clerk all Appointments of University Auditors. (*Repealed, see page* 222.)

Notice of Appointment of University Auditors.

60. The Council of the Borough shall annually appoint a Finance Committee, and every Question concerning the Payment of Money out of the Borough Fund shall be submitted to the Finance Committee Six Days at least before the same is brought under the Consideration of the Council. (*Repealed, see page* 222.)

Certain Matters to be submitted to Finance Committee before submitted to Council.

61. The University Auditors shall have Three Days' Notice of every Meeting of the Finance Committee for the Purposes herein-before mentioned, and of the Business to be transacted at such Meeting; and they or any of them shall be at liberty to attend at such Meeting, and to be heard on the Matters and Business then brought forward, but shall not have any Right of Voting. (*Repealed, see page* 222.)

University Auditors to have notice of Meeting of Finance Committee.

62. The Vice-Chancellor or his Locum tenens, and the Head of every College or his Locum tenens, shall have all the Privileges conferred on any Burgess or on any Alderman or Councillor by the Acts Fifth and Sixth William the Fourth, Chapter Seventy-six, Section Ninety-three, and Seventh William the Fourth and First Victoria, Chapter Seventy-eight, Section Twenty-two, or by this Act, and shall be deemed Persons interested in the Borough Fund within the Intent and Meaning of the Forty-fourth Section of the last-mentioned Act and of this Act.

Vice-Chancellor and Heads of Colleges to have all Privileges and Rights conferred by 5 & 6 W. 4. c. 76. s. 93., 7 W. 4. & 1 Vict. c. 78. s. 22.

63. Except as herein-after stated, all Parties shall bear and pay their own Costs of the said Reference.

Parties to bear their own Costs of Reference.

64. One equal Moiety of the Costs common to both the said University and the said Borough, and also of the Costs of and incidental to this Act, shall be paid by the Chancellor, Masters, and Scholars of the University, and the other of such equal Moieties shall be paid by the Mayor, Aldermen, and Burgesses out of the Borough Fund.

As to expenses of Act, etc.

THE UNIVERSITIES ELECTIONS ACT, 1861

24 & 25 VICT. CAP. 53.

An Act to provide that Votes at Elections for the Universities may be recorded by means of Voting Papers. [1st August 1861.]

WHEREAS it is expedient to afford greater Facilities for voting to the Electors at Elections for Burgesses to serve in Parliament for the Universities of Oxford, Cambridge, and Dublin: Be it enacted by the Queen's most Excellent Majesty, by and with the Advice and Consent of the Lords Spiritual and Temporal, and Commons, in this present Parliament assembled, and by the Authority of the same, as follows:

Electors to vote by means of Voting Papers.

1. It shall be lawful for such Electors, in lieu of attending to vote in Person, to nominate any other Elector or Electors of the same University, competent to make the Declaration herein-after mentioned, to deliver for them at the Poll Voting Papers containing their Votes, as by this Act provided. Every such Voting Paper shall bear Date subsequently to Notice given by the Returning Officer of the Day for proceeding to Election, and shall contain the Name or Names of the Candidate or Candidates thereby voted for, and the Name or Names of the Elector or Electors authorised on behalf of the Voter to tender such Voting Paper at the Poll, and shall be according to the Form or to the Effect prescribed in the Schedule to this Act annexed. Such Voting Paper, the aforesaid Date and Names being previously filled in, shall, on any Day subsequent to Notice given by the Returning Officer of the Day for proceeding to Election, be signed

by the Voter in the Presence of a Justice of the Peace, for the County or Borough in which such Voter shall be then residing; and the said Justice shall certify and attest the Fact of such Voting Paper having been so signed in his Presence, by signing at the Foot thereof a Certificate or Attestation in the Form or to the Effect prescribed in the said Schedule, with his Name and Address in full, and shall state his Quality as a Justice of the Peace for such County or Borough.

Voting Papers to be read, and Votes recorded.

2. The Voting Paper, signed and certified as aforesaid, may be delivered to the Vice-Chancellor of the University for which the Election is held, or to any Pro-Vice-Chancellor appointed by him, or, in the Case of the University of Dublin, to the Provost of Trinity College, or to any Person lawfully deputed to act for him, at any One of the appointed Polling Places, during the appointed Hours of Polling, by any One of the Persons therein nominated in that Behalf, who shall, on tendering such Voting Paper at the Poll, read out the same; and the said Vice-Chancellor, Pro-Vice-Chancellor, Provost, or Deputy shall receive the Voting Papers as the same shall be delivered, and shall cause the Votes thereby given, or such of them as may not appear to be contrary to the Provisions of this Act, to be recorded in the Manner heretofore used, in all respects as if such Votes had been given by the Electors attending in Person; and all Votes so recorded shall have the same Validity and Effect as if they had been duly given by the Voters in person: Provided always, that no Person shall be entitled to sign or vote by more than One Voting Paper at any Election, and that no Voting Paper containing the Names of more Candidates than there are Burgesses to be elected at such Election shall be received or recorded: Provided also, that no Voting Paper shall be received or recorded unless the Person tendering the same shall make the following Declaration, which he shall sign at the foot or back thereof:

'I solemnly declare, that I am personally acquainted with '*A.B.* [the Voter], and I verily believe that this is the Paper 'by which he intends to Vote pursuant to the Provisions of 'the Universities Elections Act.'

Provided also, that no Voting Paper shall be so received and recorded if the Voter signing the same shall have already voted in Person at the same Election: Provided also, that every such Elector shall be entitled to vote in Person, notwithstanding that he has duly signed and transmitted a Voting Paper to another Elector, if such Voting Paper has not been already tendered at the Poll. (*This section was repealed by S. L. R. A.*, 1875, '*as to the form of declaration thereby prescribed.*' *See also pages* 185–6.)

Voting Papers may be inspected by any Person now entitled to object to Votes.

3. It shall be lawful for any Person now by Law or Custom authorised on behalf of any Candidate to object to Votes to inspect any Voting Paper tendered at the Poll before the same shall be received or recorded, and to object to it on One or more of the following Grounds:

1. That the Person on whose Behalf the Voting Paper is tendered is not qualified to vote:
2. That the Person tendering the Voting Paper is not duly qualified in that Behalf:
3. That the Person in whose Behalf the Voting Paper is tendered has already voted at that Election in person or by Voting Paper:
4. That the Voting Paper bears Date anterior to Notice given by the Returning Officer of the Day for proceeding to Election:
5. That the Voting Paper is forged or falsified:

And the Returning Officer, his Deputy or Assessor, or any Officer having by Law or Custom Power to decide Objections in respect of Votes tendered by voters attending the Poll in Person, shall have Power to put Questions to the Person tendering such Voting Paper, and to reject, receive, and record, or receive and record as objected to or protested against, any Votes tendered by Voting Papers: Provided, that in case the Objection offered to any Voting Paper shall be that it is forged or falsified, such Returning or other Officer shall receive and record such Voting Paper, having previously written upon it, "Objected to as forged," or "Objected to as falsified," together with the name of the Person making such Objection.

4. All Voting Papers received and recorded at such Election, as well as any Voting Papers rejected for Informality or on any other Ground, shall be filed and kept by the Officer entrusted with the Care of the Poll Books or other Documents relating to the said Election; and any Person shall be allowed to examine such Voting Papers at all reasonable Times, and to take Copies thereof, upon payment of a Fee of One shilling.

Voting Papers to be filed.

5. Any Person falsely or fraudulently signing any Voting Paper in the Name of any other Person, either as a Voter or as a Witness, whether such other Person shall be living or dead, and every Person signing, subscribing, endorsing, attesting, certifying, tendering, or transmitting as genuine any false or falsified Voting Paper, knowing the same to be false or falsified, and any Person falsely making any such Declaration as aforesaid, or such Declaration as is contained in the Schedule, or with fraudulent Intent altering, defacing, destroying, withholding, or abstracting any Voting Paper, and any Person wilfully making a false Answer to any Question put to him by the Returning or other Officer as herein-before provided, shall be guilty of a Misdemeanor, and punishable by Fine, or Imprisonment for a Term not exceeding One Year.

Penalty for falsely signing Voting Papers.

6. No such Voting Paper as herein-before mentioned shall be liable to any Stamp Duty.

Voting Papers not liable to Stamp Duty.

SCHEDULE.

UNIVERSITY ELECTION, 18 .

I *A.B.* [the Christian and Surnames of the Elector in full, his College or Hall, if any, and his Degree or Academical Rank or Office, if any, to be here inserted], do hereby declare, that I have signed no other Voting Paper at this Election, and do hereby give my Vote at this Election for

And I nominate *C.D.*
E.F.
G.H.
or One of them, to deliver this Voting Paper at the Poll.

Witness my Hand this Day of 18
(Signed) *A.B.* of [the Elector's Place of Residence to be here inserted].

Signed in my Presence by the said *A.B.*, who is personally known to me, on the above-mentioned Day of , 18 , the Name [or Names] of as the Candidate [or Candidates] voted for having been previously filled in.

(Signed) *Z.M.* of [the Witness's Place of Residence to be here inserted,]
a Justice of the Peace for

THE UNIVERSITIES ELECTIONS ACT, 1868

31 & 32 VICT. CAP. 65.

An Act to Amend the Law relating to the Use of Voting Papers in Elections for the Universities. [31st July 1868.]

'WHEREAS by an Act passed in the Session holden in 'the Twenty-fourth and Twenty-fifth Years of the 'Reign of Her present Majesty, Chapter Fifty-three, intituled '"An Act to provide that Votes at Elections for the Univer- '"sities may be recorded by means of Voting Papers," it is 'provided that at the Elections for Burgesses to serve in 'Parliament for the Universities of Oxford, Cambridge, 'and Dublin Votes may be given by means of Voting 'Papers; but it is by the said Act provided that no Voting 'Paper shall be received or recorded unless the Person ten- 'dering the same shall make the following Declaration, 'which he shall sign at the Foot or Back thereof:

24 and 25 Vict. c. 53.

Sect. 2.

'"I solemnly declare that I am personally acquainted '"with *A.B.* [the Voter], and I verily believe that this is '"the Paper by which he intends to vote, pursuant to '"the provisions of the Universities Election Act."

'And whereas by virtue of The Representation of the 'People Act, 1867, the said first-mentioned Act applies 'to every Election of a Member for the University of 'London;

30 and 31 Vict. c. 102, s. 45.

'And whereas it is expedient to amend the said first- 'mentioned Act so far as respects the said recited Decla- 'ration:'

Be it enacted by the Queen's most Excellent Majesty, by and with the Advice and Consent of the Lords Spiritual and Temporal, and Commons, in this present Parliament assembled, and by the authority of the same as follows:

Alteration of form of declaration required by 24 and 25 Vict. c. 53.

1. From and after the passing of this Act the said recited Form of Declaration shall not be required, and there shall be substituted in place thereof the Form of Declaration following, that is to say,

'I solemnly declare that I verily believe that this is 'the Paper by which *A.B.* [the Voter] intends to vote 'pursuant to the Provisions of The Universities Election 'Acts, 1861 and 1868.'

Amendment of sect. 2 of first-recited Act as to University of London.

2. The Second Section of the said first-mentioned Act shall, in reference to the University of London, be construed as if the Words "in the Manner heretofore "used" were omitted therefrom.

Officers in whose presence voting papers may be signed in the Channel Islands.

3. A Voting Paper for the Election of any Burgess or Member to serve in Parliament for any Universities or University in respect of which the Provisions of the said first-mentioned Act may for the Time being be in force, may be signed by a Voter being in one of the Channel Islands in the Presence of the following Officers; that is to say,

(1) In Jersey and Guernsey, of the Bailiffs or any Lieutenant Bailiff, Jurat, or Juge d'Instruction.

(2) In Alderney, of the Judge of Alderney, or any Jurat.

(3) In Sark, of the Seneschal or Deputy Seneschal.

And for the Purpose of certifying and attesting the Signature of such Voting Paper, each of the said Officers shall have all the Powers of a Justice of the Peace under the first-mentioned Act, and a Statement of the official Quality of such Officer shall be a sufficient Statement of Quality in pursuance of the Provisions of the said Act.

Short title.

4. This Act may be cited for all Purposes as The Universities Elections Act, 1868, and the said first-mentioned Act and this Act may be cited together as The Universities Election Acts, 1861 and 1868.

THE UNIVERSITIES TESTS ACT, 1871

34 & 35 VICT. CAP. 26.

An Act to Alter the Law respecting Religious Tests in the Universities of Oxford, Cambridge, and Durham, and in the Halls and Colleges of those Universities. [16th June 1871.]

WHEREAS it is expedient that the benefits of the Universities of Oxford, Cambridge, and Durham, and of the colleges and halls now subsisting therein, as places of religion and learning, should be rendered freely accessible to the nation:

And whereas, by means of divers restrictions, tests, and disabilities, many of Her Majesty's subjects are debarred from the full enjoyment of the same:

And whereas it is expedient that such restrictions, tests, and disabilities should be removed, under proper safeguards for the maintenance of religious instruction and worship in the said universities and the colleges and halls now subsisting within the same:

Be it enacted by the Queen's most Excellent Majesty, by and with the advice and consent of the Lords Spiritual and Temporal, and Commons, in this present Parliament assembled, and by the authority of the same, as follows:

1. This Act may be cited as "The Universities Tests Act, 1871." Short title.

2. In the construction of this Act— Interpretation of terms.

The word "college" includes the cathedral or House of Christ Church in Oxford, and any hall not being a private hall established under the Act of the session of the seventeenth and eighteenth years of the reign of Her present Majesty, chapter eighty-one, nor being a hostel established under the Act of the session of the nineteenth and twentieth years of the reign of Her present Majesty, chapter eighty-eight:

The word "office" includes every professorship other than professorships of divinity, every assistant or deputy professorship, public readership, prelectorship, lectureship, headship of a college or hall, fellowship, studentship, tutorship, scholarship, and exhibition, and also any office or emolument not in this section specified, the income of which is payable out of the revenues of any of the said universities, or of any college within the said universities, or which is held or enjoyed by any member as such of any of the said universities, or of any college within any of the said universities.

Persons taking lay academical degrees or holding lay academical or collegiate offices not to be required to subscribe any formulary of faith, etc.

3. From and after the passing of this Act, no person shall be required, upon taking or to enable him to take any degree (other than a degree in divinity) within the Universities of Oxford, Cambridge, and Durham, or any of them, or upon exercising or to enable him to exercise any of the rights and privileges which may heretofore have been or may hereafter be exercised by graduates in the said universities or any of them, or in any college subsisting at the time of the passing of this Act in any of the said universities, or upon taking or holding or to enable him to take or hold any office in any of the said universities or any such college as aforesaid, or upon teaching or to enable him to teach within any of the said universities or any such college as aforesaid, or upon opening or to enable him to open a private hall or hostel in any of the said universities for the reception of students, to subscribe any article or formulary of faith, or to make any declaration or take any oath respecting his religious belief or profession, or to conform to any religious observance, or to attend or abstain from attending any form of public worship, or to belong to any specified church, sect,

or denomination; nor shall any person be compelled, in any of the said universities or any such college as aforesaid, to attend the public worship of any church, sect, or denomination to which he does not belong: Provided that—

(1) Nothing in this section shall render a layman or a person not a member of the Church of England eligible to any office or capable of exercising any right or privilege in any of the said universities or colleges, which office, right, or privilege, under the authority of any Act of Parliament or any statute or ordinance of such university or college in force at the time of the passing of this Act, is restricted to persons in holy orders, or shall remove any obligation to enter into holy orders which is by such authority attached to any such office.

(2) Nothing in this section shall open any office (not being an office mentioned in this section) to any person who is not a member of the Church of England, where such office is at the passing of this Act confined to members of the said Church by reason of any such degree as aforesaid being a qualification for holding that office.

Act not to interfere with lawfully established system of religious instruction, worship, and discipline.

4. Nothing in this Act shall interfere with or affect, any further or otherwise than is hereby expressly enacted, the system of religious instruction, worship, and discipline which now is or which may hereafter be lawfully established in the said universities respectively, or in the colleges thereof or any of them, or the statutes and ordinances of the said universities and colleges respectively relating to such instruction, worship, and discipline.

Religious instruction.

5. The governing body of every college subsisting at the time of the passing of this Act in any of the said universities shall provide sufficient religious instruction for all members thereof *in statu pupillari* belonging to the Established Church.

Morning and Evening Prayer to be used as heretofore, but an abridgement may be used on week days on request of governing body.

6. The Morning and Evening Prayer according to the Order of the Book of Common Prayer shall continue to be used daily as heretofore in the chapel of every college subsisting at the time of the passing of this Act in any of the said universities; but notwithstanding anything contained in the statute thirteenth and fourteenth Charles the Second, chapter four, or in this Act, it shall be lawful for the visitor of any such college, on the request of the governing body thereof, to authorise from time to time, in writing, the use on week days only of any abridgement or adaptation of the said Morning and Evening Prayer in the chapel of such college instead of the Order set forth in the Book of Common Prayer.

Attendance at lectures.

7. No person shall be required to attend any college or university lecture to which he, if he be of full age, or, if he be not of full age, his parent or guardian, shall object upon religious grounds.

Repeal of Acts in schedule.

8. After the passing of this Act, the Acts specified in the schedule to this Act are hereby repealed to the extent in the third column of the said schedule mentioned; and (*Repealed, S. L. R. A.*, 1883) any provision in any Act of Parliament or in any statute or ordinance of the said universities or colleges, so far as it is inconsistent with this Act, shall be repealed.

[NOTE. *A Schedule to this Act mentioning the Acts repealed by this Act was repealed by S. L. R. A.*, 1883.]

UNIVERSITIES OF OXFORD AND CAMBRIDGE ACT, 1877

40 & 41 VICT. CAP. 48.

An Act to make further Provision respecting the Universities of Oxford and Cambridge and the Colleges therein[1]. [10th August 1877.]

WHEREAS the revenues of the Universities of Oxford and Cambridge are not adequate to the full discharge of the duties incumbent on them respectively, and it is therefore expedient that provision be made for enabling or requiring the Colleges in each University to contribute more largely out of their revenues to University purposes, especially with a view to further and better instruction in art, science, and other branches of learning, where the same are not taught or not adequately taught, in the University:

And whereas it may be requisite for the purposes aforesaid, as regards each University, to attach fellowships and other emoluments held in the Colleges to offices in the University:

And whereas it is also expedient to make provision for regulating the tenure and advantages of fellowships not so attached, and for altering the conditions on which the same are held, and to amend in divers other particulars the law relating to the Universities and Colleges:

Be it therefore enacted by the Queen's most Excellent Majesty, by and with the advice and consent of the Lords Spiritual and Temporal, and Commons, in this present Parliament assembled, and by the authority of the same, as follows: (*Repealed, S. L. R. A.*, 1894.)

[1] Where the contrary is not stated the portions of this Act that have been repealed were repealed by *S. L. R. A.*, 1883.

Preliminary.

Short titles.

1. This Act may be cited as The Universities of Oxford and Cambridge Act, 1877; and the Acts described in the Schedule to this Act may respectively be cited by the short titles therein mentioned. (*Repealed, S. L. R. A.*, 1894.)

Interpretation.

2. In this Act—

"The University" means the University of Oxford and the University of Cambridge respectively, or one of them separately (as the case may require):

"The Senate" means the Senate of the University of Cambridge:

"College" means a College in the University, and includes the Cathedral or House of Christ Church in Oxford:

"Hall" means one of the following Halls, namely, St Mary Hall, St Edmund Hall, St Alban Hall, New Inn Hall, in the University of Oxford:

"The Governing Body" of a College means, as regards the Colleges in the University of Oxford, except Christ Church, the head and all actual fellows of the College, being graduates, and as regards Christ Church means the dean, canons, and senior students:

"The Governing Body" of a College means, as regards the Colleges in the University of Cambridge, except Downing College, the head and all actual fellows of the College, bye-fellows excepted, being graduates, and as regards Downing College, the head, professors, and all actual fellows thereof, bye-fellows excepted, being graduates:

"Emolument" includes—

(1) A headship, professorship, lectureship, readership, praelectorship, fellowship, bye-fellowship, tutorship, senior studentship, scholarship, junior studentship, exhibition, demyship, postmastership, taberdarship, Bible clerkship, servitorship, sizarship, sub-sizarship, or other place in the University or a College or Hall, having attached thereto an income payable out of the revenues of the University or of a College or Hall, or being a place to be held and enjoyed by a head or other member of a College or Hall as such, or having

attached thereto an income to be so held and enjoyed arising wholly or in part from an endowment, benefaction, or trust;

(2) The income aforesaid, and all benefits and advantages of every nature and kind belonging to the place, and any endowment belonging to, or held by, or for the benefit of, or enjoyed by, a head or other member of a College or Hall as such, and any fund, endowment, or property held by or on behalf of the University or a College or Hall, for the purpose of advancing, rewarding, or otherwise providing for any member of the University or College or Hall, or of purchasing any advowson, benefice or property to be held for the like purpose, or to be in any manner applied for the promotion of any such member; and

(3) As regards the University of Oxford a bursary appropriated to any College in Scotland:

"Office" has the same meaning in the sections in which "The Universities Tests Act, 1871," is mentioned as it has in that Act: 34 & 35 Vict. c. 26.

"School" means a school or other place of education beyond the precincts of the University, and includes a College in Scotland:

"Professor" includes Regius and other professor, and reader, and teacher; and "professorship" includes their several offices:

"Advowson" includes right of patronage, exclusive or alternate:

"The Charity Commissioners" means the Charity Commissioners for England and Wales:

"The Secretary of State" means one of Her Majesty's Principal Secretaries of State.

Commissioners.

3. There shall be two bodies of Commissioners styled respectively the University of Oxford Commissioners and the University of Cambridge Commissioners. Bodies of Commissioners.

The provisions of this Act referring to the Commissioners shall be construed to apply to those two bodies respectively, or to one of those two bodies separately, as the case may require.

4. The following persons are hereby nominated the University of Oxford Commissioners: Nomination of Oxford Commissioners.

The Right Honourable Roundell, Baron Selborne.

The Right Honourable John Thomas, Earl of Redesdale.

The Right Honourable Montague Bernard, Doctor of Civil Law.

The Honourable Sir William Robert Grove, one of the Justices of Her Majesty's High Court of Justice.

The Reverend James Bellamy, Doctor of Divinity, President of St John's College.

Henry John Stephen Smith, Master of Arts, Savilian Professor of Geometry.

Matthew White Ridley, Esquire, Master of Arts.

Nomination of Cambridge Commissioners.

5. The following persons are hereby nominated the University of Cambridge Commissioners:

The Right Honourable Sir Alexander James Edmund Cockburn, Baronet, Lord Chief Justice of England.

The Right Reverend Henry, Lord Bishop of Worcester.

The Right Honourable John William, Lord Rayleigh.

The Right Honourable Edward Pleydell Bouverie.

The Reverend Joseph Barber Lightfoot, Doctor of Divinity, Lady Margaret Professor of Divinity.

George Gabriel Stokes, Master of Arts, Lucasian Professor of Mathematics.

George Wirgman Hemming, one of Her Majesty's Counsel, Master of Arts.

Vacancies among Commissioners.

6. If any person nominated a Commissioner by this Act dies, resigns, or becomes incapable of acting as a Commissioner, it shall be lawful for Her Majesty the Queen to appoint a person to fill his place; and so from time to time as regards every person appointed under this section: Provided that the name of every person so appointed shall be laid before the Houses of Parliament within ten days after the appointment, if Parliament is then sitting, or if not, then ten days after the next meeting of Parliament.

Duration: Proceedings.

Duration of Commissions.

7. The powers of the Commissioners shall continue until the end of the year one thousand eight hundred and eighty, and no longer; but it shall be lawful for Her Majesty the Queen, from time to time, with the advice of her Privy Council, on the application of the Commissioners, to continue the powers of the Commissioners for such time as Her Majesty thinks fit, but not beyond the end of the year one thousand eight hundred and eighty-one.

Chairmen and meetings of Commissioners.

8. The Commissioner first named in this Act, as regards each of the two bodies of Commissioners, shall be the Chairman of the respective body of Commissioners; and in case of his ceasing from any cause to be a Commissioner, or of his absence from any meeting, the Commissioners present at each meeting shall choose a chairman.

The powers of the Commissioners may be exercised at a meeting at which three or more Commissioners are present.

In case of an equality of votes on a question at a meeting, the chairman of the meeting shall have a second or casting vote in respect of that question.

9. The Commissioners shall have a common seal, and the same shall be judicially noticed. Seals of Commissioners.

10. Any act of the Commissioners shall not be invalid by reason only of any vacancy in their body; but if at any time, and as long as, the number of persons acting as Commissioners is less than four, the Commissioners shall discontinue the exercise of their powers. Vacancies not to invalidate acts.

Statutes for University and Colleges.

11. Until the end of the year one thousand eight hundred and seventy-eight, the University and the Governing Body of a College shall have the like powers in all respects of making statutes for the University or the College respectively, and of making statutes for altering or repealing statutes made by them, as are, from and after the end of that year, conferred on the Commissioners by this Act; but every statute so made shall, before the end of that year, be laid before the Commissioners, and the same, if approved before or after the end of that year by the Commissioners by writing under their seal, but not otherwise, shall, as regards the force and operation of the statute, and as regards proceedings prescribed by this Act to be taken respecting a statute made by the Commissioners after (but not before) the statute is made, be deemed to be a statute made by the Commissioners. Power for University and Colleges to make statutes.

If within one month after a statute so made by a College is laid before the Commissioners, a member of the Governing Body of the College makes a representation in writing to the Commissioners respecting the statute, the Commissioners, before approving of the statute, shall take the representation into consideration.

In considering a statute so made by a College, the Commissioners shall have regard to the interests of the University and the Colleges therein as a whole.

The Commissioners shall not approve a statute so made by a College until they have published, in such form as to them may seem fit, a statement with respect to the main purposes relative to the University for which, in their opinion, provision should be made under this Act, the sources from which funds for those purposes should be obtained, and the principles on which payments from the Colleges for those purposes should be contributed; but nothing in this provision or in any statement published thereunder shall prevent the Commissioners from exercising from time to time according to their discretion the powers and performing the duties conferred and imposed on them by this Act.

12. From and after the end of the year one thousand eight hundred and seventy-eight, the Commissioners may by virtue of this Act, and subject and according to the provisions thereof, make, by writing under their seal, statutes for the University and for any College or Hall, and for altering or repealing statutes made by the Commissioners, and may exercise those powers from time to time with reference to the University and to any College or Hall. Power for Commissioners to make statutes for University and Colleges and Halls.

Limitation of fifty years.

13. The Commissioners shall not make a statute altering the trusts, conditions, or directions affecting a University or College emolument if the original charter, deed of composition, or other instrument of foundation thereof, not being an order in Council made under, or a statute or ordinance having effect under, any Act mentioned in the schedule to this Act, was made or executed within fifty years before the passing of this Act; but nothing in this section shall prevent the Commissioners from making a statute increasing the endowment of any University or College emolument, or otherwise improving the position of the holder thereof.

Regard to main design of founder.

14. The Commissioners, in making a statute affecting a University or College emolument, shall have regard to the main design of the founder, except where the same has ceased to be observed before the passing of this Act, or where the trusts, conditions, or directions affecting the emolument have been altered in substance by or under any other Act.

Provision for education, religion, etc.

15. The Commissioners, in making a statute for the University or a College or Hall, shall have regard to the interests of education, religion, learning, and research, and in the case of a statute for a College or Hall shall have regard, in the first instance, to the maintenance of the College or Hall for those purposes.

Objects of statutes for University.

16. With a view to the advancement of art, science, and other branches of learning, the Commissioners, in statutes made by them for the University, may from time to time make provision for the following purposes, or any of them:

(1) For enabling or requiring the several Colleges, or any of them, to make contribution out of their revenues for University purposes, regard being first had to the wants of the several Colleges in themselves for educational and other collegiate purposes:

(2) For the creation, by means of contributions from the Colleges or otherwise, of a common University Fund, to be administered under the supervision of the University:

(3) For making payments, under the supervision of the University, out of the said common fund for the giving of instruction, the doing of work, or the conducting of investigations within the University in any branch of learning or inquiry connected with the studies of the University:

(4) For consolidating any two or more professorships or lectureships:

(5) For erecting and endowing professorships or lectureships:

(6) For abolishing professorships or lectureships:

(7) For altering the endowment of any professorship or lectureship:

(8) For altering the conditions of eligibility or appointment and mode of election or appointment to any professorship or lectureship, and for limiting the tenure thereof:

(9) For providing retiring pensions for professors and lecturers:

(10) For providing new or improving existing buildings, libraries, collections, or apparatus for any purpose connected with the instruction of any members of the University, or with research in any art or science or other branch of learning, and for maintaining the same:

(11) For diminishing the expense of University education by founding scholarships tenable by students either at any College or Hall within the University, or as unattached students, not members of any College or Hall, or by paying salaries to the teachers of such unattached students, or by otherwise encouraging such unattached students:

(12) For founding and endowing scholarships, exhibitions, and prizes for encouragement of proficiency in any art or science or other branch of learning:

(13) For modifying the trusts, conditions, or directions of or affecting any University endowment, foundation or gift, or of or affecting any professorship, lectureship, scholarship, office, or institution, in or connected with the University, or of or affecting any property belonging to or held in trust for the University or held by the University in trust for a Hall, as far as the Commissioners think the modification thereof necessary or expedient for giving effect to statutes made by them for any purpose in this Act mentioned:

(14) For regulating presentations to benefices in the gift of the University:

(15) For regulating the application of the purchase money for any advowson sold by the University:

(16) For founding any office not paid out of University or College funds in connexion with any special educational work done out of the University, under the control of the University, and for remunerating any secretary or officer resident in the University and employed there in the management of any such special educational work:

(17) For altering or repealing any statute, ordinance, or regulation of the University, and substituting or adding any statute for or to the same.

Objects of statutes for Colleges in themselves.

17. The Commissioners, in statutes made by them for a College, may from time to time make provision for the following purposes relative to the College, or any of them:

(1) For altering and regulating the conditions of eligibility or appointment, including where it seems fit those relating to age, to any emolument or office held in or connected with the College, the mode of election or appointment thereto, and the value, length, and conditions of tenure thereof, and for providing a retiring pension for a holder thereof:

(2) For consolidating any two or more emoluments held in or connected with the College:

(3) For dividing, suspending, suppressing, converting, or otherwise dealing with any emolument held in or connected with the College:

(4) For attaching any emolument held in or connected with the College to any office in the College, on such tenure as to the Commissioners seems fit, and for attaching to the emolument, in connexion with the office, conditions of residence, study, and duty, or any of them:

(5) For affording further or better instruction in any art or science or other branch of learning:

(6) For providing new or improving existing buildings, libraries, collections, or apparatus, for any purpose connected with instruction or research in any art or science or other branch of learning, and for maintaining the same:

(7) For diminishing the expense of education in the College:

(8) For modifying the trusts, conditions, or directions affecting any College endowment, foundation, or gift, or any property belonging to the College, or the head or any member thereof, as such, or held in trust for the College, or for the head or any member thereof, as such, as far as the Commissioners think the modification thereof necessary or expedient for giving effect to statutes made by them for the College:

(9) For regulating presentations to benefices in the gift of the College:

(10) For regulating the application of the purchase money for any advowson sold by the College:

(11) For altering or repealing any statute, ordinance, regulation, or byelaw of the College, and substituting or adding any statute for or to the same.

Objects of statutes for Colleges in relation to University.

18. The Commissioners, in statutes made by them for a College, may from time to time make provision for the following purposes relative to the University, or any of them:

(1) For authorising the College to commute any annual payment agreed or required to be made by it for University purposes into a capital sum to be provided by the College out of money belonging to it, and not produced by any sale of lands or hereditaments made after the passing of this Act:

(2) For annexing any emolument held in or connected with the College to any office in the University, or in a Hall, on such tenure as to the Commissioners seems fit, and for attaching to the emolument, in connexion with the office, conditions of residence, study, and duty, or any of them:

(3) For assigning a portion of the revenues or property of the College, as a contribution to the common fund or otherwise,

for encouragement of instruction in the University in any art or science or other branch of learning, or for the maintenance and benefit of persons of known ability and learning, studying or making researches in any art or science or other branch of learning in the University :

(4) For empowering the College by statute made and passed at a general meeting of the Governing Body of the College specially summoned for this purpose, by the votes of not less than two thirds of the number of persons present and voting, to transfer the library of the College, or any portion thereof, to any University library :

(5) For providing out of the revenues of the College for payments to be made, under the supervision of the University, for work done or investigations conducted in any branch of learning or inquiry connected with the studies of the University within the University :

(6) For giving effect to statutes made by the Commissioners for the University :

(7) For modifying the trusts, conditions, or directions of or affecting any College endowment, foundation, or gift, concerning or relating to the University, as far as the Commissioners think the modification thereof necessary or expedient for giving effect to statutes made by them for the University.

Increase of or additional income to be regarded.

19. The Commissioners, in making a statute affecting a University or College emolument, shall take into account any prospective increase of the income of the emolument, or any prospective addition to the revenues of the University or College, and may make such provision as they think expedient for the application of that increase or addition.

Power to allow continuance of voluntary payments.

20. Nothing in or done under this Act shall prevent the Commissioners from making in any statute made by them for a College such provisions as they think expedient for the voluntary continuance of any voluntary payment that has been used to be made out of the revenues of the College in connexion with the College estates or property.

Provision for accounts, audit, borrowing, and leases.

21. The Commissioners, in statutes made by them, shall from time to time make provision—

(1) For the form of accounts of the University and of a College relating to funds administered either for general purposes, or in trust, or otherwise, and for the audit and publication thereof :

(2) For the publication of accounts of receipts and expenditure of money raised under the borrowing powers of the University or of a College :

And the Commissioners, in statutes made by them, may from time to time, if they think fit, make provision—

(3) For regulating the exercise of the borrowing powers of the University or of a College:

(4) For regulating the conditions under which beneficial leases may be renewed by the University or a College.

Union of Colleges and Halls and institutions or combination for education.

22. The Commissioners, in statutes made by them, may from time to time make provision for the complete or partial union of two or more Colleges, or of a College or Colleges and a Hall or Halls, or of two or more Halls, or of a College or Hall, with any institution in the University, or for the organization of a combined educational system in and for two or more Colleges or Halls, provided application in that behalf is made to the Commissioners on the part of each College and Hall and institution as follows:

(1) In the case of a College in the University of Oxford, by a resolution passed at a general meeting of the Governing Body of the College specially summoned for this purpose, by the votes of not less than two thirds of the number of persons present and voting, and, in case of an application for complete union, with the consent in writing of the Visitor of the College:

(2) In the case of a Hall, by a resolution of the Hebdomadal Council, with the consent in writing of the Chancellor of the University:

(3) In the case of a College in the University of Cambridge, by a resolution passed at a general meeting of the Governing Body of the College specially summoned for this purpose, and, in case of an application for complete union, the resolution being passed by the votes of not less than two thirds of the number of persons present and voting:

(4) In the case of an institution, with the consent of the Congregation or Senate of the University.

Saving respecting Hulme Exhibitions at Oxford.

23. The Commissioners shall not make a statute affecting the trusts or directions of the will of William Hulme, of Kearsley, in the county of Lancaster, deceased, or the provisions of any Act of Parliament relating thereto, except as regards so much of the funds or property of the trustees under the same as the Charity Commissioners under any scheme approved by Order in Council may assign for scholarships or exhibitions at Brasenose College or elsewhere in Oxford, without the consent in writing of the trustees under the same.

Saving respecting Snell Exhibitions at Oxford.

24. No statute or ordinance shall be made under this Act affecting the trusts, conditions, or directions of the will of John Snell, Esquire, deceased, or any scheme approved by the Court of Chancery relating thereto, without the consent in writing of the University Court of the University of Glasgow.

25. The Commissioners, in a statute made by them for the University of Oxford, or for Oriel College in Oxford, may, if they think fit, with the assent of Oriel College, signified under its common seal, and with the concurrence of the Ecclesiastical Commissioners for England, provide that the canonry in the chapter of the cathedral church of Rochester, which is now annexed and united to the provostship of Oriel College, shall, on a vacancy, be severed therefrom, and may also, with the concurrence of the said Ecclesiastical Commissioners, provide that such canonry shall be thenceforth permanently annexed and united to some office or place of a theological or ecclesiastical character in or connected with the University of Oxford, or may, with the concurrence aforesaid, make such other provisions for the future disposal and patronage of such canonry as they shall think fit; and in case any such statute shall be made annexing such canonry to such office or place as aforesaid, such canonry, or the income thereof, may, if they think fit, be reckoned and taken, in whole or in part, as a contribution of Oriel College out of its revenues to University purposes.

Provision for canonry of Rochester annexed to provostship of Oriel College, Oxford.

26. The Commissioners, in a statute or statutes made by them for the University of Cambridge, with the concurrence of the Ecclesiastical Commissioners for England, may provide for the canonry in the chapter of the Cathedral Church of Ely, which is annexed and united to the Regius Professorship of Greek, being, on a vacancy, severed therefrom, and being thenceforth permanently annexed and united to a professorship in the University of a theological or ecclesiastical character, with power, nevertheless, for the Commissioners, with the concurrence of the Ecclesiastical Commissioners, if they think it expedient, to allow the present professor to resign the professorship and to hold the canonry as if it had never been annexed to the professorship.

Severance of canonry from Greek professorship at Cambridge.

27. A statute for altering or modifying the trusts, statutes, or directions relating to the endowments held by the Regius Professor of Greek, Hebrew, or Divinity in the University of Cambridge, if affecting any statute of Trinity College touching those professors or their endowments, shall not be made by the Commissioners unless and until it receives the assent of Trinity College under its common seal.

Saving for statutes of Trinity College, Cambridge, as to Regius professorships.

28. The Commissioners, in a statute or statutes made by them for Emmanuel College in the University of Cambridge, after notice in writing to the heir of Sir Wolstan Dixie, may alter or modify the trusts, conditions, or directions of or affecting the Dixie Foundation, and as regards any right of nomination vested in the heir of the founder may commute that right in such manner, or make such other arrangement touching that right, as to the Commissioners seems just and beneficial.

Alteration of trusts of Dixie Foundation in Emmanuel College, Cambridge.

29. A statute made by the Commissioners shall not affect the right of nominating or appointing to the headship of Saint Mary Magdalene College in the University of Cambridge, unless the consent by deed of the person entitled to that right is first obtained.

Saving for headship of Magdalene College, Cambridge.

Distinction of University and College Statutes.

30. A statute made by the Commissioners may, if the Commissioners think fit, be in part a statute for the University, and in part a statute for a College or Hall.

The Commissioners shall in each statute made by them declare whether the same is a statute, wholly or in any and what part, for the University or for a College or Hall therein named; and the declaration in that behalf of the Commissioners shall be conclusive, to all intents.

If any statute is in part a statute for a College or Hall, the same shall for the purposes of the provisions of this Act relative to the representation of Colleges and Halls, and of the other provisions of this Act regulating proceedings on the statute, be proceeded on as a statute for the College or Hall.

Communication of porposed statutes for University, etc., to Council, etc.

31. Where the Commissioners contemplate making a statute for the University or a statute for a College or Hall containing a provision for any purpose relative to the University, or a statute otherwise affecting the interests of the University, they shall, one month at least (exclusive of any University vacation) before adopting any final resolution in that behalf, communicate the proposed statute in the University of Oxford to the Hebdomadal Council, to the Head and to the Visitor of the College, and to the Principal of the Hall affected thereby, and in the University of Cambridge to the Council of the Senate and to the Governing Body of the College affected thereby.

The Commissioners shall take into consideration any representation made to them by the Council, College, Visitor, Principal, or Governing Body respecting the proposed statute.

Within seven days after receipt of such communication by the Council, the Vice-Chancellor of the University shall give public notice thereof in the University.

Publication of proposed statutes for Colleges and Halls.

32. Where the Commissioners contemplate making a statute for a College or Hall, they shall, one month at least (exclusive of any University vacation) before adopting any final resolution in that behalf, communicate the proposed statute to the Vice-Chancellor of the University and to the Head, and in the University of Oxford the Visitor, of the College, and to the Principal of the Hall.

Within seven days after receipt of such communication the Vice-Chancellor shall give public notice thereof in the University.

Suspension of elections.

33. The Commissioners may, if they think fit, by writing under their seal, from time to time authorise and direct the University or any College or Hall to suspend the election or appointment to, or limit the tenure of, any emolument therein mentioned for a time therein mentioned within the continuance of the powers of the Commissioners as then ascertained; and the election or appointment thereto or tenure thereof shall be suspended or limited accordingly.

Saving for existing interest.

34. Any statute made by the Commissioners shall operate without prejudice to any interest possessed by any person by virtue of his having, before the statute comes into operation, become a member of a

College or Hall, or been elected or appointed to a University or College emolument, or acquired a vested right to be elected or appointed thereto.

35. The Commissioners, in the exercise of their authority, may take evidence, and for that purpose may require from any officer of the University or of a College or Hall the production of any documents or accounts relating to the University or to the College or Hall (as the case may be), and any information relating to the revenues, statutes, usages, or practice thereof, and generally may send for persons, papers, and records. Production of documents, etc.

Representation of Col eges and Halls.

36. Eight weeks at least (exclusive of any University vacation) before the Commissioners, in the first instance, enter on the consideration of a statute to be made by the Commissioners for a College or Hall, they shall, by writing under their seal, give notice to the Governing Body of the College, and in the University of Oxford to the Visitor of the College, and in the case of a Hall to the Principal of the Hall, of their intention to do so. Election of Commissioners by College. For Hall, Principal to be Commissioner.

The Governing Body of the College, at any time after receipt of the notice, may, at an ordinary general meeting, or at a general meeting specially summoned for this purpose, elect three persons to be Commissioners to represent the College in relation to the making by the Commissioners of statutes for the College.

But, in the case of a College, any actual member of the foundation whereof is nominated a Commissioner in this Act, no more than two persons shall be so elected, while that member is a Commissioner.

If during the continuance of the powers of the Commissioners a vacancy happens by death, resignation, or otherwise, among the persons so elected, the same may be filled up by a like election; and so from time to time.

Each person entitled to vote at an election shall have one vote for every place to be then filled by election, and may give his votes to one or more of the candidates for election, as he thinks fit.

The persons elected to represent a College, and the Principal of a Hall, shall be, to all intents, Commissioners in relation to the making by the Commissioners of statutes for the College or Hall, before and after the making thereof, but not further or otherwise, save that they shall not be counted as Commissioners for the purposes of the provisions of this Act requiring four Commissioners to be acting and three to be present at a meeting.

37. Where the Commissioners propose at any meeting, not being an adjourned meeting, to make a statute for a College or Hall, they shall give to the Governing Body of the College or to the Principal of the Hall, by writing under the seal of the Commissioners, or under the hand of their secretary, fourteen days' notice of the meeting. Notice to College or Hall of meeting.

Validity of acts as regards Colleges and Halls.

38. Any act of the Commissioners shall not be invalid by reason only of any failure to elect any person to be a Commissioner to represent a College, or the failure of any person elected to represent a College, or of the Principal of a Hall, to attend a meeting of the Commissioners.

Schools.

Notice to Governing Body of school and to Charity Commissioners.

39. If in any case the Commissioners contemplate making a statute for a College, affecting any right of preference in elections to any College emolument lawfully belonging to and enjoyed by any school, individually named or designated in any instrument of foundation, they shall, two months at least before adopting any final resolution in that behalf, give notice, by writing under their seal, to the Governing Body of the school, or to the Master or Principal of the school on behalf of the Governing Body, and to the Charity Commissioners, of the proposed statute.

Where the emolument is not a fellowship, bye-fellowship, or studentship, the Commissioners shall not make the proposed statute in either of the following cases; namely,

(1) If within two months after receipt of the notice aforesaid by the Governing Body, master, or principal of the school, two thirds of the Governing Body of the school, or two thirds of the aggregate body composed of the members of the several Governing Bodies of several schools interested (in the reckoning of the two thirds members of the Governing Body of a school who are such by virtue of membership of or election by the Governing Body of the College not being counted), by writing under their respective hands or seal, dissent from the proposed statute on the ground that it would be prejudicial to the school or schools as a place or places of learning and education; or

(2) If within two months after receipt of the notice aforesaid by the Charity Commissioners, those Commissioners, by writing under their seal, dissent from the proposed statute on the ground aforesaid.

Where fellowships or studentships are tenable in a College by undergraduates, and the fellowships or studentships of the College are divided, or proposed to be divided, into elder and younger, the elder only shall be deemed to be fellowships or studentships within this section.

Provision for case of contingent right.

40. The Governing Body of a school having a right of preference contingently only on the failure of fit objects from some other school entitled to and in the enjoyment of a prior right of preference, shall not have the power of dissent from a proposed statute under this Act.

41. Where the Governing Body of a school is a corporate body, the Governing Body of the corporation shall be deemed to be the Governing Body of the school. Governing Body a corporation.

42. The Commissioners shall send to the Secretary of State every statute relating to a school proposed by them and dissented from as aforesaid (unless another statute has been substituted), and it shall be laid before both Houses of Parliament. Statutes for schools dissented from.

43. Every right of preference retained by or for a school under this Act shall be subject to all statutes from time to time made by the Commissioners for the purpose of making the College emolument, to which the right relates, more conducive to the mutual benefit of the College and school, or for the purpose of throwing the emolument open to general or extended competition, or any vacancy for which no candidate or claimant of sufficient merit offers himself from any school entitled. Provision respecting right of preference when retained by school.

Universities Committee of Privy Council.

44. There shall be a Committee of Her Majesty's Privy Council, styled The Universities Committee of the Privy Council (in this Act referred to as the Universities Committee). Constitution of Universities Committee of Privy Council.

The Universities Committee shall consist of the President for the time being of the Privy Council, the Archbishop of Canterbury for the time being, the Lord Chancellor of Great Britain for the time being (*Repealed, S. L. R. A.*, 1894), the Chancellor of the University of Oxford for the time being, if a member of the Privy Council, the Chancellor of the University of Cambridge for the time being, if a member of the Privy Council, and such other member or two members of the Privy Council as Her Majesty from time to time thinks fit to appoint in that behalf, that other member, or one at least of those two other members, being a member of the Judicial Committee of the Privy Council.

The powers and duties of the Universities Committee may be exercised and discharged by any three or more of the members of the Committee, one of whom shall be the Lord Chancellor or a member of the Judicial Committee of the Privy Council.

Confirmation or Disallowance of Statutes.

Submission of statutes to Queen in Council.

45. The Commissioners, within one month after making a statute, shall cause it to be submitted to Her Majesty the Queen in Council, and notice of it having been so submitted shall be published in the London Gazette (in this Act referred to as the gazetting of a statute).

The subsequent proceedings under this Act respecting the statute shall not be affected by the cesser of the powers of the Commissioners.

Petition against statute.

46. At any time within three months after the gazetting of a statute, the University or the Governing Body of a College, or the trustees, governors, or patron of a University or College emolument, or the Principal of a Hall, or the Governing Body of a school, or any other person or body, in case the University, College, emolument, Hall, school, person, or body, is directly affected by the statute, may petition the Queen in Council for disallowance of the statute, or of any part thereof.

Reference to Committee.

47. It shall be lawful for the Queen in Council to refer any statute petitioned against under this Act to the Universities Committee.

The petitioners shall be entitled to be heard by themselves or counsel in support of their petition.

It shall be lawful for the Queen in Council to make, from time to time, rules of procedure and practice for regulating proceedings on such petitions.

The costs of all parties of and incident to such proceedings shall be in the discretion of the Universities Committee; and the orders of the Committee respecting costs shall be enforceable as if they were orders of a Division of the High Court of Justice.

Disallowance by Order in Council, or remitting to Commissioners.

48. If the Universities Committee report their opinion that a statute referred to them, or any part thereof, ought to be disallowed, it shall be lawful for the Queen in Council to disallow the statute or that part, and thereupon the statute or that part shall be of no effect.

If, during the continuance of the powers of the Commissioners, the Universities Committee report their opinion that a statute referred to them ought to be remitted to the Commissioners with a declaration, it shall be lawful for the Queen in Council to remit the same accordingly: and the Commissioners shall reconsider the statute, with the declaration, and the statute, if and as modified by the Commissioners, shall be proceeded on as an original statute is proceeded on, and so from time to time.

Statutes not referred, or not disallowed or remitted, to be laid before Houses of Parliament.

49. If a statute is not referred to the Universities Committee, then within one month after the expiration of the time for petitioning against it, the statute shall be laid before both Houses of Parliament, if Parliament is then sitting, and if not, then within fourteen days after the next meeting of Parliament.

If a statute is referred to the Universities Committee, and the Committee do not report that the same ought to be wholly disallowed or to be remitted to the Commissioners, then, as soon as conveniently may be after the report of the Universities Committee thereon, the statute, or such part thereof as is not disallowed by Order in Council, shall be laid before both Houses of Parliament.

50. If neither House of Parliament, within twelve weeks (exclusive of any period of prorogation) after a statute or part of a statute is laid before it, presents an address praying the Queen to withhold her consent therefrom, it shall be lawful for the Queen in Council by Order to approve the same.

Approval of statutes by Order in Council.

Effect of Statutes.

51. Every statute or part of a statute made by the Commissioners, and approved by Order in Council, shall be binding on the University and on every College and Hall, and shall be effectual notwithstanding any instrument of foundation or any Act of Parliament, Order in Council, decree, order, statute, or other instrument or thing constituting wholly or in part an instrument of foundation, or confirming or varying a foundation or endowment, or otherwise regulating the University or a College or Hall.

Statutes to be binding and effectual.

52. If after the cesser of the powers of the Commissioners (*Repealed, S. L. R. A.*, 1894) any doubt arises with respect to the true meaning of any statute made by the Commissioners for the University of Cambridge, the Council of the Senate may apply to the Chancellor of the University for the time being, and he may declare in writing the meaning of the statute on the matter submitted to him, and his declaration shall be registered by the Registrary of the University, and the meaning of the statute as therein declared shall be deemed to be the true meaning thereof.

Power in Cambridge for Chancellor to settle doubts as to meaning of University statutes.

Alteration of Statutes.

53. A statute made by the Commissioners for the University or for a Hall shall, after the cesser of the powers of the Commissioners (*Repealed, S. L. R. A.*, 1894), be subject to alteration from time to time by statute made by the University under this Act and not otherwise.

Power for University to alter Commissioners' statutes.

But where and as far as a statute made by the Commissioners for the University affects a College, the same shall not be subject to alteration under this section, except with the consent of the College.

Power for Colleges to alter Commissioners' statutes.

54. A statute made by the Commissioners for a College, and any statute, ordinance, or regulation made by or in relation to a College under any authority other than that of this Act, shall, after the cesser of the powers of the Commissioners (*Repealed, S. L. R. A.*, 1894), be subject to alteration from time to time by statute made by the College under this Act and not otherwise, the same being passed at a general meeting of the Governing Body of the College, specially summoned for this purpose, by the votes of not less than two thirds of the number of persons present and voting.

But where and as far as a statute made by the Commissioners for a College affects the University, the same shall not be subject to alteration under this section except with the consent of the University.

Confirmation or disallowance of altering statutes.

55. Every statute made by the University or a College under either of the two next preceding sections of this Act shall be submitted to the Queen in Council, and be proceeded on and have effect as if it were a statute made by the Commissioners, with the substitution only of the University or the College for the Commissioners in the provisions of this Act in that behalf.

Reference of other Statutes to Universities Committee.

Statutes awaiting submission to Queen in Council, or made before cesser of powers of Commissioners.

56. Every statute, ordinance, and regulation made as follows; namely,

(1) Every statute, ordinance, and regulation made by or in relation to the University or a College under any former Act before the passing of this Act, and required by any former Act to be submitted to the Queen in Council, but not so submitted before the passing of this Act; and

(2) Every statute, ordinance, and regulation made by or in relation to the University or a College under any former Act after the passing of this Act, and before the cesser of the powers of the Commissioners, and required by any former Act to be submitted to the Queen in Council; and

(3) Every statute, ordinance, and regulation made by or in relation to a College under any former Act or any ordinance since the

first day of January one thousand eight hundred and seventy-seven, and before the passing of this Act,

shall, in lieu of being submitted to the Queen in Council under and according to any former Act or any ordinance, and whether or not a submission to the Queen in Council is required under any former Act or any ordinance, be, with the consent of the Commissioners in writing under their seal, but not otherwise, submitted to the Queen in Council under this Act, and be proceeded on as if it were a statute made by the Commissioners, with the substitution only of the University or the College for the Commissioners in the provisions of this Act in that behalf; and the same, if and as far as it is approved by Order in Council under this Act, shall have effect as if it had been submitted and proceeded on under any former Act or any ordinance.

Tests.

57. Nothing in this Act shall be construed to repeal any provision of the Universities Tests Act, 1871. Saving for Tests Act. 34 & 35 Vict. c. 26.

58. Where the Commissioners, by any statute made by them, erect or endow an office declared by them in the statute to require in the incumbent thereof the possession of theological learning, which (notwithstanding anything in this Act) they are hereby empowered to do, provided the office be not a headship or fellowship of a College, then the Universities Tests Act, 1871, shall, with reference to that Office, be read and have effect as if the statute had been made before and was in operation at the passing of the Universities Tests Act, 1871. Operation of Tests Act as regards new theological offices. 34 & 35 Vict. c. 26.

59. The Commissioners, in statutes made by them, shall make provision, as far as may appear to them requisite, for the due fulfilment of the requisitions of sections five and six of the Universities Tests Act, 1871 (relating to religious instruction and to morning and evening prayer in Colleges); but, except for that purpose, they shall not, by a statute made by them, endow wholly or in part an office of an ecclesiastical or theological character by means of any portion of the revenues or property of the University or a College not forming, when the statute comes into operation, the endowment, or part of the endowment, of an office of that character, and in any statute made by them, shall not make directly, or indirectly through the consolidation or combination of any office or emolument with any other office or emolument, whether in the University or in a College or Hall, the entering into holy orders or the taking of any test a condition of the holding of any office or emolument existing at the passing of this Act to which that condition is not at the passing of this Act attached. Provision for religious instruction and worship in pursuance of Tests Act.

Land.

License in mortmain unnecessary on purchases under University Acts.

60. A license to aliene or to take and hold in mortmain shall be and be deemed to have been unnecessary in respect of a purchase, made before or after the passing of this Act, by the University or a College of land situate within a district or place described or named in, and required for any purpose mentioned in, the following enactments respectively:

20 & 21 Vict. c. 25. Section four of the Oxford University Act, 1857:

19 & 20 Vict. c. 88. Section fifty-one of the Cambridge University Act, 1856.

Electoral Roll, Cambridge.

Notice of objection as to Electoral Roll to be given.

61. No objection to the list of members of the Electoral Roll of the University of Cambridge, promulgated in accordance with section seven of the Cambridge University Act, 1856, made on the ground of any person being improperly placed on or omitted from that list, shall be entertained unless notice of it is given in writing to the Vice-Chancellor at least four days before the day for publicly hearing objections to that list; and the Vice-Chancellor shall, at least two days before such day, cause to be promulgated a list of all the objections of which notice has been given.

THE SCHEDULE

Short Titles for former Acts.

OXFORD.

17 & 18 Vict. c. 81.—An Act to make further provision for the good government and extension of the University of Oxford, of the Colleges therein, and of the College of Saint Mary, Winchester.	The Oxford University Act, 1854.
19 & 20 Vict. c. 31.—An Act to amend the Act of the seventeenth and eighteenth years of Her Majesty concerning the University of Oxford and the College of Saint Mary, Winchester.	The Oxford University Act, 1856.
20 & 21 Vict. c. 25.—An Act to continue the powers of the Commissioners under an Act of the seventeenth and eighteenth years of Her Majesty concerning the University of Oxford and the College of Saint Mary, Winchester, and further to amend the said Act.	The Oxford University Act, 1857.
23 & 24 Vict. c. 91.—An Act for removing doubts respecting the Craven Scholarships in the University of Oxford, and for enabling the University to retain the custody of certain testamentary documents.	The Oxford University Act, 1860.
32 & 33 Vict. c. 20.—An Act to remove doubts as to the validity of certain statutes made by the Convocation of the University of Oxford.	The Oxford University Statutes Act, 1869.

CAMBRIDGE.

19 & 20 Vict. c. 88.—An Act to make further provision for the good government and extension of the University of Cambridge, of the Colleges therein, and of the College of King Henry the Sixth at Eton.	The Cambridge University Act, 1856.

(*This Schedule is repealed by S. L. R. A.*, 1894.)

CAMBRIDGE LOCAL GOVERNMENT ACT, 1889

52 & 53 VICT. CAP. CXVI.

An Act to confirm certain Provisional Orders of the Local Government Board relating to the Boroughs of Banbury and Cambridge.

[26th July 1889.]

WHEREAS the Local Government Board have made the Provisional Orders set forth in the Schedule hereto, under the provisions of the Public Health Act, 1875, and the Local Government Act, 1888:

38 & 39 Vict. c. 55.
51 & 52 Vict. c. 41.

And whereas it is requisite that the said Orders should be confirmed by Parliament:

Be it therefore enacted by the Queen's most Excellent Majesty, by and with the advice and consent of the Lords Spiritual and Temporal, and Commons, in this present Parliament assembled, and by the authority of the same, as follows:

Orders in Schedule confirmed.

1. The Orders as altered and set out in the Schedule hereto shall be and the same are hereby confirmed, and all the provisions thereof shall have full validity and force.

Short title.

2. This Act may be cited as the Local Government Board's Provisional Orders Confirmation (No. 15) Act, 1889.

SCHEDULE[1]

BOROUGH OF CAMBRIDGE

Provisional Order made in pursuance of Section 52 of the Local Government Act, 1888, and under Section 297 of the Public Health Act, 1875.

To the County Council for the Administrative County of Cambridge ;—

To the Chancellor, Masters, and Scholars of the University of Cambridge ;—

To the Mayor, Aldermen, and Burgesses of the Borough of Cambridge ;—

To the Commissioners appointed for putting into execution certain Local Acts of Parliament of the reign of His late Majesty King George the Third, and respectively intituled "An Act for the better "paving, cleansing, and lighting the Town of "Cambridge ; for removing and preventing ob- "structions and annoyances ; and for widening the "streets, lanes, and other passages within the said "Town," and "An Act to amend and enlarge the "powers of an Act passed in the twenty-eighth "year of the reign of His present Majesty, intituled, "An Act for the better paving, cleansing, and "lighting the Town of Cambridge, for removing "and preventing obstructions and annoyances, and "for widening the streets, lanes, and other passages "within the said Town," being the Sanitary Authority for the Urban Sanitary District of Cambridge, in the said administrative County ;— 28 Geo. III, c. lxiv. 34 Geo. III, c. civ.

To the Guardians of the Poor of the Cambridge Union, in the same County ;—

And to all others whom it may concern.

[1] The first part of the Schedule relates to the Borough of Banbury and is here omitted.

51 & 52 Vict. c. 41.

WHEREAS by Section 52 of the Local Government Act, 1888 (which Act is herein-after referred to as "the Act"), it is enacted that the Local Government Board shall make Provisional Orders for dealing with every case where the Council of a Borough is not the Urban Sanitary Authority for the whole of the area of such Borough, and the area of the Borough is either co-extensive with or is wholly or partly comprised in any Urban Sanitary District, and that such Order shall determine whether the area of the Borough or of the Sanitary District, or an area comprising both the Borough and the Urban Sanitary District, or a portion of such united area, shall, whether with or without any adjoining area, be the area of the County District for the purposes of the Act, so, however, that in either case the Order shall provide for the Council of the Borough becoming the District Council, and that the Order may for that purpose alter the boundaries of the Borough; and that where certain members of the Sanitary Authority for any such Urban Sanitary District are appointed by a university or any colleges therein, the Order may provide for the appointment by such university or colleges of members on the District Council;

And whereas the Borough of Cambridge is a Borough within the meaning of the Act, and the inhabitants of the Borough are a body corporate, by the name of the Mayor, Aldermen, and Burgesses of the Borough of Cambridge, and act by the Council of the Borough, which now consists of the Mayor, ten Aldermen, and thirty Councillors;

And whereas the Borough is, for the purpose of the election of Councillors, divided into five wards, to each of which six Councillors are assigned;

28 Geo. III, c. lxiv. 34 Geo. III, c. civ.

And whereas under the provisions of certain Local Acts of Parliament of the reign of His late Majesty King George the Third, and respectively intituled "An Act for the better "paving, cleansing, and lighting the Town of Cambridge; "for removing and preventing obstructions and annoyances; "and for widening the streets, lanes, and other passages "within the said Town," and "An Act to amend and enlarge "the powers of an Act passed in the twenty-eighth year of "the reign of His present Majesty, intituled, An Act for "the better paving, cleansing, and lighting the Town of "Cambridge, for removing and preventing obstructions and "annoyances, and for widening the streets, lanes, and other "passages within the said Town," (which Local Acts are herein-after respectively referred to as "the Act of 1788" and "the Act of 1794,") certain magistrates and officers for the time being of the University of Cambridge, and of the colleges and halls therein, certain magistrates and persons of the Corporation, together with the persons therein mentioned and certain other persons to be elected as therein prescribed, were appointed Commissioners (herein-after referred to as "the Commissioners") for putting those Acts into execution within the Town of Cambridge;

And whereas by another Local Act of Parliament of the reign of Her present Majesty Queen Victoria, intituled "An "Act to amend the Cambridge Improvement Acts, and to "exempt the Eastern Counties Railway Company from "certain Tolls thereby imposed" (herein-after referred to as "the Act of 1846"), provision was made for the payment by the Eastern Counties (now the Great Eastern) Railway Company to the Commissioners of a fixed annual sum in lieu of certain tolls payable by them under the Acts of 1788 and 1794; 9 & 10 Vict. c. cccxlv.

And whereas by the River Cam Navigation Act, 1851 (herein-after referred to as "the Act of 1851"), certain persons (including three persons to represent the University of Cambridge, and three persons, being members of the Council, to represent the Borough) were appointed Conservators of the River Cam; 14 & 15 Vict. c. xcii.

And whereas by the Cambridge Award Act, 1856 (herein-after referred to as "the Act of 1856"), provision was made with respect to certain differences that had arisen between the University of Cambridge and the Corporation; 19 Vict. c. xvii.

And whereas by Section 6 of the Public Health Act, 38 & 39 Vict. c. 55.

1875, it is enacted that, for the purposes of that Act, the Borough of Cambridge should not be deemed to be a Borough, and should be deemed to be an Improvement Act District, and by virtue of that section, that Improvement Act District became an Urban Sanitary District (herein-after referred to as "the Sanitary District"), of which the Commissioners are the Urban Sanitary Authority;

And whereas by a Provisional Order of the Local Government Board dated the Eighteenth day of March, One thousand eight hundred and eighty-one, and duly confirmed by the Local Government Board's Provisional Orders Confirmation (Bath, etc.) Act, 1881 (which Order and Act are herein-after respectively referred to as "the Order of 1881" and "the Confirming Act of 1881"), the Act of 1788 and the Act of 1794 were partially repealed and altered;

44 Vict. c. xv.

And whereas the Council of the Borough is not the Urban Sanitary Authority for the area of the Borough, and the Borough is co-extensive with the Sanitary District, and the University is represented on the said Urban Sanitary Authority in manner aforesaid:

51 & 52 Vict. c. 41.

38 & 39 Vict. c. 55.

Now therefore, We, the Local Government Board, in pursuance of the powers given to Us by Sections 52 and 59 of the Act, by Section 297 of the Public Health Act, 1875, and by any other enactments in that behalf, do hereby Order that, from and after the date of the Act of Parliament confirming this Order, the following provisions shall take effect:—

Commencement of Order.

Art. 1. This Order shall come into operation on the Ninth day of November, One thousand eight hundred and eighty-nine, except so far as is otherwise herein expressly provided.

Definitions.

Art. 2. The several terms in this Order shall have the same meanings respectively as are assigned to them by Section 100 of the Act, and the term "Colleges and Halls" shall be taken to include public hostels.

County District.

Art. 3.—(1) The area bounded as herein-after mentioned (being the area both of the Borough and of the Sanitary

District) shall be the area of the County District for the purposes of the Act, and the Mayor, Aldermen, and Burgesses of the Borough, acting by the Council of the Borough, constituted and elected in the manner herein-after provided, shall become the District Council for such County District.

(2) The boundary of the County District and Borough shall be that shewn by a red line on the maps, each marked "Map of the Borough of Cambridge, 1889," and sealed with the official seal of the Local Government Board, one of which shall be deposited in the office of the said Board, and the other of which shall be deposited by the town clerk of the Borough at his office within seven days after the date of this Order. Map of the Borough

Art. 4.—(1) Copies of the said map deposited with the town clerk, certified by him, shall be sent within one month after the date of the Act of Parliament confirming this Order to the clerk of the County Council for the administrative County of Cambridge, to the Director-General of Her Majesty's Ordnance Survey at Southampton, and to the Registrary of the University. Copies of map to be deposited and to be evidence.

(2) Copies of or extracts from the said map deposited with the town clerk, certified by him to be true, shall be received in all courts of justice and elsewhere as primâ facie evidence of the contents of such map so far as relates to the boundaries of the Borough; and such map shall at all reasonable times be open to inspection by any person liable to any rate leviable within the Borough, and any such person shall be entitled to a copy of or extract from such map, certified by the town clerk, on payment of a reasonable fee for every such copy or extract. All sums received under this Article shall be carried to the credit of the Borough fund.

Art. 5. The number of Councillors of the Borough shall be increased from thirty to thirty-six, of whom thirty shall continue to be elected by the Burgesses of the Borough, and six shall be elected to represent the University in the manner herein-after directed. Number of Councillors. Election of Councillors by the University.

Art. 6. With respect to the election of Councillors to represent the University the following provisions shall apply :—

(1) Two of such Councillors shall be nominated by the Council of the Senate of the University, and be elected by grace of the Senate, and the remaining four shall be elected by the colleges and halls of the University situated within the Borough, in such manner as shall be from time to time determined by grace of the Senate. The Vice-Chancellor of the University or his deputy shall be the returning officer at all elections of such Councillors.

(2) Every member of the Senate of the University (whether a Clerk in Holy Orders or the regular minister of a dissenting congregation or not) who is resident in a college or hall of the University situated within the Borough, or is resident in the Borough, and every person who is enrolled and entitled to be enrolled as a Burgess of the Borough, shall be qualified to be elected such Councillor, and every such Councillor shall be qualified to be elected Alderman or Mayor. (3) The annual election of such Councillors shall be held on such day or days, not earlier than the Fifteenth day of October and not later than the First day of November, as may from time to time be appointed by the Vice-Chancellor.

(4) The Registrary of the University shall forward to the town clerk immediately after the election has been completed, and not later than the Third day of November, a statement of the persons elected as such Councillors, and, in the case of the first election, of the term of office for which each of them was elected.

(5) Any vacancy among such Councillors, whether occurring in the regular course or casually, shall be filled up by the election of a Councillor by the body which elected the Councillor whose place has become vacant, and any Councillor elected to fill a casual vacancy shall hold office until the time when the

person in whose place he is elected would regularly have gone out of office, and he shall then go out of office. An election to fill a casual vacancy among such Councillors shall be held as soon as practicable after the vacancy occurs. The town clerk shall give notice to the Registrary of vacancies among such Councillors.

(6) The provisions of Sections 11, 12 (1) (*b*), 51 to 59 (both inclusive), and 66 of the Municipal Corporations Act, 1882, shall not apply to elections of such Councillors. 45 & 46 Vict. c. 50.

(7) Six Councillors shall be elected as in this Article mentioned at the annual election in the year One thousand eight hundred and eighty-nine; and for the purposes of that election this Order shall operate from the date of the Act of Parliament confirming the same.

Number of Aldermen.

Art. 7. The number of Aldermen of the Borough shall be increased from ten to twelve, of whom two shall be elected from among the Councillors elected to represent the University; and the provisions of the Municipal Corporations Act, 1882, relating to the election of Aldermen, shall be modified accordingly. The first election of the two additional Aldermen shall be on the Ninth day of November, One thousand eight hundred and eighty-nine.

Terms of office of Councillors first elected by University

Art. 8.—(1) At the first election of Councillors to represent the University, they shall be elected for the following terms of office; that is to say,—

One of the Councillors elected by grace of the Senate, and one of those elected by the Colleges and Halls, for a term ending on the First day of November, One thousand eight hundred and ninety;

The other Councillor elected by grace of the Senate, and one of the Councillors elected by the Colleges and Halls, for a term ending on the First day of November, One thousand eight hundred and ninety-one;

The other two Councillors elected by the Colleges and Halls for a term ending on the First day of November, One thousand eight hundred and ninety-two;

Retirement of additional Aldermen.

(2) Of the two Aldermen elected in pursuance of Article 7, one shall go out of office on the Ninth day of November, One thousand eight hundred and ninety-two, and the other on the Ninth day of November, One thousand eight hundred and ninety-five; and the Council of the Borough shall, on the Ninth day of November, One thousand eight hundred and eighty-nine, or at the next following quarterly meeting, and not later, by a majority of votes, or in case of an equality of votes by the casting vote of the chairman, determine which of the said Aldermen shall go out of office on the dates above specified respectively.

Byelaws, etc. to continue in force.

Art. 9. All byelaws and regulations made by the Commissioners which, on the Ninth day of November, One thousand eight hundred and eighty-nine, are in force within the Sanitary District shall continue in force within and apply to the Borough, except in so far as the same may hereafter be altered or repealed; and save that the Corporation shall be substituted for the Commissioners throughout the byelaws and regulations.

Town clerk and other officers continued.

Art. 10. The town clerk and all other officers and servants of the Corporation of the Borough who hold office on the Ninth day of November, One thousand eight hundred and eighty-nine, shall continue to be the town clerk and officers and servants of the Corporation of the Borough, and shall hold their offices by the same tenure as at that date.

Compensation to existing officers. 51 & 52 Vict. c. 41.

Art. 11. The provisions of sub-section (13) of Section 118 and of Sections 119 and 120 of the Act shall apply to the persons who on the Ninth day of November, One thousand eight hundred and eighty-nine, hold office as officers or servants of the Commissioners, with the substitution of "district fund and general district rate" in sub-section (8) of Section 120 for "county fund as a payment for general "county purposes," and with such other modifications as are necessary to make those provisions applicable to the said officers and servants and to the Corporation.

Property, etc. of Commissioners.

Art. 12.—(1) All property, powers, duties, and liabilities which immediately before the Ninth day of November, One thousand eight hundred and eighty-nine, are vested in or attached to the Commissioners shall be transferred to, vested in, and attached to the Corporation as Urban Sanitary Authority, and all arrears of rates which at the date aforesaid are due or owing to the Commissioners may be collected and recovered by the Corporation.

(2) The Commissioners shall on the Ninth day of November, One thousand eight hundred and eighty-nine, be abolished and cease to exist. **Commissioners abolished.**

Art. 13. The accounts of the Commissioners and their officers up to the Ninth day of November, One thousand eight hundred and eighty-nine, shall be audited by the proper officer of the Local Government Board in like manner and subject to the like right of appeal as if this Order had not been made. **Audit of accounts of Commissioners.**

Art. 14.—(1) The unrepealed provisions of the Act of 1788 (except Sections 63, 74, 76, 77, 87, 88, 89, 92, and 101), and of the Act of 1794 (except Sections 21 and 25), shall be wholly repealed except so far as the same may have been acted upon, and except so far as it may be necessary to continue the same for the purpose of recovering any rate made prior to the Ninth day of November, One thousand eight hundred and eighty-nine. **Repeal and alteration of Local Acts.**

(2) The Act of 1788 and the Act of 1794, as altered by the Order of 1881 and this Order, shall be further altered so that the unrepealed provisions thereof shall apply to the Corporation instead of the Commissioners, and so that they may hereafter be respectively referred to as the Cambridge Improvement Act, 1788, and the Cambridge Improvement Act, 1794.

(3) The Act of 1846 shall be wholly repealed except so far as the same may have been acted upon.

(4) Sections 19, 20, and 22 of the Act of 1851 shall be altered so as to provide that the Councillors representing the University, and the Aldermen chosen from among such Councillors, shall not be eligible for election to represent the Borough as Conservators of the River Cam or as auditors of the accounts of those Conservators.

(5) Sections 23, 25 to 31, 37, 38, 50, and 56 to 61 (all inclusive) of the Act of 1856 shall be wholly repealed except so far as the same may have been acted upon.

(6) Section 35 of the Act of 1856 shall cease to apply to the service of any municipal office by Councillors elected to represent the University, and Aldermen elected from among such Councillors.

Rating, etc. of University property.

Art. 15. The Act of 1856 shall be further altered so as to provide as follows:

(1) From and after the Ninth day of November, One thousand eight hundred and eighty-nine, the general law applicable to rateability, valuation, and rating of property for the purposes of the rates for the relief of the poor, the rates leviable under the Public Health Act, 1875, the Borough rate, and all other rates shall apply also to the property of the University and of a college or hall therein without any exemption or distinction of or in favour of the same, except that a chapel of a college or hall shall be deemed to be an episcopal chapel within the meaning of the Act relating to the exemption of churches and chapels from rates, and shall be exempt accordingly.

Union Assessment Committee.

(2) The Assessment Committee of the Cambridge Union (herein-after referred to as the Assessment Committee) shall be constituted in accordance with the following provisions:

(3) The Assessment Committee shall consist of twenty-four members, twelve of whom shall be annually appointed by the Guardians of the Poor of the Cambridge Union (herein-after referred to as "the Guardians"), four by the University, in such manner as may be from time to time determined by grace of the Senate of the University, and eight by the Council of the Borough from among themselves. The appointments by the University and by the Council of the Borough shall be forthwith certified to the clerk to the Guardians.

(4) The first appointments shall be made as soon as practicable after the Ninth day of November, One thousand eight hundred and eighty-nine, and the Assessment Committee so appointed shall continue in office until the appointment of a new Committee in the year One thousand eight hundred and ninety, 25 & 26 Vict. c. 103. at the time prescribed by the Union Assessment Committee Act, 1862.

(5) No member of the Assessment Committee shall be precluded from acting and voting on that committee by reason only of his being a member of any body corporate or shareholder in any company, and thereby interested in property subject to the operation of the powers of the committee.

(6) Any casual vacancy among the members appointed by the University and the Council of the Borough shall, with all convenient speed, be filled by the University or by the Council of the Borough respectively in such manner as may be from time to time determined by grace of the Senate of the University and by the Council of the Borough respectively.

(7) The Assessment Committee appointed under this Article shall hold their first meeting on the Twenty-second day of November, One thousand eight hundred and eighty-nine, at twelve at noon, at the Guildhall in the Borough, or at such other time or place as shall be appointed by the Guardians.

(8) The provisions of the Union Assessment Committee Act, 1862, and of the Acts amending the same, shall, so far as is consistent with the provisions of this Order, apply to the Assessment Committee constituted under this Order, and to the powers, functions, and duties of such committee.

(9) Subject to any directions given by the Assessment Committee, the overseers of each parish within the Cambridge Union shall, within two months after the first meeting of the Assessment Committee appointed

under this Order, make a new valuation of all the rateable hereditaments in such parish, and a new valuation list in substitution for the valuation list then in force ; and the Assessment Committee may, in relation to such new valuation and the making of such new valuation list, from time to time give and make all such or the like directions and provisions, and exercise all such powers in relation thereto as Assessment Committees are authorised, to give, make, and exercise under the Union Assessment Committee Act, 1862, and the Acts amending the same.

Expenses of Commissioners and Corporation, how to be defrayed.

Art. 16.—(1) For defraying expenses incurred by the Commissioners before the Ninth day of November, One thousand eight hundred and eighty-nine, in the execution of the purposes of the Act of 1788 and the Act of 1794, and of the Public Health Act, 1875, or to be incurred after that date by the Corporation in the execution of the purposes of the unrepealed provisions of the Act of 1788 and the Act of 1794, and of the Public Health Act, 1875, the Corporation shall have power to make and levy from time to time, when and as often as occasion requires, a general district rate under and in accordance with the provisions of the Public Health Act, 1875, and all the provisions of that Act relating to district funds and general district rates (including the provisions relating to appeals against rates) shall apply to the Corporation and the Borough as if the purposes of the Act of 1788 and the Act of 1794 were purposes of the Public Health Act, 1875.

Existing mortgages.

(2) All moneys owing by the Commissioners immediately before the Ninth day of November, One thousand eight hundred and eighty-nine, on the security of the improvement rate leviable by them under the Act of 1788 and the Act of 1794, either alone or with some other security (the liability for the repayment of which moneys will, by virtue of Article 12 of this Order, attach to the Corporation), shall be deemed to have been borrowed on the security of the general district rate leviable under the Public Health Act, 1875, either alone or together with such other security, as the case may be, and

the general district rate shall be substituted for the improvement rate in every mortgage or other instrument of security granted or issued by the Commissioners before the Ninth day of November, One thousand eight hundred and eighty-nine, so that mortgagees and other creditors may have the like rights and remedies to all intents against the general district rate as they would have had against the improvement rate if this Order had not been made.

Saving for rights and privileges of University.

Art. 17. Nothing in this Order contained shall affect the exclusive rights and privileges of civil and criminal judicature and trial in the courts of the University as the same may have been granted by the charters of the University and confirmed by divers Acts of Parliament to the University and to all persons matriculated therein or being members thereof, nor any other of the respective rights, privileges, and franchises of the University and their successors, and the several bodies politic, corporate, collegiate, or sole of the University, and their successors, except so far as the same are hereby expressly altered.

Modification of Municipal Corporations Act, 1882.

Art. 18. Sub-section (4) of Section 257 of the Municipal Corporations Act, 1882, shall cease to apply to the Borough in so far as concerns the offices of Councillors elected to represent the University and Aldermen elected from among such Councillors; and sub-section (5) of that section shall altogether cease to apply to the Borough and the University, and the Colleges and Halls therein, and the members thereof; and the remaining provisions of the said Act relating to the University shall be construed with such modifications as may be necessary for carrying this Order into effect.

Art. 19. This Order may be cited as the Borough of Cambridge Order, 1889.

Given under the Seal of Office of the Local Government Board, this Fourth day of June, One thousand eight hundred and eighty-nine.

CHAS. T. RITCHIE, President.
HUGH OWEN, Secretary.

(L S)

CAMBRIDGE UNIVERSITY AND CORPORATION ACT, 1894

57 & 58 VICT. CAP. LX.

An Act to amend the Law relating to the jurisdiction of the Chancellor Vice-Chancellor and other authorities of the University of Cambridge over persons not Members of the University and to make better provision for the use of commons the management of markets and fairs and in other respects for the local government and improvement of the borough of Cambridge and for other purposes. [3rd July 1894.]

WHEREAS by a charter dated or purporting to be dated the twenty-sixth day of April in the third year of Her reign Her Majesty Queen Elizabeth granted (among other things) "That the Chancellor Masters and Scholars "of the University of Cambridge by themselves or their "deputies officers servants and ministers from time to time "as well by day as by night at their pleasure might make "scrutiny search and inquisition in the town and suburbs "and in Barnwell and Sturbridge for all common women "bawds vagabonds and other suspected persons coming or "resorting to the town and suburbs or the said fairs and "punish all whom on such scrutiny search and inquisition "they should find guilty or suspected of evil by imprisonment "of their bodies banishment or otherwise as the Chancellor "or his vice-gerent should deem fit. And the mayor bailiffs "and other officers and ministers of the town and all other "persons whatsoever were commanded not to impede such "scrutiny search and inquisition but on request of the "Chancellor or his vice-gerent aid and assist therein under "pain of contempt and incurring the indignation of the "Queen Her heirs and successors":

And whereas by an Act passed in the thirteenth year of the reign of Queen Elizabeth chapter twenty-nine intituled "An Acte for Thincorporatōn of bothe Thunyversities" (section 2) the said charter was declared to be good effectual and available in law to all intents constructions and purposes:

And whereas by section 3 of an Act of Parliament passed in the sixth year of His Majesty King George the Fourth intituled "An Act for the better preservation of the peace "and good order in the Universities of England" it was enacted "that every common prostitute and night-walker "found wandering in any public walk street or highway "within the precincts of the said University of Oxford and "not giving a satisfactory account of herself shall be deemed "an idle and disorderly person within the true intent and "meaning of the Act 5 Geo. IV, cap. 83 intituled 'An Act "'for the punishment of idle and disorderly persons and "'rogues and vagabonds in that part of Great Britain called "'England' and shall and may be apprehended and dealt "with accordingly": 6 Geo. IV, c. 97.

And whereas it is expedient to repeal the recited portion of the charter and so much of the first recited Act or any other Act as confirms or preserves the same and to extend to the University of Cambridge the recited section 3 of the said Act 6 Geo. IV, cap. 97 and to confer further powers on the proctors and pro-proctors of the University of Cambridge for the maintenance of discipline among its members:

And whereas by section 10 of the Theatres Act 1843 no theatre or other place of public resort can be licensed for the public performance of stage plays within the precincts of the University of Cambridge or within fourteen miles of the town of Cambridge without the consent of the Chancellor or Vice-Chancellor of the University: 6 & 7 Vict. c. 68.

9 Vict. c. xvii. (*sic*).

And whereas by section 16 of the Cambridge Award Act 1856 no occasional public exhibition or performance (whether strictly theatrical or not) other than performances in theatres regulated by the Theatres Act 1843 can take place within the borough of Cambridge (except during the period of the Midsummer Fair or in the Long Vacation) unless with the consent in writing of the Vice-Chancellor and the mayor:

And whereas the mayor aldermen and burgesses of the borough of Cambridge (in this Act called the Corporation) are the local authority within the meaning of the Public Health Acts Amendment Act 1890 and a resolution of the council of the borough was duly passed on the 13th day of July 1893 for the adoption of Part IV (music and dancing) of that Act and fixing the 1st day of October then next for the coming into operation of the same within the borough:

And whereas it is not necessary or expedient to maintain the aforesaid jurisdiction of the Chancellor and Vice-Chancellor as it now exists and it is desirable to make such provisions relative thereto as this Act contains:

* * * * * * * * * * * *

May it therefore please Your Majesty that it may be enacted and be it enacted by the Queen's most Excellent Majesty by and with the advice and consent of the Lords Spiritual and Temporal and Commons in this present Parliament assembled and by the authority of the same as follows (that is to say):—

Part I.—Preliminary.

Short title.

1. This Act may be cited as the Cambridge University and Corporation Act 1894.

Interpretation.

2. In this Act the following words and expressions have the meanings hereby assigned to them unless the subject or context otherwise requires:—

"The Corporation" means the mayor aldermen and burgesses of the borough of Cambridge;

"The borough" means the municipal borough of Cambridge;

"The council" "the borough fund" and "the borough "rate" "the district fund" and "the general district "rate" mean respectively the council borough fund and borough rate district fund and general district rate of the borough;

"The joint committee" means the joint committee constituted by section 5 of the Act of 1889;

"The commons" means the commons and open spaces mentioned or referred to in the preamble to this Act and shewn on the map of the commons herein-after mentioned;

"Daily penalty" means a penalty for each day on which any offence is continued after conviction therefor.

Execution of Act.

3. This Act shall so far as it relates to the powers and duties of the Corporation be carried into execution by the Corporation acting by the council.

Part II.—University Jurisdiction.

Limits of Part II of this Act.

4. This part of this Act shall (unless otherwise expressed) extend and apply to the whole of the borough and to any area beyond the borough situate within two miles and a half from the church of St Mary the Great in the borough and the said limits shall for the purposes of this part of this Act be deemed to be the precincts of the University of Cambridge.

Partial repeal of charter.

5. So much of the charter as is recited and set forth in the preamble to this Act and so much of the Act of the thirteenth year of the reign of Queen Elizabeth chapter twenty-nine intituled "An Acte for Thincorporatōn of bothe "Thunyversities" and so much of any other Act as confirms or preserves that portion of the recited charter is hereby repealed without prejudice to anything already done and suffered.

S. 3 of 6 Geo. IV to apply to University of Cambridge.

6. The recited section 3 of the said Act 6 Geo. IV, cap. 97 shall extend and apply to the University of Cambridge and subject to the provisions of this Act shall have effect within the precincts of the said University as if the words "either of the said Universities of Oxford and Cambridge" were inserted therein in lieu of the words "the "said University of Oxford."

Proctors to have powers of constables.

7. For the maintenance of discipline among the members of the University of Cambridge the proctors and pro-proctors of the University shall by virtue of their respective offices have the powers vested in constables duly appointed and sworn under or by virtue of section 1 of the said Act 6 Geo. IV, cap. 97 and shall for the same purpose have power with or without any constables appointed under the same Act to enter any premises licensed for the sale of intoxicating liquors or any premises kept or used for public entertainment of any kind during the performance of such entertainment or so long as any of the public are assembled there.

Partial repeal of 6 & 7 Vict. c. 68, s. 10.

8. Section 10 of the Theatres Act 1843 is hereby repealed so far as it relates to the University or town of Cambridge or the neighbourhood thereof.

Power to revoke theatrical licences.

9. The county council for the county of Cambridge may at any time revoke any licence for the public performance of stage plays within the borough on the complaint in writing of the Vice-Chancellor or the mayor sent to the clerk of the said council who shall forthwith upon the receipt of such complaint summon a special meeting of the county council to consider the same and give written notice of the complaint to the person complained of in order that he may make his answer or defence at such special meeting.

Power to revoke licences for other public entertainments.

10. The licensing justices for the borough may at any time revoke any licence within the borough granted in pursuance of Part IV of the Public Health Acts Amendment Act 1890 on the complaint in writing of the Vice-Chancellor or the mayor sent to the clerk to the justices who shall forthwith upon the receipt of such complaint summon a

special session of the licensing justices to consider the same and give written notice of the complaint to the person complained of in order that he may make his answer or defence at such special session.

Amendment of section 16 of Award Act.

11. Section 16 of the Cambridge Award Act 1856 shall henceforth be read and have effect as if the words "(except "during the period of Midsummer Fair or in the Long Vaca- "tion)" and the words "Vice-Chancellor and the" were expunged and omitted therefrom.

Saving for rights and privileges of University.

12. Nothing in this part of this Act contained shall affect any right power or privilege of the University or of any court or officer of the University except so far as the same is hereby expressly abolished or modified[1].

[1] Parts III, IV, V, and VI of this Act and a Schedule are here omitted.

INDEX

CAMBRIDGE: PRINTED BY JOHN CLAY, M.A. AT THE UNIVERSITY PRESS

For EU product safety concerns, contact us at Calle de José Abascal, 56–1°,
28003 Madrid, Spain or eugpsr@cambridge.org.

www.ingramcontent.com/pod-product-compliance
Ingram Content Group UK Ltd.
Pitfield, Milton Keynes, MK11 3LW, UK
UKHW010341140625
459647UK00010B/743

* 9 7 8 1 1 0 8 0 0 3 7 9 7 *